RAINBOW OF EDUCATIONAL PHILOSOPHIES

METHODS AND MODELS

FORBI STEPHEN KIZITO, sj.

authorHOUSE

1663 LIBERTY DRIVE, SUITE 200
BLOOMINGTON, INDIANA 47403
(800) 839-8640
www.authorhouse.com

First published by AuthorHouse 06/18/04

ISBN: 1-4184-2421-8 (e)
ISBN: 1-4184-2420-X (sc)

Library of Congress Control Number: 2004094925

This book is printed on acid free paper.

Printed in the United States of America
Bloomington, IN

ACKNOWLEDGEMENT

I am indebted to Sr. Lucille Coldrick, RDC who gave me the opportunity to mingle and discuss educational philosophy issues with the students and faculty of Preston High School. My gratitude also goes to the following Jesuits - Norrie Clarke, Joseph Koterski, Gerald McCool, and Thomas Hennessy – whose valuable suggestions gave shape to this book at every point. Finally, thanks to the Jesuit Provinces of West Africa and New York for providing me with the space and time necessary to put this volume together.

DEDICATION

To the students and faculty of
Preston High School, Bronx, New York

Table of Contents

List of Tables

List of Figures

INTRODUCTION

Educational systems are responsible institutions whose specificity is to initiate young and other members into intellectual and social life. The intellectual and social heritage offered for the initiation of the young are chosen, developed, and emphasized in educational programs and aims following deliberately chose, dominant, and prevailing values in the society. Hence, education is an interested and purposeful venture. Wingo makes the point thus:

> Ideas about education do not develop in a cultural vacuum. Men's perceptions of any aspect of social life are conditioned by their total background of experience… A person who believes that the ultimate end is eternal salvation is likely to see the function of school in a different light from the person who subscribes to a naturalistic view of man and his place in the world.[1]

If education is a socialization process what is the use of philosophy in such a process? The basic concern of educational practitioners is with educational objectives, curriculum, pedagogy, and administration. What has philosophy to do in these areas? The role of philosophy of education is neither to establish educational objectives nor rules of pedagogy and administration. Rather, philosophy of education guarantees the intelligibility of educational practices by establishing its ultimate causes (experience and associations that led to the system) and grounds (necessary evidence that supports the validity of the system). Philosophy of education asks fundamental questions about educational practices. As Edward Power has it, "it is the business of educational philosophy to probe the fundamental issues of education and to supply some direction with respect to what ought to be done in order to achieve and maintain educational decency."[2] Some of the drawbacks in the practice of education are not due to the fact that educational practitioners are thinking the wrong question. Rather, the errors are due to the lack of profound and clear thinking about the problem themselves. Philosophy is that obstinate discipline that enables the educational questions to be pushed as far as it is philosophically possible. Philosophy of education, therefore, does not volatize educational matters into pure philosophy. Rather it is an application of philosophic methods and principles to education. It is concerned with the development and experience of human beings. So, philosophical inquiry into the ultimate question of educational experience necessarily involves an analysis of human nature and development as constitutive elements of that experience.

As afore mentioned education does not take place in a vacuum. As such, there cannot be an atemporal philosophy of education. Every philosophy of education is a philosophy of this or that system of education. No educational philosophy can be considered a proto-type or pure exemplification of philosophy of education. There are philosophies of education that are not necessarily mutually exclusive. This book is a presentation of myriad ultimate beliefs and their implication for education. Some of them are partly contradictory, partly overlapping in their trends and emphases.

The beauty of presenting such systematic educational philosophies is that it will provide guidance for those engaged in education. First, the systematic presentation familiarizes educators with authors, their points of view, and the fresh insights they bring to educational problems. Also, the insights of these authors will assist educators in a radical reexamination and reassessment of their educational structure, fundamental propositions, ultimate objectives, and basic procedures. Furthermore, the exposition of different educational philosophies provides an opportunity to appreciate contrasting or similar educational philosophies, their inertia, and development. In other words, this book should draw educators out of their educational ghetto or parochialism into the rainbow of educational philosophies. It should assist them in clarifying their educational philosophies.

This book presents a spectrum of educational philosophies influenced by religion, politics, culture, theory, national consciousness. Chapters 1, 2, and 3 introduce the reader to the dynamics of philosophy of education. It presents a definition of philosophy of education, traces its history in broad strokes, and outlines some of the building blocks of educational philosophy. Each chapter brings to light the ultimate questions in the practice and study of education. As such, they constitute good starting points for organizing the theories and philosophies that enlighten them. Chapter 4 presents an educational philosophy that is crafted from activities of an interest group, namely, feminism. Feminism, like multiculturalism and post-colonialism, challenges the traditional emphases of educational philosophy. Chapter 5 introduces the reader to a faith inspired philosophy of education, that is, an educational philosophy with a spiritual vision. It integrates elements of religion or faith with the elements of secular education. The aim is not to change the dynamics of one or the other but to give education a spirituality. Chapters 6, 7, and 8 present traditional philosophies of education, namely, idealist, existentialist, and Marxist philosophies of education, respectively. They show how educational philosophies are elaborated from systems of thought.

[1]Wingo, G. M. (1965). *The philosophy of American education*. Lexington, MA: Heath.

[2]Power, E. J. (1982). *Philosophy of education. Studies in philosophies, schooling, and educational policy*. Englewood Cliffs, NJ: Prentice-Hall, p. xii.

CHAPTER 1

GENERAL PHILOSOPHY OF EDUCATION

General philosophy and philosophy of education are closely related in purpose in that both are concerned with ultimate reality and meaning. Also, both disciplines are brought into direct relationship in that both use the same methods. Philosophy of education postulates a strong link between philosophy and education as is evident in the history of philosophy and the overall praxis of education. There is philosophy behind every educational system inasmuch as philosophy concerns itself with the views and values of the educators and the society that is sponsoring the education. To explain this connection the present section will look at the nature and aims of philosophy, education, and philosophy of education.

NATURE AND AIM OF PHILOSOPHY

Philosophy is a term that cannot be easily captioned in a unique formula. This is because philosophy is an umbrella term used to cover myriad intellectual inquiries that rely quasi exclusively on reason alone rather than other sources of knowledge such as tradition, divine revelation, etc., and strives after generalities rather than particulars. "It is a paradox faced by all of those who attempt to write the history of philosophy that the 'philosophy' of the history they write probably would not have been defined exactly alike by any two of the major figures whom they judge fitting to include in their accounts. For throughout its long and varied history in the West, 'philosophy' has meant many different things."[1] Examples of these variations in the definition of philosophy abound. For Greek Socratics philosophy is "the love of wisdom." Wisdom stands for any exercise of overall integrating intelligence in any sphere. For idealism philosophy is a through examination of the origin, extent, and validity of people's ideas. Honer, Hunt, and Okholm also suggest other uses of the term: "Some regard philosophy as the name for a subject area of study; some prefer to use the term to identify an individual's general approach to life; others see philosophy as the identification of the presuppositions underlying a subject matter."[2] Amidst this diversity of definitions, is there any possible thread that runs through all of them? Is there any core meaning that can serve as an all-inclusive definition of philosophy? A tentative attempt in this direction is to define philosophy as "the rational, methodical, and systematic consideration of those topics that are of greatest concern to man."[3] From the above definition we have a first aspect of the composite definition of philosophy as an activity.

Philosophy As A Cognitive Activity

Philosophy is a rational activity in the sense that it strives to arrive at knowledge and truth through reason rather than through empirical confirmation. Philosophy is a rational discipline because it looks for logical connections. The requirements for logical connections include: consistency (ideas forming part of an answer are not conflictual), coherence (ideas forming part of an answer hang together and are relevant to each other rather than just co-existing), and adequacy (ideas forming part of an answer apply to all phenomena under consideration and not just to some). Philosophy is systematic in that once the foundations of a discipline have been identified it begins to understand complex and dynamic situations in broad outlines, always defining these realities at levels of abstraction or as concepts. Berlin makes the point thus: "Philosophy is a critical examination not of what exists or has existed or will exist – this is dealt with by ordinary opinions and the natural sciences – but of the ways in which they are viewed or conceived; not of the items of experience but of the categories in terms of which they are conceived and classified."[4] Hence, philosophy is that mental activity of creating categories, frames, spectacles, and models by which human beings and their experiences can be understood in depth. Philosophy is a methodical activity in the sense that it specifies procedures in its inquiry in order to establish the ultimate foundations of any discipline.

The reasoned techniques employed by philosophy are clarification and rational justification. The clarificatory role of philosophy lies in proffering the rules for clear thinking about an issue or a problem at hand. Rational justification means that philosophy grounds the issue by giving reasons for a proposed solution of the problem at hand. Is the public's constant demand for justification of educational policy and practice not a familiar refrain? Justification is subjecting one's educational beliefs and practices to rational scrutiny. Pratte (1992) underscores a usefulness of philosophical clarification and justification in education as follows: "A close examination of selected educational concepts may lead teachers, administrators, and laypersons to a deeper understanding necessary for the attainment of sound and justified educational policy and practice. A clear understanding of the concept of education, for example, can have a powerful influence on the making of judicious educational decisions."[5] Philosophy that clarifies and justifies makes practitioners advance in their subject inquiry in a promising way.

Philosophy as such is unique in that it has the whole of reality and the place of human beings within it as its subject matter, unlike other disciplines which limit themselves to particular areas of inquiry. But philosophy does have a special point of view on this broad subject matter, namely, to inquire into the universal foundational principles and laws governing all of reality, what makes it ultimately intelligible as a coherent whole, especially regarding the nature and meaning of human beings in the universe.

This general philosophy can then become applied philosophy when it takes on the limited subject matter of other disciplines and applies its own general conclusion to a deeper more critical analysis of them to other areas of inquiry. This is the case of when a subject is expressed in a way that it includes the preposition 'of', for example, philosophy of history, philosophy of religion, and in our case, philosophy of education. The task of Philosophy "is not to add to our knowledge of the primary subject matter explored by various branches of substantive inquiry... The task of Philosophy is to be a critique of cognitive claims, with the intent, in part, to purge our ideas and beliefs of unclear and dubious assumptions, in part, to make us self-conscious about the nature and grounds of our intellectual commitments, and in part to enlarge the angle of our vision by suggesting alternative ways to unreflective habitual ones and for organizing and bringing into mutual relationships various detailed portions of our knowledge."[6]

Philosophy, therefore, establishes the foundations of any discipline, groups the findings into a system of concepts by establishing logical connections between and among the concepts. Thus the specific task of philosophy "is to examine categories, concepts, models, ways of thinking or acting… images and systems of categories."[7] Berlin further specifies that "the task of philosophy, and it is often a difficult and painful one, is to extricate and bring to light the hidden categories and models in terms of which human beings think, to analyze clearly what is obscure or contradictory in them, to discern the conflict between them that prevent the construction of more adequate ways of organizing and explaining experience… and then at a still more abstract level, to examine the nature of this explaining activity itself, and to bring to light the concealed models that operate in the second order activity itself."[8]

What possible explanation can be offered to the lack of consensus among philosophers concerning the definition of philosophy? A plausible reason is that those who find it necessary to philosophize come from different backgrounds and fields, and are motivated by different interests and concerns. St. Thomas Aquinas, a Catholic Dominican of 13th century, George Berkeley, Bishop of the Irish Church in 18th century, and Søren Kierkegaard, a Danish divinity student of 19th century all saw philosophy as a way of defending the intelligibility of the truths of religion and fighting the rationalistic and materialistic challenges that belittled religious truths. Pythagoras in ancient Italy, René Descartes of late Renaissance, and Bertrand Russell of the 20th century are primarily mathematicians whose reasoning about the world and human knowledge has been influenced by the distinctive concepts and modes of reasoning of mathematics as the science of numbers. Plato, Thomas Hobbes, and John Stuart Mill are primarily interested in political arrangement. Whatever they have done for philosophy is motivated by the desire to ultimately affect the political behavior of humans. From the above, it follows that the shades in the definition of philosophy come about because philosophers reflect on and reason from their peculiar worldviews. The lack of consensus concerning the content of philosophy is not to be taken tragically. Rather, it should be considered as a suggestion that philosophy has different hypotheses to explore in its search for the adequate intelligibility of human life and the world as a coherent whole.

From the above presentation it can be concluded that philosophy is an activity of inquiry: wondering, criticizing, questioning, synthesizing. Philosophy is an activity of inquiry which is undogmatic, open-minded, and willing to be guided by reason, persistent search, reflective unemotional inquiry, and disinterested interest. Philosophy is also a method of inquiry which is logical, deductive, inductive, abductive, and dialectical. Philosophy is not a body of knowledge of a positive kind such as law, biology, or history but an activity of clarifying, a technique of thinking, a search for ultimate foundational principles for understanding anything.

Philosophy As Content: Fields of Philosophy

Philosophy in general has traditionally been divided into the following areas of investigation: metaphysics, anthropology, natural philosophy, epistemology, and axiology which includes ethics.

The first field of philosophy is metaphysics. Metaphysics asks the question: What is real? Metaphysics inquires into the nature of existence. Hence, answers to the metaphysical question are sine qua non for the other specific questions about reality. If the metaphysical question remains unanswered then it is impossible to answer questions about knowing the reality let alone talking about its value. Metaphysical inquiry about existence focuses on general characteristics that are universal in what is real, including the laws of interaction between beings and the ultimate categories into which reality is divided. Metaphysics, as a subject that deals with that which is 'beyond physics,' can be defined as a study of ultimate reality. 'Beyond physics' is what is first and last. Hence, metaphysics studies the origin and destiny of realities as part of knowing the nature of the reality.

Metaphysics has four branches – cosmology, ontology, anthropology, and natural theology – which address different problems. Cosmology is a persistent inquiry into the origin, structure, and purpose of the universe in which human beings find themselves and of which they are part. It seeks to discover what is true about the universe. Ontology studies being, that which is. It analyzes being with the aim of discovering valid relationships and distinctions. Anthropology studies the nature and fundamental properties of human beings and seeks to avoid or go beyond approaches that regard humans as mere scientific objects. Natural theology is a reasoned discourse about God. It deals with the existence and nature of God and God's relationship with the universe and especially the human beings that dwell within it.

Metaphysics is crucial in decisions about education. For example, from the anthropological perspective "it makes a great deal of difference for education," states Knight "if a student is viewed as 'Desmond Morris' 'naked ape' or as a 'child of God'. Likewise, it is important to know whether children are essentially good as is asserted by Rousseau's Emile, or whether their goodness has been radically twisted by the effects of sin as Christian thinkers think. Variation in anthropological positions leads to significantly different approaches to the educational process."[9] Ward's questions go in a similar line: "In the enterprise of education, what is the most important factor? What has most of all to be taken into account? Man, of course."[10] Ward later concludes, "in short, the general philosophy of man and mind and life and nature is sure to influence philosophy of education and the practice of education."[11] The cosmological aspect will in part define the purpose of education. Isn't the distinction between confessional and public schools rooted in the philosophy of God?

In brief, philosophy has far reaching effects on the nature of the educational system, defining expectations for the educational community, and determining the content of curriculum. Philosophy will probe the nature and general characteristics of any educational system. As such, the office of philosophy in education is to explain the facts or reality about a given educational system. Enshrined in this role is an implied office of guaranteeing recommendations for education based on the facts. For example, if corruption is the real cankerworm that erodes an educational system metaphysical reflection will ponder and state the fact of educational corruption and recommend solutions for the problem. Besides explaining the facts and guaranteeing the recommendations of education, philosophical theories also supplement the facts in a way. The supplementation of educational facts by theory provides the basis for recommendations made about the system. Furthermore, the philosophical view chosen has important bearings on the explanation of the facts of education and the recommendations proffered. Such an inquiry is not an idle curiosity but a critical challenge undertaken to understand and improve the educational system.

The next main field of philosophy is *epistemology*. Epistemology designates inquiries into the origin, nature, and limitation of knowledge. It answers the question: How do we know? Implicit in this question are other questions: Can knowledge be gained from pure reason or experience or both or neither? Must knowledge always be a logical derivation? Are there foundational truths that constitute the basis for knowledge? Also, epistemology wants to know what can be known. That is, epistemology studies theories of knowledge. Epistemology wants to know if there is anything that can be known with certainty. It wants to know the nature of the relationship between things as they are perceived and as they are in themselves. Epistemology seeks to separate what is true from what is false. Finally, epistemology attempts to answer the question: What counts as knowledge? That is, it wants to know the definition of knowledge. It seeks to understand what justifies the appellation knowledge. In sum, other disciplines and sciences equally shed light on the question: What is known? As such, they overlap with epistemological inquiry. However, what distinguishes epistemology as a philosophical discipline different from others that seek to explain the knowledge is that epistemology is interested in the criteria to be used to determine what is known from what is unknown.

What is the importance of epistemology for education? Classroom teachers who evaluate students daily are interested in the question: What does it mean for a student to know? When should a student be credited with knowing? Should teachers insist that the material they are teaching is true? Can an epistemological argument be made for making knowledge accessible to all students? What is the relationship between knowledge and power? Epistemology is the subject in which the teacher has to find guidance. Theories and sub-theories abound in epistemology. It is important for teachers to know some of them so as to evaluate the material they teach and the methods that are recommended to them.

Also, the choice of philosophy determines what is taught (content) and how it is taught (pedagogy). In other words, epistemology is preoccupied with the nature of knowledge and the nature of the procedures necessary to acquire such knowledge. By reflecting on the method by which knowledge can be secured "some philosophers have derived from epistemological reflection a theory of learning and instruction, and a consequent recommendation of it, from the methods epistemology lays down… Epistemological reflection on education attempts to derive from a study of the method of knowledge and of their nature a description for procedure by which learning may be furthered, and a consequent recommendation that such course, should be pursued in schools."[12] Hatcher makes the point in the case of Plato as follows:

That there is a close relationship between one's favored epistemology and educational practice is not a new idea. In some cases, epistemology seems to determine to a large degree the person's educational philosophy. For example, Plato's Republic can be understood as an attempt to work out an educational system that will best equip students to achieve Plato's specific epistemological goals; these are the understanding of the general ideas or "Forms" necessary for intelligent judgment in both theoretical and practical matters.[13]

The attainment of 'Form' determines the way Plato structured education. In early childhood he programmed subjects like art, music, and poetry that sharpen the appreciation of reasoned arguments. After this, students are offered subjects like math, astronomy, and geometry which deal with abstractions which is the realm of the 'Forms'. Hence, Plato's epistemology determines how education is structured as well as his pedagogy.

The third main field of philosophy is axiology. Axiology is an inquiry into the nature of values and valuation. The axiological question with which philosophy deals is: What is valuable? Which values should society uphold? Axiology, therefore, begins by defining values, how they are determined, and the standards for value. Axiological inquiry is not interested in the denotation of valuable things (listing valuable things) but in their connotation (characteristics of valuable things). There are myriad sets of values such as aesthetic values, economic values, moral values, economic values, and acts and/or objects of art that have high or low value. Axiology, as a philosophical discipline, confines itself to aesthetic values (inquiry into the nature of beauty and ugliness) and ethical values (inquiry into the nature of right and wrong).

Value is a concept that complements but also stands in contrast to the concept of fact. A fact is simply recognized, impersonal, objective, and real. A value is selected, personal, and subjective. For something, an attitude, an ideal, a purpose, or a goal to be of value it must be an object of preference or judged as important. In this case values are defined by human interest. Educational values define educational preferences, underline educational patterns of meaning, and determine the disposition of the educational system towards persons and situations (who should be admitted into the system?).

Axiology describes the preferences of an educational system. It informs others what the educational system is all about. Immanuel Kant wrote that "institutions without concepts are blind."[14] However, axiology does not stop at the revelation of educational intentions but also advances a theory of justification for the choice. Justification means advancing reasons for the validity of the choice of values. As such, axiology can be an important criteria for classifying educational systems or discerning differences in educational systems according to their dominant value-orientation. In light of values as indicators of preferences the thought of educational neutrality or value-free-education is a myth. Value-free-education is not only impossible but it also means that the values held by the stakeholders are not being taught. Every educational system is tendentious and for any person to be operational in it it is imperative to be familiar with the dynamics of that system. Axiology, therefore, offers a comprehensive view of a system like an educational system. The importance of axiology for education cannot be overemphasized. An exposition of the value preferences of an educational system will enlighten parental choice and expectations concerning the system with which they want to be part. Also, value preferences are important for self-realization in that they are polaristic, organic, and serve as normative goals. They are important for evaluation in that they constitute the criteria for appraising a given educational system by serving as guides for investigation and indicators of frustration or satisfaction with the system.

The fields of philosophy – metaphysics, epistemology, anthropology, natural, and axiology – are not written in stone since they overlap. If philosophy is considered as a pursuit of values (axiology) a rational pursuit of such a value system must depend on a general conception of the world in which the values are sought. Such a conception of the world is the subject matter of metaphysics. Metaphysics, for its part, presupposes an investigation into various knowledge claims and methods of thinking from which and by which a general picture of the world can be formulated. Such a knowledge base is the subject matter of epistemology. Hence, the fields of philosophy are convenient distinctions not hard and fast demarcations. The fields of philosophy outline four main lines of philosophical inquiry: inquiry into the ground of existence (metaphysics), inquiry into the nature of the human person (anthropology), and inquiry into the origin and limitations of knowing and knowledge (epistemology), and inquiry into the problem of the purpose and, therefore, of value (axiology).

Philosophy As Attitude:
Methods

Philosophy is also distinguished as method. The question then arises: With regard to method, what is the philosopher's home ground? In which area of method is a philosopher's expertise unique? Philosophy, like other disciplines such as science, analyzes and conceptualizes. However, the peculiarity of philosophy is that it is critical and speculative.

Philosophy is a meta-inquiry (an inquiry about inquiry). "Critical philosophers also accept responsibility for examining and criticizing the fundamental beliefs or basic assumptions held by people as they organize their worlds and express their convictions."[15] Two examples as remarks generally considered as clinching statements will drive home the point. First, the statement 'I saw it with my own eyes' is usually considered a statement to ascertain fact. A philosopher's task here may be that of questioning the reliability of sensory perception. Plato's Theaetetus questions whether 'perception is knowledge' or whether perception is a decisive arbiter for solving a problem. Plato then went on to build a profound theory of perception. A second example, is the commonly held assumption of a necessary connection between cause and effect. It was not until David Hume that this seemingly obvious fact came under fire. Hume wanted to know if cause and effect are the same, different, or both; continuous, discontinuous, or both; independent, dependent, or interdependent. Hume's analysis led him to abandon the cause-effect vocabulary and embrace that of a conjunction or regular sequence of events. Hume's analysis in turn is strongly criticized and reflected by many philosophers.

Philosophy is critical because it proceeds in an intellectually disciplined manner to actively and skillfully analyze, synthesize, and/or evaluate any information. It transcends the subject matter by looking for sound reason, clarity, consistency, and relevance. Critical philosophy examines the structures of thought implicit in all reasoning process: question-at-issue, purpose, concepts, assumptions, implications, and consequences. Critical thinking, therefore, is the skill for processing and generating information. Critical philosophical method is an intellectual commitment to clarify meaning and relate concepts. Critical philosophy contrasts itself with the mere acquisition and retention of knowledge alone. The aim of critical philosophy is not justification but criticism, not to prove theories but to subject them to critical review. Criticism does not make the philosopher a mere fear-dispeller. Rather, the purpose of a philosopher's questioning is a search for profound understanding. Philosophy advances toward a better understanding not by adding any new propositions to its list. Rather philosophy transforms the intellectual scene through analysis thus enabling the problem to be seen in a new way. Through criticism philosophy enables a problem to be seen in a new light, from an alternative perspective. Critical philosophy offers an alternative 'vision' of a problem. The usefulness of philosophy, therefore, as a critical discipline is that it dispels the fear associated with blind adherence to outworn notions, elucidates any irrational suspicion on one's ability to self-examination by assisting people to understand themselves and by so doing operate knowledgeably.

Critical philosophy looks at fundamentals. Its collateral, speculative philosophy, pieces together the fundamentals in order to create the big picture. Speculative philosophy looks at reality synoptically. However, synopsis is not an end in itself. It furnishes the basis for what is called a synthesis. The purpose of the synthesis is to supply a set of concepts and principles which shall cover satisfactorily all the various regions of fact which are being viewed synoptically. Whitehead makes the point sublimely as follows: "Speculative philosophy is an endeavor to frame a coherent, logical, necessary system of general ideas in terms of which every element of our experience can be interpreted".[16] Speculative philosophy, unlike the practical sciences which seek knowledge in order to produce a product or an act, seeks knowledge of the truth for its own sake.

> It is right also that philosophy (speculative science) should be called knowledge of the truth. For the end of theoretical (i.e. speculative) knowledge is truth, while that of practical knowledge is action.[17]

Albeit the knowledge obtained from speculative philosophy is theoretical, such knowledge may be used for practical ends later. Since speculative philosophy has the reason why it can help practical science explain their practical applications. Also, since practical sciences have the reason for which they facilitate the leisure for the speculative. Hence, in the expression speculative philosophy is a germ for praxis.[18]

Critical philosophy analyzes whereas speculative philosophy integrates. Although the methods and the certainty each aims at are different, both methods are not exclusive but complementary. Speculative philosophy, quite clearly, builds on the findings of critical philosophy. Critical philosophy, in turn, tacitly supposes speculative philosophy because any analysis to understand parts is undertaken as a prelude to understand the whole. In light of this, critical philosophy and speculative philosophy can be considered as two extremes of a philosophical methodic continuum. The degree to which their interdependence is thrown in fresh combinations determines the intermediary stages.

Philosophy As A Way Of Life

Etymologically philosophy comes from two Greek words φίλος (philos) meaning love of and σοφία (sophia) meaning wisdom. However, during the course of the centuries, the meaning attached to wisdom has undergone many changes and even present-day thinkers are not completely agreed as to the aims and content of philosophy. For example, according to Pythagoras, a Greek scientist and philosopher, wisdom included know-how in mathematics and astrology, and peculating about the fundamental elements of the universe. For Plato the object of philosophy was the discovery of ultimate truths and reality. In the hands of Socrates the search for wisdom still retained its practical component but changed its focal area. Philosophy was more "interested in the problems of human life and conduct than in scientific speculation. Wisdom was regarded as knowledge for the conduct of life and philosophy was viewed as a way of life, as providing a means of enabling the individual to live the best kind of life."[19]

Philosophy is that discipline that investigates underlying reality, inquires into the nature of basic beliefs, and synthesizes all learning. Philosophy is theoretical (metaphysics, epistemology) in that it seeks to discover the truth not because of its usefulness but for the sake of truth itself. Philosophy also has a practical component (axiology) which is the search for truth in order to act on it. As such philosophy becomes a way of life. The critical and speculative methods are its choicest methods. The philosophical cube below summarizes the complex reality that goes on in any philosophical unfolding.

Nature And Aim Of Education

Education is an activity "that happens in and over time; it is something that people engage in, more or less, deliberately. It is something that people try to achieve by doing other things (for example, going to college) and in doing things to others."[20] Four elements of education stand out from this definition: education is a human growth process, an instruction, an art and discipline, and a product.

Education As Process Of Human Growth

Questioning educators about what they are doing with their students the refrain that runs through their answer is that they are aiding their students to develop their talents and capacities. 'To develop' is not a growth process to be understood malignantly in the comparative sense as an absence of adult maturity in the students or regarding their talents and capacities as dormant and awaiting reawakening. 'To develop,' in a benign educational sense, is considered positively and intrinsically as the ability to grow, to acquire effective intellectual habits and dispositions. Bertrand Russell makes the point poignantly: "Education, in the sense in which I mean it, may be defined as the formation, by means of instruction, of certain mental habits and a certain outlook on life and the world."[21] Education, in light of the above, answers the question: what is the nature of the process one undergoes as one acquires effective intellectual habits and dispositions?

The kinds of things that go on in education as a developmental process are limited to human becoming through learning. Human growth and learning are, therefore, crucial in defining the process of education. Education is learning in that "what is learnt is worthwhile to the learner and usually (in contrast to training) where it is learned in such a way that the learner can express his own individuality through what he learns and can subsequently apply it, and adapt it flexibly to situations and problems other than those he considered in learning it."[22] This is where education, as learning a process, departs from rearing, training, and indoctrination. Education is enabling "individuals to continue their education – the object and reward of learning is the continued capacity for growth."[23] Education bears traces of self-education whereas training and indoctrination depict the mind as a receptacle into which knowledge can be poured. This falsifies the authentic nature of education as process.

Ward reinforces this stance when he says that "the view that education is self-education, no matter how much and how well education is prompted by teachers and other extrinsic aids, is a doctrine common to all who have ever tried to say a philosophical word on what it is to learn and to educate."[24] Alfred North Whitehead affirms the idea of education as a process of enabling self-development by flagging a danger of rote learning: Education "must beware of what I call 'innate ideas,' that is to say, ideas that are merely received into the mind without being utilized, or tested, or thrown into fresh combinations."[25] Education, as a process of intellectual growth, is characterized by an increasing capacity of the student to deal with several alternatives simultaneously. Education is also a transition from a one-track mind to dealing with complex reality. It is, therefore, not grotesque to say that learning, getting educated happens within the student not in the teacher. Also, education is restricted to humans, creatures with minds, rational creatures, people. Animals can be taught, they can learn, but they cannot be educated. It would be more appropriate to call the learning undergone by human beings instruction.

From the point of view of the learner, therefore, education is growth because it deals with acquired characteristics and not inherent or innate characteristics. As such, it is the task of education to *'update'* people. The etymology of education includes elements of the growth process. Etymologically 'to educate' means to lead or bring out. That which is brought out and developed are human capabilities which education awakens, nourishes, and exercises. Education is a conscious evolution. Education is characterized by increasing self-independence, self-accounting, and a transition from mere orderly behavior to an eventual recognition of a logical necessity. Education leads students to accept certain values as important. Education, in a narrow sense, means the development of capacities that are valuable, not pernicious. Education is a personal and transformative venture because its end result is to take care of an individual's well-being.

Education As Instruction

From the point of view of teachers education means instruction, that is, an effort to assist or shape the growth process of the learner. Hence, it is the flip side of learning. Instruction is both an art and a discipline. The assistance that instruction offers in the educational process can be considered from four vantage points: predisposing, structuring, sequencing, and reinforcing.

Predisposing is understood as the manner in which instruction facilitates and regulates the exploration of alternatives by the learner. Instruction must do something to get the learning started (activation), to keep it going (maintenance), and to keep it focused (direction). Also, it is the task of instruction to present the body of knowledge to be learned in a recognizable form to the learner. This is what is described as optimal structuring. Optimal structuring involves a particular mode of presenting the material to be learned, economy of presentation (amount of knowledge to be held in mind and processes to achieve growth), and effective power of structuring (generative value of learned dispositions). Furthermore, instruction involves sequencing. Sequence focuses on leading the learner through problems or a body of knowledge that increases the learner's ability to grasp, transform, and transfer what has been learned. Finally, instruction must take into consideration pacing reinforcements (rewards/punishments).

Education, from the standpoint of the instructor, is the art and discipline of predisposing students to learning, structuring, and sequencing the material to be learned, and reinforcing the learning. "Education is not a transfer of knowledge; it is to guide the learning process, to put the responsibility for study into the student's own hands. It is not a piecemeal merchandization of information; it is the provision of the keys that will allow people to unlock the vault of knowledge on their own."[26] Instruction is not a retail of information or fact feeding but assumes a supporting role in students' learning experience. In this case the teacher is a thinking expert who guides students. As the popular adage has it, the instructor is a guide by the side not a sage on the stage.

Education As A Sociopolitical Instantiation

Education can also be defined from the point of view of the principal educational provider or agency. The education enterprise is not a haphazard process. It is a deliberate mode of activity oriented toward producing certain kinds of results. As a purposive enterprise education is realized through particular molds or schools cast by the organizers. Hence, education, in a secondary sense, is a sociopolitical institution dependent on the primary sense which is the process of human learning. Institutions or instantiations are dependent because what they are or should be is derived from what that education pursues or is supposed to pursue. Hence, there can be a Christian education, public education, liberal education, Cameroonian education, and American education. Institutions bear the responsibility for education, hence education policy. Institutions decide who should be educated (admission policies), the content of education (curriculum), and the role the school should play (cultural option).

From the social function of education as a sociopolitical institution it follows that education is normative because it harbors the standards for what is desirable and acceptable as education. In light of this education is "systematic socialization" as David Emil Durkeim defines it.[27] Educational institution formulates and clarifies the purpose of education. The institutional consideration of education emphasizes the social task of education because education searches for educational values within the local environment.

Education As Product Or Aim

The deadlock in which education finds itself today in many countries is a result of the fact that politicians and national leaders feel that it is enough to state the goals of education. Most of them never consider concretely how these goals are to be met. Hence, to define education as aims one must also tackle the question of means as inherent in aims. Every process or institution has its peculiar ends not achieved or achievable by any other institution but that institution alone. Such ends make the institution an institution sui generis and autonomous.

Education, as a human growth process and as a sociopolitical institution, focuses on the shaping and maturing of persons in society, by society, and for society. Students deliberately undertake the task of education because they want to acquire, through learning, desirable dispositions and habits. Societies establish and support schools because there is something they wish the schools to accomplish. Aims for education are, therefore, quintessential in any definition of education because one will "decline to call anything education unless it fosters or is intended to foster desirable dispositions and not undesirable ones, and this is the usage which is important for the philosophy of education."[28] Dewey reinforces this point by saying that "the net conclusion is that acting with an aim is all one with acting intelligently. To foresee a terminus of an act is to have a basis upon which to observe, to select, and to order objects and our own capacities."[29] Aims of education are, therefore, expressions of broad human concerns or desires.

To sum up, education is a personal and transforming venture because its end result is to nourish an individual's well-being. Also, education is a social and normative institution because it is a great concern for society requiring special instruments and organization like schools which justify its claim to be regarded as an institution. The above elaboration of education presents a three-fold definition of education: the nature of education (growth and instruction), the orientation of education (sociopolitical institution), and the aims of education (desired results and means to them).

NATURE OF PHILOSOPHY OF EDUCATION

Philosophy of education is concerned with applying the general conclusions of philosophy to the field of education. This involves building systems of ideas concerning the nature of education, investigating the purpose of education as a social institution, and with clarifying the meaning of educational concepts.[30]

Defining Philosophy Of Education

Philosophy of education lends to a belief that there is a necessary relationship between the two disciplines. But "just what this relationship is constitutes one of the controversies in educational theory today."[31]

To the question: What is philosophy of education? McClellan hesitates to offer a definition because "many otherwise sensible men and women turn quite silly when they try to answer the question. I've no reason to think that I shall succeed where others have failed, but I am obliged to make the effort."[32] Price offers one reason for this pessimism concerning the definition of philosophy of education. "This vagueness of the phrase 'philosophy of education' consists in the absence of a boundary marking off philosophies of education from other theories."[33] According to Price, philosophy of education has no subject matter of its own since it takes the narrated educational experience of other educational disciplines as given and reflectively inquires into their meaning. As a mixed science philosophy of education has no clear contours. Smith mentions another difficulty stemming from many definitions of philosophy and education. "If there are many ways of conceiving philosophy and many ways of conceiving education, it follows that there must be many, many ways of conceiving philosophy of education. It might prove interesting and rewarding to develop systematically the possible permutations."[34] Despite the seeming optimism of this approach Smith is quick to note that the number of topics and permutations makes this approach impossible to manage.[35]

Since defining the contours of philosophy of education and interfacing philosophy and education have not yielded significant progress in the definition of philosophy of education defining it by discrimination may prove useful. This is a way of understanding philosophy of education by highlighting what it does differently from other humanities of education like psychology, pedagogy, sociology, history, and administration.

Psychology of education "deals with the specific qualities of human beings as they manifest themselves in the learning process in schools and in life itself. As education is organized it is necessary to understand, too, the part the teacher plays in the process."[36] Psychology of education answers questions like: Is experience necessary in education? What is rationalization, intelligence, common sense, imagination and its relationship to memory? Psychology of education differs from philosophy of education in focus and scope. Concerning focus psychology of education is a systematic observation of and experimentation on human behavior in educational settings and subjecting these findings to theoretical scrutiny. Philosophy of education, on the contrary is not a fact-gathering process but a coordination and clarification of data already collected by other disciplines. With regard to scope educational psychology restricts itself to well-defined behavioral theories whereas educational philosophy crosses boundaries and borrows the theories of other disciplines like sociology to establish itself. Hence, educational philosophy is more far-ranging in the use of theories than educational psychology.

Sociology discusses social factors in education and answers questions like: does education aim at direct social results? What are the socio-educational institutions? What are the social problems and questions that have a direct bearing on education? The difference between educational sociology and educational philosophy is the same as what was said about educational psychology. History of education wants to know what education was in the past. What is the significance of social inheritance for education? The historian and philosopher of education are interested in an analysis of past educational experience. However, they differ in the kind of report they want to present from such an analysis. The historian wants to produce a more factual and accessible report whereas the philosopher is interested in constructing a conceptual report. The historian wants to know what happened in the experience called education. The focus is on events, particulars. The philosopher asks depth questions and the focus is on basic patterns, categories, ideas, generalities, and the implication thereof which underlie and render meaningful the whole process of education.

Pedagogy of education grapples with questions of methods and means such as: What is meant by teaching and learning method? Administration of education is busy with the educational machinery: organization and finance. It answers questions like: What is the nature of the educational system? Who pays for education? Are experts necessary in this educational system? Pedagogy and administration of education analyze the principles of education primarily to provide guidance for educational practitioners. The primary purpose of philosophy of education is interpretation and understanding of educational practice; application is only a secondary purpose. Also, pedagogy and administration are interested in principles designated as the best by educational theory. Educational philosophy, on the contrary, is not immediately interested in the best principle but in the assumptions or premise that underlie the best practices.

Philosophy of education attempts "to find the meaning of the whole educational process as it takes" shape in history, sociology, administration, and the other humanities.[37] Philosophy of education attempts to give an inclusive answer to the question: What is the precise meaning of all these fragmented aspects of education? What is the final truth that does justice to all the other aspects of education? Philosophy of education is interested in the ends and purposes of education. Hence, the answer given by philosophy of education must give unity to the truths of the other disciplines of education. Philosophy of education has no new facts of its own about education to consider. Rather it considers the old facts of the other disciplines of education in its own way. Philosophy of education questions the significance of the facts already discovered in other disciplines of education in the light of the ends of education. Philosophy of education wants to know what the discoveries of other fields of education suggest about the ultimate nature of education. In a way, philosophy of education demands consistency of purpose in the educational arrangement.

In brief, what does it mean to philosophize in education? It means a reasoned and systematic engagement in a meta-analysis and synthesis of educational findings with the hope of understanding the ultimate meaning of the educational system. Philosophy of education is a systematic discussion of educational problems at a philosophical level, that is, probing educational problems until they are reduced to their ultimate meaning – what is really true, valuable, and real about the system. Philosophy of education takes educational reflection beyond the common sense level by correcting and refining it. It encourages the educational community not merely to hold its nose to the grindstone. According to Thomas Moore, "philosophers of education, then, are concerned with a scrutiny of what is said about education by those who practice it and those who theorize about it."[38] So if one considers educational practice and theory as groundwork, philosophy of education is a higher-ordered activity based on it. Philosophy of education also aims at presenting the overall objectives, content, and strategy of education in terms of a consistent and integrated organization. Philosophy of education offers a reasoned panoramic view of education.

Educational Philosophy is Theoretical and Applied

Conventional theoretical or speculative disciplines busy themselves with the nature of reality. The theoretical discipline of metaphysics describes what is. For example, it may tell us something about the reality of the school, learning process, and curriculum. History of education is also theoretical and describes these same realities in terms of what they were. Theoretical disciplines fall short of any immediate practical relevance because they only describe educational reality, offer information about the real state of educational affairs without any interest in stating guidelines for practical action. Normative philosophy develops from obtained speculative knowledge and asks questions about what is good, beautiful, and the best organization for the educational enterprise described. Hence, prescriptive philosophy focuses on what ought to be without any interest in the steps necessary to translate this knowledge to action.

Philosophy of education does not stop with the description of the ultimate causes and principles of education. Philosophy of education is not only interested in theoretical knowledge about education but it is also interested in the difference that this kind of knowledge can make in the practice of education. Hence, philosophy of education can be described as an applied discipline because it puts into practice or uses practically the principles and concepts derived from and based on theoretical and normative educational philosophy. Philosophy of education is an applied discipline because it uses the theories and principles of first-order and second-order knowledge to study educational practice.

Philosophy of education generates three hierarchical levels of knowledge. First-order knowledge is produced by answering fundamental questions about an educational enterprise. Examples of such questions are: what is real, true, and factual about this system of education? First-order knowledge constitutes the foundation of the educational system in question. From the foundational knowledge principles can be developed concerning the good and the beautiful in the educational enterprise. This is second-order knowledge. From the educational principles educational policies and practices can be constructed. Policy and practice are third-order knowledge because they are dependent on previously established theories and principles. Wherever educational philosophers work they navigate the spheres of theory, principle, and practice. Theory establishes general foundations of education. Principles translate the general theories into particular educational systems. Policy and practice bring the principle into the classroom to affect the teaching-learning process. By balancing theory and practice educational philosophy takes seriously the dictum that: theory without practice is lame; practice without theory is blind. Sometimes the establishment of practical knowledge may be the preponderant focus of an educational philosophy. In this case practical knowledge is the immediate cause. At other times the focal interest may be to establish evidence concerning the educational enterprise. In this case, theory is the immediate final cause and practice the remote final cause of the educational enterprise.

Philosophy of education is not only a theoretical discipline. It is not the private domain of philosophers who have only a tangential interest in education. Neither is philosophy of education only an applied discipline carried out by educators disinterested in philosophy. Philosophy of education is both a theoretical and applied discipline. Educational problems and issues are neither that commonsensical nor do they depend on trial and error in a way that they do not need the enlightenment of philosophy. Philosophy of education is the domain of "philosophers who really work at education, and educators who really work at philosophy."[39] Proficiency in education and philosophy are indispensable to do philosophy of education.

Approaches To Philosophy of Education

How can students be introduced to a study of philosophy of education? This section proposes the following approaches: historical, thematic, typological, and systematic.

Historical Approach

The historical approach to educational philosophy is not a naïve narrative of past educational events. Rather it is an interpretation or reconstruction of past educational practices. This approach explores educational arrangements and the thoughts of acknowledged philosophers concerning basic educational issues. The study is usually chronological in order and focuses on the major works of philosophers who have made significant contributions to education. One purpose of this approach is to familiarize students with the valuable contributions of each philosopher to education. This approach is exemplified in Chapter III of this book entitled *Philosophy of Education in Historical Perspective.* In galloping pace the chapter studies the evolution of educational thought, plans, theories, and organization through the works of Plato, Rousseau, and Dewey. Three authors who have privileged this route are William Frankena in *Three Historical Philosophies of Education,* Adrian Dupuis in *Philosophy of Education in Historical Perspectives,* and Edward Power in *Educational Philosophy: A History from the Ancient World to Modern America.* Educational historians are interested in the scope, forms, approaches, and assumptions underlying educational practice. Their particular focus is on the aims and purposes of education.

An advantage of the historical approach is that it offers students an opportunity to develop a sense of the historicity or long-range perspective of educational problems. That is, it gives students an understanding of where an educational system is coming from, where it is now, and where it is heading. Following on this the student will understand the roots, forms, continuities and discontinuities, and shades of current educational problems and past solutions. A historical reconstruction of past educational practice brings with it new insight and better understanding of the forces at work in an educational system.

A setback of the historical perspective is that it requires the beginning student to acquire a solid historical and philosophical background. This disadvantage becomes even more acute if the interest of the beginning student is to acquire basic educational principles that are necessary to be an effective practitioner here and now.

Thematic Approach

The thematic approach is an engagement of philosophical methods to study issues and problems of education. Examples of issues that can be analyzed are the goals of education, social role of schools, school types, and nature of the educational process. Since the problems are approached philosophically it is to be expected that the thematic approach will touch on assumptions that make the educational system meaningful or the concepts that constitute the framework for understanding the system. The specificity of this approach is that each problem is treated with a certain amount of independence. That is, the educational problem is allowed to stand on its own authority without reference to a specific system or historical context.

The philosophical interest in the thematic approach is to explain why the problem is problematic. Educational philosophy may do this by producing relevant evidence relating to the problem. In this light educational philosophy is synoptic. Educational philosophy may probe the adequacy of the evidence thus making it a critical discipline. Finally, educational philosophy may establish logical connections between evidence and problem; hence, it is systematic. This approach is exemplified in Chapter II of this book entitled *Developing a Philosophy of Education*. The chapter outlines educational problems that form the building blocks for constructing a philosophy of education. Philosophers who have embraced the problem approach include Philip Phenix's *Philosophy of Education*, Harry Broudy's *Building a Philosophy of Education*, and Thomas W. Moore's *Philosophy of Education. An Introduction*.

An advantage of the thematic approach is that it challenges students to get involved in thinking about educational issues with an open mind and an inquiring perspective. This attitude is crucial in developing any philosophy of education. For an educational practitioner the problem approach has immediate practical relevance in that it clarifies educational problems. Such a clarification is an important first step in thinking out solutions to such problems. A drawback of this approach is that it offers the student only a myopic view of education. It fails to give the student a systemic or overall view of the educational enterprise of which the problem is part.

Typological Approach

The typological approach is a study of philosophy of education which takes the provider or educational agency as a criterion for classification. This is the approach of Chapter Four of this book. This chapter deals with faith-inspired philosophy of education. The typological approach is similar to the problem-solving approach with a difference in that the typological approach attaches a name to the problem under review. Hence, the problem is proper to Catholic educational philosophy or the like.

A merit of this approach is that it provides an opportunity for a comparative study of educational issues thus putting them in a broader perspective and light. An example of this approach is Brian Holmes' *Problems in Education. A Comparative Approach* in which he undertakes a national comparative study of education in the United States of America, England, Wales, Russia, and Japan. The danger of this approach is that a label of an educational provider may be attributed to a problem as its peculiar problem whereas it is a problem that cuts through educational types. This danger can be described as artificial forcing.

Systematic Approach

The systematic approach is a study of 'schools of thought' or movements in educational philosophy. It focuses on the fundamental questions and concepts elaborated by these 'schools'. Hence, there are 'schools' like Philosophical Anthropology in Education which question the necessity of education for life or Existential Philosophy of Education which want to know the human condition that is important for education. The systematic approach is the conventional manner in which textbooks and courses of educational philosophy are organized. Systematic philosophy of education develops a tenuous educational position by introducing coherence into educational ideas that would otherwise remain uncoordinated. Hence, the approach has the advantage of providing the beginning student with insight into a coherent system of thought and to the basic assumptions, principles, and concepts that are consequential on it. The systematic approach then may be a good window of opportunity for the beginner. However, the advantages of the systematic approach may backfire when the orientation that a 'school of thought' offers becomes a source of prejudice for the beginner. Philip Phenix highlights this danger thus, "the other reason for not using the traditional systems is that they sometimes tend to arrest rather than stimulate thought. When educational problems are analyzed in the light of certain standard philosophies, undiscriminating readers may easily confuse labels and stereotypes with real understanding."[40]

Practically, it is quasi impossible to have an educational philosophy rooted exclusively in one approach. It is not possible to have a history of education, for example, which is not thematic, systematic, or both. This book, as is already evident, is a compounded approach to educational philosophy.

SUMMARY

An adequate philosophy of education embraces and works with all truths that determine the educative process since its principal objective is to scrutinize these educational truths. The end result of the scrutiny is that philosophy of education determines (theoretical) or supplies (applied) basic principles that guide the choice of educational aims, selection and management of curriculum content, and selection of appropriate educational method in the case of conflict. In a way, philosophy of education can be likened to a *clearinghouse* that establishes the ultimate nature, meaning, and guiding principles of educational reality.

[1] *The History of Western Philosophy in Encyclopedia Britannica, vol. V.* (1994). Chicago: Encyclopedia Britannica, Inc. p; 733.

[2] Honer, S., Hunt, T. & Okholm, D. (1991). *Invitation to philosophy. Issues and options.* California: Wadsworth Publishing Company. p. 1).

[3] *Encyclopedia of Britannica, Vol. V. p. 733.*

[4] Berlin, I. (1969). *A 'dangerous but important activity'.* In M. van Cleve (Ed.). *Modern movements in educational philosophy (pp. 9-11).* Boston, MA: Houghton Mifflin Company.

[5] Pratte, R. (1992). *Philosophy of education: Two traditions.* Springfield, IL: Charles C. Thomas Publishers.

[6] Nagel, E. *'Philosophy in educational research'. in The theory and practice of education.* Vol. II. By Hartnett, A. & Nish, M. (eds.).(1976). London: Heinemann Educational Books Ltd.

[7] Berlin, *op. cit.,, p. 10.

[8] Berlin, *op. cit.,, p. 10.

[9] Knight, G. R. (1998). *Philosophy and education. An introduction in Christian perspective.* Berrien Springs, MI: Andrews University Press.

[10] Ward, L. R. (1963). *Philosophy of education.* Chicago: Henry Regnery Company. p. 11.

[11] Ward, L. R. *op. cit.,, p. 23.

[12] Price, K. (1962). *Education and philosophical thought.* Boston, MA: Allyn & Bacon. pp. 14-5.

[13] Hatcher, D. L. [online] *Epistemology and education: A case for fallibilism.* www.bekeru.edu/html/crit/litereature/dlh_ct_epistemology.htm.

[14] Kant, I. *Critique of pure reason.* P. 51.

[15] Honer, Hunt, & Okholm, *op. cit.,, p. 8

[16] Whitehead, A. N. (1969). *Process and Reality: An Essay in Cosmology.* New York: Free Press. p. 5.

[17] Aristotle. *Metaphysics II.* 993a, 15.

[18] Cf. Conway, P. H. (1960). *Principles of Education. A Thomistic Approach.* Washington, D. C.: The Thomist Press.

[19] Curtis, S. J. (1968). *An introduction to philosophy of education.* 2nd Ed. London: University Tutorial Press, p. 5

[20] McClellan, J. E. (1976). *Philosophy of education.* Englewood Cliffs, NJ.: Prentice-Hall, Inc. p. 17.

[21] Russell, B. (1917). *Mysticism and logic.* London: George Allen and Unwin. p. 37.

[22] Rowntree, D. (1982). *A dictionary of education.* Totowa, NJ.: Barnes & Noble Books. p. 75.

[23] Dewey, J. *op. cit.,,* p. 117.

[24] Ward, L. R. *op. cit.,,* p. 55.

[25] Whitehead. *Aims of education.* P. 1.

[26] Makiguchi, T. (1989). *Education for creative living: Ideas and proposals.* Trans. By Alfred Birnbaum. Ames: Iowa State University Press. p. 16.

[27] Makiguchi, T. (1989). *op. cit.,* p. 29.

[28] Frankene, W. K. (1965). *Three historical philosophies of education.* Chicago: Scott, Foresman and Company. p. 6.

[29] Dewey, J. *op. cit.,,* p. 120.

[30] Rowntree, D. *op. cit.,,* p. 215.

[31] Depuis, A. M. (1966) *Philosophy of education in historical perspective.* Chicago, IL: Rand McNally and Company. p. 4

[32] McCleelan, J. E. (1976). *Philosophy of education.* Englewood Cliffs, NJ: Prentice-Hall. p. 1.

[33] Price, *op. cit.,,* p. 16.

[34] Smith, P. G. (1965). *Philosophy of education.* New York: Harper & Row. p. 51.

[35] Ibid. p. 52.

[36] Fitzpatrick, E. A. (1953). *Philosophy of education.* Milwaukee, WI: The Bruce Publishing Company. p. viii.

[37] Horne, H. H. (1927). *The philosophy of education.* New York: The Macmillan Company. p. 7.

[38] Moore, *op. cit.,,* p. 7.

[39] Broudy, H. (Spring 1956). *Philosophy of education.* The Harvard Educational Review. 26(2), p. 288.

[40] Phenix, P. H. (1959). *Philosophy of Education.* New York: Henry Holt and Company. p. vi.

CHAPTER 2

DEVELOPING A PHILOSOPHY OF EDUCATION

In Chapter 1 the task of philosophy of education was described as scrutinizing educational practice and theory in order to establish the foundations of the educational enterprise. Educational practice is a complex activity and deals with areas such as teaching and learning, curriculum, administration, ethics, aims, nature of the learner and knowledge. Each of these practice areas contains theories that assist in their interpretation and explanation. But the question of interest for philosophy of education is: which of these areas generates a philosophical interest that merits the attention of a philosopher-educator?

Thomas Moore defines an area of "philosophical interest" as "one which gives rise to question of a conceptual nature, about relationships... or one which reveals certain assumptions proposed in an argument, assumptions which, being the basis for the argument, need to be established before the argument can be evaluated... Concepts, assumptions, and the arguments based on them are possible sources of philosophic interest."[1] The job of the philosopher at this point is to analyze or compare concepts in order to obtain clarity, to understand the phenomenon better, and to evaluate the arguments that validate the logical structure of the concept. Chapter II answers the question: What is the scope of philosophy of education? What is the content of philosophy of education? Is philosophy of education necessary? What is the purpose of philosophy of education?

SCOPE OF PHILOSOPHY OF EDUCATION

The scope of any discipline defines the limits or the range of its competence, what it can and cannot do. It is a truism that not every problem in education calls for a philosophical answer. For example, questions in special education – education of students with learning disabilities – falls squarely in the domain of educational psychology not philosophy. Hence, it is important to establish the contours of philosophy of education. This section outlines the debate on what philosophers and educators advance as the competence of educational philosophy. A synthesis will be worked out of the various stances.

The debate

According to Sidney Hooks only the study of values constitute the specific domain of philosophy of education. "A philosophy of education, worthy of consideration," writes Sidney Hooks, "will not develop as a result of philosophers applying their philosophy to questions of education. It will develop when philosophers and educators, as well as other intelligent citizens, concern themselves with questions of education, explore their bearing on conflicting value commitments and seek some comprehensive theory of human values to guide us in the resolution of conflict."[2] Sidney Hooks rejects theories of reality and epistemology as domains of philosophy of education. "There is a great deal of nonsense talk about philosophy of education. This is particularly true of claims that a metaphysical or epistemological position has logical implications for educational theory and practice."[3] Sidney Hooks describes any entertainment of the position that the establishment of curriculum must depend on a prior establishment of the reality as "almost comical."[4] Sidney Hooks characterizes Harry Broudy's position that educational activities be derived from philosophic positions such as Thomism or Existentialism as a perpetration of "garrulous absurdities."[5] Concerning Price's stance that the epistemology of philosophers should recommend an epistemology for educators by suggesting school courses Sidney Hooks says that this is putting "the cart before the horse."[6]

Sidney Hooks arguments are based on two premises. The first argument is based on what may be called democracy in education. According to Sidney Hooks there are many areas of value in education "in which substantial agreement has been reached… by educators who are at odds with each other in their metaphysics and epistemology."[7] Conversely, "educators who agree about the desirability of certain educational aims and methods may disagree profoundly in their world outlook."[8] Hence, the educational democracy on which Sidney Hooks' arguments are based is founded on the assumption of a possibility of agreement. The second argument from history fortifies Sidney Hooks' rejection of metaphysics and epistemology as domains of philosophy of education. "There is considerable historical evidence," writes Sidney Hooks, "to show that Dewey reached his characteristic educational insights before he elaborated his characteristic philosophical views."[9] Hence, Sidney Hooks contends that philosophy of education should be an investigative-inductive process rather than a deductive-applied process.

Elizabeth Flower rejects Sidney Hooks' choice of ethics as the unique scope of philosophy of education. Examining the work of educators Elizabeth Flower finds two significant tendencies. First, there are the statisticians. Second there are those involved in evaluating educational programs and "tend to identify philosophy of education with pronouncements of values and aims held to be of prime importance, of overall objectives, or of social significance of educational institutions."[10] Elizabeth Flower makes a choice as to which of these is the domain of philosophy of education proper. "Now the kind of philosophy of education I should be interest in must, at least if it is to be successful, speak to the concerns of the first, and offer a rather different notion of philosophy to the second."[11] According to Elizabeth Flower philosophy of education should be classified as a social science because it is engaged in "describing certain phenomena and establishing systems of concepts which combine empirical import with theoretical significance."[12] Elizabeth Flower opts for the statistical approach because it examines ultimate norms critically and describes them disinterestingly. This dispassionate approach is the office of metaphysics.

On the other hand, Elizabeth Flower rejects ethics as the domain of educational philosophy because it prescribes hence is dogmatic. According to Elizabeth Flower "the only moral is caution lest convictions… become converted into credos."[13] Another view, which Elizabeth Flower rejects, is the view which holds that philosophy of education is deduced from the work of philosophers. Elizabeth Flower arrives at this conclusion after a historical examination of the philosophy of education of Plato, Locke, and Compte.

With Richard Morris a synthesis of the foregoing domains of philosophy of education began to emerge. According to Richard Morris philosophy of education should be concerned with questions of epistemology, metaphysics, and ethics. However, while endorsing a synthesis Morris introduces a hierarchy in the scope of educational philosophy. According to Richard Morris epistemology is central and quintessential to educational philosophy. As such, "students of philosophy of education will do well to begin here."[14] Primacy is given to epistemology because of the centrality of knowledge in the educative process. Richard Morris' argument in favor of epistemology at the center is rooted in the fact that knowledge is a sine qua non for the educative process. Next in the hierarchy is metaphysics. According to Richard Morris knowledge does not exist in a vacuum. Knowledge is always knowledge about the world, ends, freedoms, and so on. It is always knowledge about something. Hence, metaphysics is constitutive of knowledge as the 'factual part' of the educative process. The appreciation of these facts produces variety in what is known, thus calling for a choice. Richard Morris draws the conclusion that "the early division of the course is necessary preparations for the final stage… Here the search for ethics of education culminates. In fact, philosophy's ethical and aesthetic inquiries are replaced by strictly educational ones: the aims, values, methods, and practices of education which are consistent with the findings in stages one and two."[15]

The Synthesis

From the debate three areas of in education stand out as major preoccupations for philosophy of education, namely, educational values, educational foundations, and knowledge.

In studying educators, philosophy of education is interested in their value commitments. Aim in education is defined as that which is valuable and desired. Education, as a process of development of persons, presents alternative directions, which call for moral considerations and choices. It is the job of philosophy to shed light on the various alternatives. It is, therefore, obvious that an area of expertise of philosophy of education is the question of values. The branch of philosophy that studies values is ethics. Ethical theory inquires into the nature of moral choices that determine the character and quality of the educational experience provided by educators, the attitudes and dispositions that constitute learning, and the values that epitomize an educational system and gives it its specific identity. Ethics is an inquiry into desirable ways of educational activity.

Educational philosophy considers education as a moral enterprise. The moral activity in education, which is of interest to philosophy of education, is not limited to the subject area of moral instruction. Philosophy of education operates in those areas where educational decisions are made. Philosophy of education takes a more pervasive conception of ethics. It is involved in the clarification of values wherever alternative values are concerned. For example, philosophy of education is speculative where decisions have to be made about what shall be taught, how and when, by whom and for whom. Philosophy of education engages in analysis of values in the work of teachers, counselors, administrators, and students. Basically educational philosophy clarifies and justifies the decision making process. It answers questions like: how are decisions about values made? What are the grounds on which the educational values are chosen? What criteria support the choice? Educational aims, for example, are neither self-evident nor is there unanimous agreement on them. This is thus an area of potential conflict in education. Ethical theory clarifies such conflicts by going beyond what is apparent value to a demonstration of accepted value. Ethical theory also renders justifications for values by demonstrating their connectedness to already accepted and significant choices.

The second area of interest of philosophy of education is in the ultimate questions of education. This is what goes on when educational phenomena are defined or analyzed. The philosophical task of inquiring into the ultimate nature of things is metaphysics. Metaphysics, therefore, is concerned with the foundations of education. The function of metaphysical inquiry in education is not to propose assumptions that should underlie any educational enterprise. "The purpose of metaphysical discussion is to criticize and clarify what is already assumed about an educational system."[16] Metaphysics inquires into the pervasive and fundamental concepts in which the foundations of an educational enterprise are couched. What metaphysics hopes to accomplish is to go beyond the appearances of an educational enterprise, from what it seems to be to what it really is. The importance of establishing educational foundations is that it makes it possible to appraise the educational outlook of everyone involved in the educational enterprise.

The quintessence of any educational enterprise is the acquisition of knowledge, which is essential for human development. Since educational philosophy is interested in human development it is invariably interested in knowledge. The branch of philosophy that probes into knowledge is epistemology or theory of knowledge. Philosophy of education proposes no new knowledge for any educational enterprise. Rather, philosophy of education examines what constitutes knowledge, the meaning of knowledge, the activities involved in building knowledge, and the concepts in which they are expressed. "The main goal is simply to increase understanding of what knowledge is in itself and in its various branches, and to give insight into some of its complexities, ramifications, and connections, thus providing a critical comprehensive view rather than a limited conventional view."[17] The clarification that philosophy of education brings sets the stage for appreciating what a system considers as knowledge and the criteria for such a claim. The importance of such an elucidation is that it informs teachers what to emphasize in their teaching.

THE CONTENT OF PHILOSOPHY OF EDUCATION

What makes philosophy of education a discipline? What is its distinct and independent focus?

Educational Aims

Philosophy of education approaches education as a moral institution. Some axiological areas of interest that constitute the content of philosophy of education are educational finality and philosophy of teaching.

Educational finality

An important question of philosophical interest to the philosopher-educator is the assumptions that underlie any educational enterprise. Educational assumptions are logical prerequisites for any educational practice or theory. An educational system exists because it assumes certain values to be worthy of pursuit. One of the assumptions of interest to the philosopher-educator is educational aim.

The philosophical import of educational ends is that they provide the raison d'être or rational justifications for the educational enterprise. That is, educational ends show the permissibleness of the educational enterprise, provide legitimacy for the enterprise, validate or invalidate educational activities. Another significance of educational ends is that they provide intelligibility.

According to Dewey educational ends constitute the criteria by which educational activities are selected and observed. The realization of such ends through selected activities "signifies that an activity has become intelligent."[18] Intelligibility also supposes continuity and direction. Implicit in the concept of ends is the idea of order and progression. Hence, aim is important in ascribing intrinsic continuity to educational activities or the lack of aim simply qualifies these activities as serial aggregate acts. An end is not mere utopia but a foreseen result that organizes and gives direction to educational activities.

Two kinds of educational ends – intrinsic and extrinsic – are of special interest to the philosopher-educator. Thomas Moore designates the intrinsic ends as educational aims and the extrinsic ends as educational purpose. Educational purpose answers the question: What is this educational enterprise for? Purposes are always expressed in instrumental terms and "point to ends external to an activity."[19] The purpose of any education is the end product that lies outside the real practice of education. For example, a student may be asked: What are you studying biology for? The answer may come as: so that I may be a medical doctor. Becoming a medical doctor has no direct concern with studying biology now. However, it can be a remote final cause since is it removed from the actual and present benefits of studying biology. Educational purpose probes the remote future end product when the activity of education is completed. Purposes refuse to make education its own reward. Educational purposes broaden educational ends and provide added rationale to the educational enterprise.

Educational aim answers the question: What are you doing? What is this educational enterprise about? The answer to the aim question brings out the good *per se* of educational instruction. For example, the aim of studying biology is to have mastery of human anatomy. In this case there is no reference to the benefit of the study of biology outside of itself. In the case of education, the aim of the educational enterprise may be for moral and intellectual development, for example.

Dewey uses the term aim and purpose interchangeably. However, he maintains the distinction between extrinsic purpose, which he describes as "ends outside of the educative process" or "ulterior ends", and intrinsic aims, which he describes as "aims belong[ing] within the process" or "nominal aims."[20] In a lecture to the Philosophy of Education Society in 1995, Patrick Suppes of Stanford University designates educational aim as "the restricted aims of instruction" on the one hand, and educational purpose as "a sounder structure of education aims" on the other hand.

Philosophers are not agreed as to which of these educational ends is the turf of the philosopher-educator. According to Dewey philosophers should ponder the intrinsic aims of education. "In our search for aims in education," writes Dewey, "we are not concerned, therefore, with finding an end outside of the educative process to which education is subordinate… We are rather concerned with the contrast which exists when aims belong within the process in which they operate."[21] The reason why Dewey opts for the intrinsic ends is because of his preference for the autonomy of education. Education aims primarily at individual human growth and only peripherically is it a provision for the reconstruction of social habits. Extrinsic purpose is "an externally dictated order… rendering the work of both teacher and pupil mechanical and slavish."[22]

Arguing from an observation of the long-term use of education Thomas Moore characterizes options similar to that of Dewey as "an unfortunate result."[23] "There is, however, no warrant for this kind of exclusiveness," explains Thomas Moore. There is a sense in which education is good per se, and is its own reward. But it makes good sense to ask: why do we want well-developed, sensitive, intellectually equipped, and useful people? The educated person needs also to be a good citizen, a good worker, a good colleague, and being educated may be and indeed should be, a great help in achieving these worthwhile external ends. Education has important purposes as well as important ends."[24] Thomas Moore, therefore, advocates an inclusive simultaneous stance to intrinsic and extrinsic ends of education.

Patrick Suppes, like Thomas Moore, endorses the inclusive approach to educational ends. However, unlike Thomas Moore who proposes a simultaneous treatment of both ends, Suppes proposes a sequential treatment of intrinsic aims and extrinsic purpose. "We must make good use of the wide agreement on the restricted aims of instruction and of the possibility of building from this base a sounder structure of educational aims… A systematic formulation of aims should build as thoroughly as possible on this wide factual basis of agreement."[25] For Patrick Suppes reflection on extrinsic purpose of education is dependent on reflection on the intrinsic aims. For Thomas Moore reflection on educational aims and purposes should be on an equal footing.

The question of aims in education is a question of choice of educational values. Aims are values in that they constitute objects of human desire and interest. The study of values belongs to the axiological domain of philosophy and, therefore, is of interest to the philosopher-educator. Inasmuch as the choice of educational aims is a question of value preferences and discrimination it is incumbent on the philosopher-educator to offer reasons regarding the choice of values to be made. Philosophy of education, therefore, enlightens the discussion and decision about the aims. The philosopher-educator does not only shed light on the nature of the values concerned but also pushes the question further to enlighten the status of the value. In discussing the status of educational values philosophy of education answers questions like: Are the educational ends simply goals that have to be reached at one point in time (push) or are they like magnets pulling the development of the student to itself? Are educational goals in serial succession (immediate, mediate, and ultimate)? Are educational goals tied to specific persons and/or circumstances (relative) or independent of them (absolute)? Are the aims subjected to periodical revision (variable) or are they constant? Do aims control the educational process here and now (immanent) or do they prepare for some future actuality (transcendent)? Has the educational enterprise one or many aims? Are the aims implicit or explicit?

It is the work of the philosopher to make a pillar of cloud by day and a pillar of fire by night of the hidden assumptions that give pace to any educational enterprise. Philosophy of education must bring intelligibility to bear when educational aims are obscured through clarification and criticism. Clarification can be cast in a metaphysical question of whether educational goals are causes or effects. The importance of this question is crucial in the management of educational motivation.

Principles of good aims

There is no one clear-cut road to establish educational aims. However, certain guidelines will be in place.

First, any study of the aims of education must state clearly what part of the aims is the direct responsibility of the educational institution and which is only attendant or an indirect responsibility. To talk intelligibly about what education ought to be doing it is crucial to specify the level of educational ends under discussion. If the difference in levels of ends is overlooked confusion will set in and controversy will become muddled. "The first prerequisite to intelligent discussion of educational aims is an understanding of the hierarchy of such aims and a willingness to identify the level of the hierarchy of such aims and a willingness to identify the level of the hierarchy on which the discussion is to take place."[26] Agreement about educational ends is an invariable determinant of the educational means and process. The work of the philosopher of education is not to conjure or fabricate educational goals. The professional touch of the philosopher-educator is to examine already built-in goals in an educational enterprise and to put order into that scrambled heap of educational goals. The philosopher-educator does this by discovering levels of goals and their interaction.

Second, the philosopher-educator must establish guidelines for developing criteria for good aims. These criteria should constitute the rational framework for current educational practice and theory.

Philosophy of teaching

Educational philosophy is also interested in the role of the teacher. However, the interest is not to suggest the best pedagogy for teachers. Rather educational philosophy focuses on teachers' philosophy of teaching. The philosophical interest in teaching is with the teachers' commitment. Educational philosophy studies commitment as benchmarks of the teachers' personal values in teaching and as a representation of stable beliefs, ideas, and assumptions that affect the teachers' behavior. Hence, the philosophical interest in the role of the teacher is not in the appropriateness or inappropriateness of the teacher's method but his/her in teaching as a value-laden activity.

Examples of specific areas in the role of the teacher that will interest the educational philosopher are the teacher's personal vision of teaching, rationale for teaching, and purpose for teaching. The educational philosopher asks questions like what goals has the teacher set for the class and why? What professional growth goals does the teacher set for the self? How is the teacher's philosophy operationalized? How does the teacher perceive the values of the educational system? Are there system values to which the teacher needs to connect when teaching?

Apart from probing the value commitment of the teachers educational philosophy also takes interest in clarifying the role of the teacher. Educational philosophy would like to know what the teacher understands by learning. What does the teacher understand by teaching? How does the teacher want to make a difference? What is important for philosophy of education is not the question asked but the answers proffered. The answers given by teachers to these questions are often metaphorical. Examples of metaphors used to describe learning are filling the container, journey to a horizon, and discipleship. Metaphors used to describe the role of the teacher include coach, gardener, midwife, evangelist, and tour-bus driver. Metaphors are heuristically illuminating and also have their limitations. The duty of the philosopher-educator is to clarify these metaphors. Doing so entails examining the concepts within each metaphor and establishing their educational implication. A metaphor is only a tool, a locus of inference with which educational philosophy must labor in order to establish educational meaning.

Knowledge In Education

Philosophy of education is interested in what constitutes knowledge in an educational set up. Two areas of knowledge that capture the interest of educational philosophy are the nature of knowledge and knowledge as a reconstruction.

The Nature Of Knowledge

Philosophy of education is interested in the content of knowledge produced in an educational establishment. Educational philosophy is particularly interested in the nature, sources, validity, and organization of knowledge.

Philosophy of education is interested in what constitutes knowledge. It asks the question: what skills and behavioral capacities are considered signs of knowledge? Is what constitutes knowledge always only a direct and immediate knowledge *of* something or only an indirect and mediate knowledge of something, or both? Is the knowledge perceptual (primary and immediate) or is it conceptual (secondary and derived), or both? Contrasts such as these indicate the clarifying interest that educational philosophy brings to bear on knowledge.

Philosophy of education is also interested in what an educational enterprise recognizes as legitimate sources of knowledge. It seeks answers to the following questions: What does the learner do to obtain knowledge? Where does the learner seek understanding? Philosophy of education investigates the possible answers, the activities involved, and the emphasis of each. Some conventional sources of knowledge that educational philosophy has analyzed include sense perception, reason, intuition, tradition, and revelation.

Sense perception acknowledges bodily sensation (sight, touch, taste, smell, and feeling) as a source of knowledge. In this case philosophy of education will study the criteria of appropriateness of the educational stimuli (content taught) presented and the criteria of physical, mental, and emotional soundness of those involved in the learning process. Stimuli and persons are important ingredients for sense perception to be possible. A distinct but related source of knowledge akin to sense perception is reason. Reason is important in the organization of the knowledge obtained by self-perception. It is a systematic reflection on data obtained by senses. Hence, it is *a posteriori* (follows experience). Philosophy of education also wants to know if *a priori* (precedes experience) knowledge is possible.

Intuition, as a source of knowledge, is characterized by direct, immediate, and inward learning. It is learning without mediation. The task of philosophy of education is not to establish the truth or falsity of intuitive knowledge. Its office is to establish the criteria for accepting intuitive knowledge as true or false. Tradition is a source of knowledge in the sense of receiving ready-made knowledge from others. Tradition is a source of knowledge in that it contains within itself knowledge ready to be handed-on. Educational philosophy is interested in the concepts through which the knowledge is handed-on. Revelation is considered a source of knowledge mostly in religious circles. In revelation God communicates knowledge to the beneficiary of the revelation.

Philosophy of education is not only interested in the sources of knowledge but also in the criteria for validating knowledge. Validity is a test that ascertains the truth or falsity and adequacy or inadequacy of the knowledge obtained. Standards may be developed that determine the adequacy of knowledge from each source. For example, reverence and devotion may be the standards for judging knowledge from revelation; obedience the standard for tradition; reflection and logical orientation as standard for reason.

Another way in which philosophy of education clarifies knowledge produced by an educational establishment is to evaluate how it is organized. In doing this it is looking out for the classes, methods, and theories involved as well as the thread that holds such knowledge together. The classes give concreteness and simplicity to the knowledge. Organization of method offers procedural clarity. Classification by theory offers a framework for developing insight into the established knowledge. The unity of knowledge has the advantage of creating a community of people who understand one another.

Intellectual Reconstruction

Chapter 1 outlined methods of philosophy of education among which are analytical and comparative approaches. The process of analysis involves piecemeal activity in order to discover the component parts of an educational system. Then there is interpretation that is rebuilding the system into varied and alternative ways for a fuller understanding. The comparative approach is a fusion (comparison) and differentiation (contrast) of previous meanings in order to come up with a modified meaning that may enhance understanding of the educational systems being compared. Analytical and comparative philosophies of education are intellectual reconstructions of meaning inasmuch as they abstract and conceptualize new meaning from previous meaning. This is the job of philosophy.

Also, today's definition of school goes beyond teachers, students, and parents to include the local community – media, health, insurance, and other professionals. The result of this new inclusive concept of school necessary brings into the school environment discrepant and maybe incompatible views of learning, human nature, educational aims, and educational process. The local community brings into the school different norms and ideals that may be conflictual at times. In order to harness the beauty and contribution which each of the views has in the educational arena it is necessary to decipher the emphasis of each view and then reconstruct new meaning that will be meaningful to the educational enterprise in question. It falls within the job description of the educational philosopher to analyze and adjudicate the varying emphases.

EDUCATIONAL FOUNDATIONS

Philosophy of education deals with the ultimate questions of education. Examples of ultimate questions that may be of interest to philosophy of education include the structure and function of education, and activities and event in education. However, this section will look at other two ultimate questions: educational anthropology, and human development.

Educational Anthropology

Any educational enterprise logically begins with a specification of the ends it has to achieve. This is to avoid the enterprise becoming a haphazard venture. Inherent in the goals or objectives is an implicit description of an educated person. To realize these goals certain means are employed and they are deemed necessary and adequate. Any elaboration of ends and means must take cognizance of human nature and assume that it can be modified. "There would be no point in trying to teach children if whatever was done could make no difference to them."[27] Since education aims at modifying human conduct it follows that an understanding of human nature is a logical prerequisite or assumption of education and, therefore, is of philosophical interest.

According to Abraham Edel "when an educational theory is brought into the philosophical workshop one of the first parts to be unpacked is its implicit theory of human nature. This is diagnosed and sorted."[28] The philosophical interest in educational anthropology is in the malleability of human nature. The history of educational philosophy abounds with examples, which indicate that part of its business has been to unpack this human nature. Locke's empiricism concludes that human beings are born tabula rasa, completely empty. In this anthropological model students are raw materials to be stamped into assigned designs. The importance of this approach is the affirmation of the equality and homogeneity of human nature, and the equality of educational opportunities. The importance for education is Locke's affirmation that human nature is malleable.

John Dewey, for example, writing within the backdrop of materialistic evolutionism expounded a human nature that is continuous with nature. "Experience," wrote Dewey, "knows no division between human concerns and a purely mechanical physical world. Man's home is nature; his purposes and aims are dependent for execution upon natural conditions. Separated from such conditions they become empty dreams and idle indulgences of fancy… This philosophy is vouched for by the doctrine of biological development which shows that man is continuous with nature, not an alien entering her processes from without."[29] Beyond their physical nature human beings also have native endowments that Dewey variously calls inchoate and scattered impulses, native powers, and instincts and they are unlearned, original, and uninformed.[30] According to Dewey it is possible to pattern these powers. "The inchoate and scattered impulses of an infant do not coordinate into serviceable powers except through social dependencies and companionship."[31] What is important here is that Dewey is concerned with human nature as that which can be altered, adapted, improved "and since some of Dewey's severest criticisms of other schools of thought are based on their theories of human alterability, it will be useful to approach Dewey's attitudes toward other concepts of human nature from that angle."[32]

The philosophical interest in the study of human nature is usually stated as a metaphysical question of potentiality versus actuality. Potentiality is the capacity to become. Actuality is that which has already become. Philosophy of education, therefore, is interested in the ability of students to become educated. The assumption about human potency calls for a study of sub-concepts like reason, memory, language, imagination, and self-transcendence because these are the aspects of human nature directly involved in education.

So, the task of philosophy is not to condemn or honor the concepts in which human nature is expressed. The point for educational philosophy is to explore, analyze, and refine the concepts and assumptions underlying the model. By so doing philosophy of education brings out the philosophic character of educational anthropology. Hence, philosophy of education brings to fuller consciousness and sharper focus a fundamental dimension of education. After probing into the implicit human outlook the educational philosopher can now elaborate the task of education and suggest criteria for evaluating it. The educational philosopher does not invent the human nature implicit in any educational theory. The educational philosopher clarifies the human nature in question and posits its logical consequences in terms of educational means and goals.

Human Development

The previous section indicated that philosophy of education is interested in the ability of human nature to be modified. However, philosophy is not only interested in the ability but also in the process of human becoming. The concepts used to describe human becoming in education are growth and development. The question can then be asked: What is the interest of the philosopher-educator in the process of human development?

Growth through education is a process of realizing chosen educational values. The growth process may be examined by identifying the periods, stages, or phases of development. Thus one may speak of the different stages of education such as kindergarten, elementary, secondary, university, and adult. The job of analyzing these phases is proper to psychology of education not philosophy. Another possible approach is to look at the factors that affect the development such as environment and heredity. Again these studies are strictly the domain of educational sociology. Another study may undertake to clarify the dominant trends of development. In this case the following developmental patterns may be found: education as unfolding, molding, self-creation, interaction, or divine creation. However, the study of trends belongs to the descriptive science called educational phenomenology.

What then is the particular interest of the philosopher in the process of human developmental? Philosophy of education is interested in education as a process characterized by changes that lead to a particular result. Philosophy of education addresses the question: In the process of education what has become different and what has remained the same in the student? Change, understood as a process of self-realization, is a fundamental theme of philosophy of education. The question for educational philosophy is: What constitutes educational growth or self-realization? What is the criterion of growth? This is the crucial question in Dewey's educational philosophy. According to Dewey an experience is considered educative or growth if it contributes to the disposition or ability to secure a good life and avoid bad ones. Without going into the details of Dewey's criterion for deciding what is growth, it suffices to say that it is the duty of philosophy of education to clarify the criteria for growth. By so doing it sets the stage for evaluating the educational enterprise. Another question that the philosopher may grapple with is whether the development is fate. Educational growth comes about through learning. It is the job of the philosopher to further refine the learning process by linking it to determinism and freedom, for example.

The study of philosophy of education focuses on three areas of philosophical interest, namely, the foundation of education (metaphysics), educational values (ethics), and knowledge (epistemology). To these three domains can be added two critical elements of education, namely, the student and the teacher. Hence, philosophy of education must answer five rudimentary questions:

1. What is the ultimate end of education?
2. Why a preferred method of instruction?
3. What is the nature of the student?
4. What is the role of the teacher?
5. What ought to be taught?

NECESSITY OF PHILOSOPHY OF EDUCATION

What makes philosophy of education useful to educational stakeholders? What is the task of philosophy of education? Many educators contend that philosophy of education supplies no skills to teachers. What, therefore, is its usefulness? This section outlines the competence of philosophy of education and anticipates what students should expect when they study the subject. It discusses the necessity of philosophy of education by outlining some benefits that accrue from it as well as indicate the people susceptible to benefit from it.

Philosophy of Education Maintains Roots

The argument has been advanced that because philosophy of education has no specific inventory of aims and content it is not a necessary discipline.

Against such an argument one can advance the usefulness of philosophy of education in times of change. In an era of change rules are not enough to guarantee continuity. One always has to fall back to foundational outlooks, that is, to philosophy. Also, education will always stand in need of the imaginative-speculative sense of philosophy to figure out alternative education, of its comprehensive-integrative sense to relate education to other areas of life, and philosophy's critical sense of responsibility to probe educational assumptions and test educational objectives.

Philosophy Of Education Enlightens

Philosophy of education has a practical importance. In any ordinary educational enterprise teachers, students, and parents question the educational enterprise: what is the aim of their local education? What is the role of teachers in the local school? What knowledge and learning is adequate in order to achieve the aim of the educational system? What is the nature of school-community relationship? What is the relationship of education to local politics, religions, and morality?

The above questions are practical philosophical probes into the foundation and logical relationships of local education. The answers to these questions are offered by philosophy. Hence, it can be said that educational philosophy enlightens the school community. For teachers, for example, answers to the above questions imply that philosophy of education has given them direction for and confidence in their work. The answers provided by philosophy of education will be useful for students insofar as the answers enable students to anticipate the promises of learning. Because of philosophy of education students can perceive the coherence between educational goals and educational means. For legislators and politicians the answers may constitute pointers and suggestions to the kind of climate to be establish that will favor the educational enterprise.

The training of educators today is largely centered on leadership skills, organization, and methodology. Many educators lack a formation in philosophic thinking hence are deficient in the tools necessary for questioning the larger purposes of educational systems. This lack contributes, to a certain extent, to the failure of the educational enterprise in many countries. Lawrence Cremin makes the case against education in the United States as follows:

> Too few educational leaders in the United States are genuinely preoccupied with educational issues because they have no clear ideas about education. And if we look at the way these leaders have been recruited and trained, there is little that would lead us to expect otherwise. They have too often been managers, facilitators, and politicians in the narrowest sense. They have been concerned with building, balancing budgets, and pacifying parents, but they have not been prepared to spark a great public dialogue about the ends and means of education. And in the absence of such a dialogue, large segments of the public have had, at best, a limited understanding of the whys and wherefores of popular schooling.[33]

Intrinsic, therefore, in the formation of educators is the recipe for the collapse, destruction, and sterility of the educational enterprise. For education to thrive educators need courses that emphasize the humanities of education such as history, literature, and philosophy. Knight underscores the usefulness of philosophy of education as follows:

> The task of educational philosophy is to bring future teachers, principals, and superintendents, counselors and curriculum specialists into face-to-face contact with the large questions underlying the meaning and purpose of life and education… Thus the major task of educational philosophy is to help educators think meaningfully the total educational and life process so that they will be in a better position to develop a consistent and comprehensive program that will assist their students in arriving at the desired goal.[34]

Philosophy of education and the other humanities of education will acquaint educators with the problems that plague education, offer alternative insights into these problems, clarify the aims of education, and guide the development of local philosophies of education. Philosophy of education is an arbiter inasmuch as it assists in the decision of what should be considered as education and what should not be considered as education. The primary focus of philosophy is in theoretical problems. However, the educator's interest is in the secondary activity of philosophy or applied philosophy. Applied philosophy is the educator's use of philosophy as a practical vehicle emphasizing not the theoretical principles per se but their significance for education. "The educator, however, is not a person who pursues knowledge for its own sake. His activity lies within the sphere of what Aristotle termed practical sciences, and he looks to philosophy to provide him with principles so that he can place his work on a sound basis."[35]

An anticipated objection from a practitioner concerning the clarificatory role of philosophy in education can be stated as follows: The practitioner may reject rationality on the basis that his/her work is to care for students' self-esteem and academic achievement. To this objection a philosopher of education may reply as follows: philosophy can clarify the practitioner's present practice as well as offer alternative ways for planning a course of action.

In brief, it is only because of philosophical enlightenment that a responsible judgment can be made concerning the advantages and disadvantages of the existing state of education and specific reforms that will make it function satisfactorily. Philosophy of education provides the wisdom that underpins any understanding of the educational system. It provides the theoretical and intellectual basis for the guidance of educational practice and analysis of the data of educational experience. A succinct and terse philosophy of education provides educators with a meaningful matrix of reference on which they can construct and give meaning to their teaching activities and interpret the learning behavior of the students. A lack of such a reference means that educational decisions are taken arbitrarily or because of expediency without any regard for long term educational planning or prediction.

Philosophy Of Education Critiques

Proposed educational objectives and practices may be based on warranted conclusions from other branches of inquiry – culture, politics, and sociology. The task of philosophy of education is to criticize these assumptions and conclusions to ascertain that they are solidly grounded. The purpose of the critique is to ascertain if the objectives can render vital service to the educational enterprise. An indispensable prerequisite for such critique is competent familiarity with the field of education, logical maturity, and sensitivity to shifts in meaning of words. For example, the word development is used differently in biology (development of an embryo), psychology (development of an idea), and moral (development of human individuality).

As a critique philosophy of education can also reveal the elements of sterile utopianism and of an ineffective sentimentalism that may be present in actual or proposed educational goals. It does so by examining current assumptions concerning the relationship of ends to means and the coherence of envisaged ideals. Educational objectives are often proposed with a consideration of human capacities of students while neglecting the social mechanisms other than schools that are in operation to carry forward the ideals. Philosophy of education needs to examine the compatibility of educational objectives with what is presumably known about the capacities and aspirations of those for whom the objectives are being proposed.

In short, as a science that critiques philosophy of education can throw light on educational practices and reform by removing inconsistencies, suggesting new developments, and raising questions. By so doing it paves the way for a rational rather than doctrinaire or emotional evaluation of such activities.

Philosophy Of Education Integrates

Philosophy of education also integrates in that it coherently relates the contributions of other fields like philosophy, politics, and morality to education.

Educational specialization has led to a breakdown of relationships in various branches of education (balkanization). This is the tower of Babel effect of specialization. Educational administration, curriculum, and educational psychology have been estranged from one another. A holistic view of education needs an integrating perspective that brings together these compartmentalized educational inquiries. Philosophy of education can make a contribution in this area. The aim of philosophy, as mentioned earlier, is to evaluate evidence, explicate concepts, and systematize knowledge. Philosophy of education can serve as an integrating discipline by assessing, articulating, and organizing the logical principles and claims of each discipline and later showing their logical interactions.

In brief, philosophy of education can play a purgative role of philosophic criticism and an integrative role of logically connecting. Competent philosophical inquiry in education requires considerable familiarity with the substantive content and procedures of education as well as mastery of the techniques of logical philosophical analysis.

Beneficiaries of Philosophy of Education

The necessity of philosophy of education can be established not only from what it does but also by identifying its beneficiaries. It is, therefore, important for philosopher-educators to answer the following questions: To who is philosophy of education addressed? Who does the philosopher-educator hope to influence?

Historically, philosopher-educators clearly designated their clientele. The philosophy of education of Plato and Aristotle targeted the citizen-leader of Greek communities. Rasenkranz, who coined the expression 'philosophy of education', wrote his educational philosophy for university professors and university trained schoolteachers. In the preface to his book intended to serve as an introduction to philosophy of education Phenix designates college and university students as his primary target group. A secondary group which he expects would draw profit from his book are those "who wish to engage in serious reflection about issues of education."[36] These include parents, teachers, administrators, and concerned citizens. For Lucas, his book on philosophy of education is expected to be a valuable document for those preparing to be professional teachers and for those in countries that require such a course for certification.

In sum, the educational landscape in many countries is fraught with confusion and bewilderment. Educators have lost the sense, if not given up to find out, where the system is going and why. Economic hardships leave educators with little room to think these out. Success in life is no longer linked to educated life but to astuteness in becoming a celebrity. Education is no longer at the center stage of government action. Before, educational budget was a priority. Today it is not so. Finally, no one is sure of the finality of most educational systems. The reason for this is that politicians, educators, and concerned citizens are not agreed on these issues. Amidst such confusion the science of education needs to extricate itself. Philosophy of education can prove a useful guide and orientation by providing criteria for differentiating the true and false in education. Philosophy of education offers new avenues for serious inquiry and thought concerning educational ideas and traditions. Philosophy of education can also develop new insights into educational problems by critically examining intellectual disputes and expressions.

Methods of Philosophy of Education

Educational philosophies can be distinguished by their dominant purposes, what they hope to achieve. Any purpose supposes a means to attain it. In conjunction with purpose, method – how a body of educational discourse is handled – is important in classifying of philosophies of education.

Normative Philosophy Of Education

Philosophy of education "is normative insofar as it is concerned to propose ends or values for education to promote, principles for it to follow, excellencies for it to foster, or methods, contents, programs, etc., for it to adopt and employ, in general or specific situations."[37] Two lines of pursuit

– theoretical and practical – stand out in this definition of normative philosophy of education. Theoretically, philosophy of education is normative in that it determines standards of education by stating the criteria for what counts or does not count in education. Educational philosophy prescribes what education ought to be and defines educational ideals. It appears "to be pointing upward to the 'heights' to be reached through education."[38] The task of the prescriptive approach is, therefore, judgmental. Normative philosophy of education contains parameters concerning desirable ends, principles, and subject matter of education. Normative philosophy of education also has a practical dimension. It recommends the means and methods that should be followed to attain educational ends. The business of normative philosophy of education, therefore, is the promotion of certain ends – 'producing' people of a certain sort. Practical normative philosophy of education searches ends and values that give direction to the educational enterprise. The task of the practical dimension is to identify and describe appropriate goals and means of education.

Prescription alone does not make educational philosophy normative. What accounts for the philosophical dimension is the philosopher's interest is justifying the prescriptions. Hence, normative philosophy of education contains practical precepts about what should be done in education and how, as well as providing reasons for these conclusions. Normative philosophy of education designs an educational enterprise by providing answers to the what, how, and why of education. It is akin to architectural design.

Two ways of establishing normative patterns of education, which are not exclusive but complementary, are through empirical and rational constructs. "An empirical approach would involve collecting information by the use of opinion pools, attitude tests, questionnaires, and similar techniques largely developed by psychologists and sociologists."[39] Such tests provide valuable and specific information about the selected aspect of education under consideration. From the information acquired specific norms for that specific educational situation can be developed. Also, developing and refining the norm of the specific situation can elaborate general norms for other and similar situations. The second method of establishing normative patterns is one "in which philosophical techniques and sources (particularly the writings of representative thinkers) are employed [and] has the advantage of reversing the emphasis from the specific to the most general statement of norms. A pattern resulting from this approach could be described as a rational construct of the Weberian type."[40] In this approach, basic sources provide the educational system with ideal patterns to be pursued.

Normative philosophy of education does not take up every norm existing in the educational agency sponsoring an educational system. Rather, rational normative educational philosophy selects norms around which to design its educational philosophy. The selection and arrangement of the norms will depend on the area of education being philosophized upon. The rationale behind norm selection and arrangement or normative construct is to "facilitate the presentation of an otherwise immensely multifarious subject matter."[41] Another importance of the normative approach is that the norm provides the legal framework or basis on which the educational system operates. Also, the norm is a useful criterion for classifying any educational institution or system as private, public, or confessional, for example.

Normative philosophy of education is concerned with value. It is present wherever the goal of education is character formation. Historical incarnations of normative philosophy of education are possible where education is considered as a sociopolitical institution. For example, Hitler discussed his educational theory in Mien Kampf as a prescription of Nazi ideals. Marxism is literally the directive for educational arrangement. Marxism is ultimately and doctrinally conceived to direct the practicalities of education. "In Italy, Giovanni Gentile, a professional philosopher, was commissioned to explore dialectically the meaning for education of the principles of Fascistic social organization."[42] Also, Christian philosophy of education which, is Bible based, is normative. That is, the Bible is the skeleton around which practical applications of Christian educational philosophy are arranged. A Christian school's educational philosophy, therefore, will be Biblically inspired with implications for the teaching-learning process, role of the education, and the role of student. Concerning the use of aim in normative philosophy Dewey writes, "an aim denotes the result of any natural process brought to consciousness and made a factor in determining present observation and choice of ways of acting."[43] Alfred North Whitehead is a practical example of how aims can be used normatively in philosophizing about education. According to Whitehead one aim of education is to fight "what I call 'inert ideas' – that is to say, ideas that are merely received into the mind without being utilized, or tested or thrown into fresh combinations."[44] From this stated aim prescriptions are made about educational arrangements to avoid 'inert ideas'. "Let us now ask how in our system of education we are to guard against this mental dry out. We enunciate two educational commandments, 'Do not teach too many subjects,' and again, 'What you teach, teach thoroughly.'" The goal of normative philosophy of education is to develop and prescribe educational aims and practices that are in harmony with a particular worldview.

Analytical Philosophy Of Education

Philosophy of education "is analytical insofar as it is concerned merely to analyze, clarify, or elaborate, or to criticize and evaluate our thinking about education – the concepts, the terms we employ, the arguments we use, the assumptions we make, the slogans we proclaim, the theories we formulate."[45] Analytical philosophy of education assesses educational concepts, definitions, clarifications, and distinctions carefully. It pulls educational concepts apart then reconstructs them in order to attain depth meaning. Such analysis may include empirical statements and factual claims about the educational system whose veracity can be ascertained by experiment or empirical observation. The aim of analytical philosophy of education is to better understand the current educational practice. Analytical philosophy of education is not speculative but a critical clarification of educational confusion or sloppiness. It does so by establishing the validity of education, and unfolding its underlying assumptions, and underpinning logic.

Analytical philosophy of education describes, explains, and predicts. Using the historical method, which surveys documents and statistical data, analytical philosophy describes the state of an educational system or institution. Proponents of descriptive educational philosophy are Victor Cousin[46] and Herbert Barnard.[47] Examples of excellent educational descriptive studies are provided today by educational yearbooks. The descriptive data provides the basis for a better understanding of the educational environment – demographics or climate, for example – of the system or institution.

The descriptive analysis can be taken a step further by searching and identifying causes or determinants of educational policy, for example. In this case the analysis is explanatory. It is used to explain the operation of the educational system. Hans[48], Isaac Kandel[49], and Schneider[50] are prominent educators of this extra mile in educational analysis. William Harris[51] and Francis Sadler[52] contend that the descriptive data can also be used for educational prediction and planning educational development. Donald O'Connor in his *Introduction to the philosophy of education* is very critical of the synthetic and prescriptive approaches as philosophies that promised more than they were able to deliver. Explanation and prediction add a sociological dimension to analytical philosophy of education.

Analytical philosophy of education provides a method for understanding not only the operation of an educational system or institution but also how that system transforms the larger local environment. Analytical philosophy of education is a construct. The composite picture it provides describes, provides explanations, and makes it possible to predict the system or institution. The goal of analytical philosophy of education is conceptual clarity and methodological understanding. This approach to education makes the philosopher-educator more sensitive and critical of fossilized educational judgments hidden in educational clichés, slogans, and ready-made answers.

Analytical philosophy is common among those who study philosophies or philosophers of education as well as those who conceive education as a growth process or instruction. In the latter case the philosopher of education is evaluating and reporting the progress of students or method of the teacher. The philosopher is doing the same kind of analysis and synthesis carried out by philosophers. The purpose is to expose the facts of the learning activity of the students or teaching experience of the teacher.

Inspirational Philosophy Of Education

Educational philosophy is described as inspirational when an educational artifact is judged as an ideal piece and proposed as a model. Also, to be labeled inspirational such works must acquire a classical stature and pass the test of time.

Inspirational philosophy was popular prior to the 20th century when the writing of one philosopher dominated the educational arena for decades. This is the case with Plato's (427-347BC) *The Republic* and Rousseau's (1712-1778) *Emile*. These writings are treated in greater detail in Chapter III. It suffices here to mention that in *The Republic* Plato set out to propose a superior educational arrangement that will effectively form a responsible citizen. Rousseau's *Emile* was intended to be an elaboration of an ideal education. However, the proliferation of philosophies of education since the beginning of the 20th century has dampened the role of inspirational philosophy of education. Also, inspirational philosophy of education is not popular with educational philosophers because the setting of a utopia is synonymous to stagnation and the end of the educational enterprise.

However, when education is viewed from the point of view of educational agency then inspirational philosophy of education is still en vogue. Faith-inspired and National philosophies of education are examples of inspirational philosophies of education. In the former, Christian humanism is proposed as utopia. In the later responsible citizenship is utopia.

Comparative Philosophy Of Education

Comparative philosophy of education is a multi-track analytical philosophy of education with its own fascination. It brings together educational traditions that have developed in isolation and along regional lines. It has been variously called cross-cultural studies, dialogue in education, educational globalization. The impetus for educational comparison has come about with the breaking down of narrow provincialism that reigned prior to the 1960s and the rise of aggressive internationalism in the 1980s and 1990s. Also, modern forms of communication (distant learning) and unprecedented mingling of people due to faster travels have aroused expectations in comparative education. The comparison may be across nations, across epochs, or across educational agencies and systems.

Despite the promises of comparative education some risks present themselves. The first difficulty is commensurability. The amount and variety of factual information encountered in a comparative study of education can become unmanageable. Some people may compare the dominant administrative, cultural, legal, or fiscal aspect of the system. Philosophy of education must delineate a specific line of comparison. Comparative philosophy of education is not intended to be an encyclopedic collection of educational information around the world. Another risk of comparative education is assimilation. Assimilation refers to an unreflective importation of the assumption, frameworks, and agenda of another educational tradition. Comparative philosophers of education are not out for a hunting expedition nor are they dissidents of one educational or philosophical tradition who think that another tradition has 'got-it-right'. Comparative educational philosophy seeks to develop philosophical insights concerning an educational system. "Since the dominant social commitment of a group plays the determining role in education, introductory studies in comparative education must begin with an inquiry into the social philosophies of the supporting groups."[53] The purpose of such an inquiry for philosophy of education is not to give general descriptions of educational systems or to decipher patterns of significance. The purpose of such an inquiry is to explain why educational systems are the way they are.

The advantages that may accrue from such comparisons are many. Comparison forces the philosopher-educator to reflect on the most deeply entrenched and otherwise unquestionable agendas and assumptions of their educational system. Such a reflection may lead to a better understanding of the system thus providing a real opportunity for an appropriate and real contribution to the system. Also, as philosophies interact they may enrich one another (fecundation). Comparative education seeks to discover the forces that differentiate educational systems. Its focus is on form not details. It seeks explanations of particular 'forms' or educational systems. This approach imposes the challenge to examine the roots of the educational systems in question. Comparison brings into sharper focus the foundation of each educational system as it explores the differences and similarities between them. With this knowledge also emerges certain sensitiveness to common educational problems and solutions. The bottom-line contribution of the comparative approach to philosophy of education is that it deals with fundamental principles and fosters the acquisition of a philosophic attitude in analyzing and formulating a clearer understanding of the problems of education. Lastly, such comparisons may contribute to the preparation of participants for international careers like working for UNESCO or World Council of Comparative Education Societies (WCCES) whose primary purpose is to bring comparative studies to bear on major educational problems.

SUMMARY

Chapter 2 delimited the study of the reality of education, knowledge in education, and educational values as the three basic contours of philosophy of education. Out of these contours several foci like educational aims, anthropology, and the nature of knowledge were deciphered as topics of interest for philosophy of education. Another conclusion from this chapter is that philosophy of education makes use of the resources of general philosophy and the theory of education but it cannot be reduced to any of them. The breath and depth of educational philosophy and what it achieves gives it its special character. Philosophy of education may set out to recommend something, discover and interpret, clarify, or understand an aspect of an educational enterprise. Whatever the specific purpose of educational philosophy it enlightens, critiques, or integrates the educational process. It is concerned with educational vision. Philosophy of education is a specialized inquiry into the educational process. The approaches indicate different perspectives and levels on which educational philosophy operates.

[1] Moore, T. W. (1982). *Philosophy of education. An introduction.* London: Routledge & Kegan Paul, pp. 21-2.

[2] Hooks, S. (Spring 1959). *Scope of Philosophy of Education.* The Harvard Educational Review. 26(2) p. 148

[3] Hooks,. *op. cit.,,* p. 145

[4] Hooks,. *op. cit.,,* p. 145

[5] Hooks, *op. cit.,,* p. 148

[6] Hooks, *op. cit.,,* p. 148

[7] Hooks, *op. cit.,,* p. 145

[8] Hooks, *op. cit.,,* p. 145

[9] Hooks, *op. cit.,,* p. 147

[10] Flower, E. F. (Spring 1956). *In two keys.* The Harvard Educational Review 26(2) p.99.

[11] Flower, *op. cit.,,* p.99.

[12] Flower, *op. cit.,,* p.100.

[13] Flower, *op. cit.,,* p.100.

[14] Morris, R. K. (Spring 1956). *The philosophy of education: A quality of its own.* The Harvard Educational Review. 26(2), p. 143.

[15] Morris, *op. cit.,,* p. 143-4.

[16] Phenix, P. (1958). *Philosophy of education.* New York: Henry Holt and Company. p. 507.

[17] Phenix, *op. cit.,,* p. 298

[18] Dewey, J. (1916). *Democracy and education.* New York: p. see summary.

[19] Moore, *op. cit.,,* p. 27.

[20] Dewey, *op. cit.,,* p. 71.

[21] Dewey, *op. cit.,,* p. 71

[22] Dewey, *op. cit.,,* p. summary.

[23] Moore, *op. cit.,,* p. 29.

[24] Moore, *op. cit.,,* pp. 29-30.

[25] Suppes, P. (1966). *The aims of education.* In A. Neiman (Ed.) *Philosophy of education 1995.* Urbana, IL: University of Illinois at Urbana-Champaign, p. 10.

[26] Broudy, H. S. (1954). *Building a philosophy of education.* New York: Prentice-Hall, p. 32.

[27] Moore, *op. cit.,,* p. 30.

[28] Edel, A. (1956). *What should be the aim and content of philosophy of education?* Harvard Educational Review 26(2), 119-26, p. 119.

[29] Dewey, *Democracy and education.* p. 333

[30] Dewey, J. (1922). *Human nature and conduct.* New York: Henry Holt Company, p. 85.

[31] Dewey, *Human nature and conduct.* p. 94.

[32] Brown, J. N. (1940). *Educational implication of four concepts of human nature.* Washington, DC: The Catholic University of America Press, p. 17.

[33] Cremin, L. A. *The genius of American Education.* in Knight, G. R. (1998). *Philosophy and Education.* Berrien Springs, MI.: Andrews University Press. p. 4.

[34] Knight, G. R. *op. cit.,,* pp. 4-5.

[35] Curtis, *op. cit.,,* p. 7.

[36] Phenix, *op. cit.,,* p. v.

[37] Frankena, *op. cit.,,* p. 8.

[38] Soltis, J. F. (1973). *Philosophy of education. A fourth dimension.* In A. C. Ornstein & W. E. Hedley. (Eds). *Educational foundations. Ideas and Issues.* Columbus, OH: Charles. E. Merrill Publishing Company. p. 154.

[39] Holmes, B. (1965). *Problems in education. A comparative approach.* New York: The Humanities Press.

[40] Holmes, *op. cit.,,* p. 55.

[41] Gerth, H. H. & Mills, C. W. (1948). *From Max Weber. Essays in Sociology.* London: Routledge & Kegan Paul, p. 324.

[42] Smith, *op. cit.,,* p. 51.

[43] Dewey, *Democracy and education.* p. 333

[44] Whitehead, *Aims in education.* p. 3

[45] Frankena, *op. cit.,,* p. 8.

[46] Cousin, V. (1836) *Report of the state of education in Prussia.* 2nd Ed. Trans. S. Austin. London: Effingham.

[47] Barnard, H. (1872). *National education. Systems, institutions, and statistics of public instruction of different countries,* Part II. New York: E. Steiger.

[48] Hans, N. (1949). *Comparative education.* London: Routledge.

[49] Kandel, I. L. (1933). *Comparative education.* New York: Houghton Mifflin.

[50] Schneider, F. A. (1947). *Triebkráfte der Pádagogik der Vólker. Salzburg: Otto Muller.*

[51] Harris, W. T. (1891). *Annual report of the Commissioner of education for the year 1888-1889.* Washington DC:

[52] Sadler, M. E. (1902). *The unrest in secondary education in Germany and elsewhere. In Education in Germany.* London: HMSO

[53] Thut, I. N. & Adams, D. (1964). *Educational patterns in contemporary societies.* New York: McGraw-Hill. p. 9.

CHAPTER 3

PHILOSOPHY OF EDUCATION IN HISTORICAL PERSPECTIVE

Every civilization has some form of education by which its heritage is meaningfully transmitted from one generation to another. For example, African traditional initiation is a sacred ritual of inculcating African traditional wisdom to younger generations. This form of education is also alive in Christianity where Sacred Scripture, which embodies the source of Christian wisdom, is taught to every generation. Jewish rabbinical schools played and still play an important role in the education of Jewish children. The above forms of education have their support structures that give them meaning as well as forces that offer compelling explanations of them. Christianity has Scripture, tradition and the magisterium as three sources of meaningful educational development. Judaism, because it develops within the backdrop of a theocentric religion, does not need a philosophy as such to guide it. A theocentric life and Jewish laws and customs are enough to ground the educational system.

Philosophy of education had an intellectual standing long before becoming a recognized curricular discipline. On the one hand, philosophy of education is as old as Plato (427-347 BC) since this philosopher was the first to thematically and systematically devote considerable attention to the nature, purpose, and content of education in the light of reason. The works of Plato are considered the first fully developed philosophy of education because in them are found the first explicit, philosophical justification of the theory of education. On the other hand, philosophy of education is a new discipline because it only began to emerge as an independent discipline in the works of the American philosopher, John Dewey (1859-1952).[1] Dewey is credited for popularizing the term philosophy of education by making a distinction between philosophy of education (study of the fundamental principles of the theory of education), science of education (study of the educational process), and the art of education (the method or techniques of educational practice).

Before Dewey philosophy of education had only an intermittent importance. That is why the subject has no regular historical epochs. Before Dewey teachers and writers of education were content to follow common sense in matters of education. This is evident in the Institutio oratoria of the Roman educator Quintilian (AD 35-95) for whom the goal of education is the formation of 'a good man skilled in speaking.' 1500 years later the Ratio Studiorum (1599), the Jesuit educational bible, was written. It is basically deductions from the experience and practice of Jesuit teachers. About 50 years later John Locke (1632-1704) wrote Some Thoughts Concerning Education in which he confined himself to the narrative description of his experience as tutor rather than considering it theoretically.

ROOTS IN CLASSICAL GREECE

Plato the Educator

Plato is not only a brilliant philosopher and writer but also a practical educator. Plato is the first Greek philosopher who attended to education in a systematic way by bringing philosophical theory to bear on common sense educational notions. His *The Republic* stands as a landmark of educational philosophy.

Context of Plato's educational philosophy

Born and nurtured in an Athenian family with distinguished political connections Plato had the ease of seeking a civic career. However, educated at the foot of Socrates Plato refrained from seeking a political career because of prevailing political abuse and disturbance. The peak of Plato's career coincided with the decline of Athenian democracy. The political abuse that brought disillusionment to Plato concerning the political scene was the trial and death of Socrates on charges of impiety, subversion, and corruption of the youth. According to Plato the charges were downright false and calculated misuse of political power for gains by those whose conventional morals were ruffled by the questions that Socrates asked. Also, Plato was disgusted with those who sought safe haven in authoritarianism and dogma. According to Plato this is dangerous. Appalled by the wickedness of his times and the dangers of unreflective social life, Plato came to the conclusion that most states are badly governed. The only prospect for justice for individuals and the society is rooted in a properly husbanded educational process that only philosophy can offer. Plato, therefore, wanted an aristocracy of talent, a ruling intellectual *élite*. Plato has Socrates remark:

> Until philosophers are kings, or the kings and princes of this world have the spirit and power of philosophy, and political greatness and wisdom meet in one, and those commoner natures who pursue either to the exclusion of the other are compelled to stand aside, cities will never have rest from their evils – no, nor the human race, as I believe – and then only this our State have a possibility of life and behold the light of day.[2]

The philosopher-king incarnates the highest wisdom humanly possible. He rules not for the purpose of dominating but to lead other citizens to share his vision and love. His approach is dialectic not indoctrination. Here lies the genesis of Plato's educational philosophy.

The Peloponnesian War (431-404 BC) between the Athenian democracy and the Spartan oligarchic tribalism had lasting negative effects on Plato. The victory by the Spartans meant humiliation for the Athenians, the breakdown of the Athenian confederation, a deterioration of the Athenian constitution, and an establishment of Spartan oligarchic supremacy. The effects of the war led Plato to put a halt on any political ambition he may have had until such a time when the reforms he envisioned would be attainable.

The purpose of Platonic educational philosophy goes beyond mere pedagogy. It is set in the larger context of social improvement and education for leadership. Plato's school, the Academy of Athens (387-386 BC), was a symbol of revolt against political egoism and self-seeking. It was an institution in which Plato hoped to disseminate his ideas. The objective of the Academy was to train a new breed of politicians who might become the sort of philosopher-king envisioned in The Republic. The trajectory of Plato's career points out clearly that he is a philosopher of education par excellence. His abandonment of a political career in favor of a pursuit of what goes into the formation of an effective leader eloquently portrays Plato's sublime conviction that education cannot be divorced from a broader context of social convictions and political considerations. The Academy plunged Plato into school design and administration. By the time of his death he was finishing another book, the Laws, a model civic code, in which he devotes a whole section (Book VII) to education. In light of the educational reasoning elaborated here "Plato's stature as a philosopher and his genius for practical embodiment of ideas in educational programs and institutions placed him in the first rank in the history of education; he knows from experience what he is talking about, he cares about it, and he proposes to do something original with education."[3]

Plato's philosophy of education

Plato was a prolific writer. Only a herculean effort can extract a philosophy of education from all his volumes. However, in his *The Republic*, we have the broad strokes of Plato's educational philosophy. It covers topics like teaching methods, epistemological theory, curriculum development, analysis of human nature, and social role of education.

The Republic is a statement of aims involved in training the philosopher-king and the means to be employed. Hence, one topic of interest in Platonic educational philosophy is about aims of education. The issue facing education according to Plato is political virtue – producing responsible and just citizens. Plato, therefore, recommends education as a means for reforming individual character and society. Another question concerns the nature of the philosopher-king and the relationship that exists between society and education. Since Plato envisioned the formation of a political *elite,* he also elaborated a theory of educational soundness based on his understanding of the Two Worlds (the world of phenomena and the world of the Forms). According to Platonic epistemology knowledge of ultimate truth is knowledge of the eternal and unchanging world of the Forms. So, education can be defined from the epistemological standpoint as a path to the Forms. Plato developed a scheme for attaining knowledge based on his philosophical theory that included conjecture (forming images), beliefs (grasping ideas), understanding (developing hypothesis), and pure vision (grasping ideas). The purpose of knowledge is to provide educands with a vision of Goodness or eternal Forms. A propos of the epistemological method Plato advanced that since truth is innate the teacher can only awaken the student or open the doors of the student's perception by questioning and personal example.

Also, in The Republic Plato deals with the organization of education into two stages. This is later developed in his The Laws in which education is organized into more stages: Nursery (3-6 years), primary (6-10 years), and secondary (10-16 years). Plato's epistemological system outlines a gradual ascent of the mind from traditional and popular opinions to a wisdom based on a vision of eternal principles of truth. In a nutshell, education in Platonic educational philosophy is a process of reviving innate knowledge of unchanging reality. Reasoned questioning or critical dialectic sustains this process. This intellectual scheme also has a moral component. The revival is not for its own sake but so that the educand can be equipped for the service of justice in society.

Plato's The Republic is a paradigm of his educational theory. It outlines the principles that govern his elaboration of curriculum, method, and education administration, all of which are considered means to a just and good citizenry as well as to a just and good society. However, the whole edifice of Plato's educational philosophy is founded on his Two-world metaphysics, his facts on human nature and society (ethics), and an epistemology that ties his metaphysics and ethics together. In Plato's metaphysics the Forms or Ideas that exist in the realm of the supernatural are good. The Form of humanity is good. The Form of society is good. It is because of this goodness that Plato recommends knowledge of the Forms as worthy of any educational pursuit. In a way, then, Plato's ethics and metaphysics are indissoluble although they can be conceptually distinguished. The epistemological foundation of Plato's theory states that the whole purpose of life is to become a copy of the Form. A better guide to the process of becoming a form is knowledge not opinion. This knowledge can only be acquired through learning, that is, discovery of the truth.

The roots of all later philosophy of education are found in classical Greece. Whereas some authors like Aristotle undertook thinking about education only as an aspect of a larger project like politics Plato is the first to embark on educational thinking, per se. "Among the few who have given major attention to refining common sense educational notions by philosophical theory the first, and perhaps the greatest was Plato."[4] Another reason for considering Plato as the origin of systematic philosophy of education is because his work eclipsed all others for a long time. "Plato was educational philosophy's first architect. The citadel he constructed was both sturdy and ornamental... Plato heads the list but Isocrates (436-338 BC) and the Sophists are on it too, although their contribution to educational philosophy is dwarfed by Plato's monumental stature."[5] Brambaugh and Lawrence corroborate this point. "Plato's dialogues, because of their extraordinary quality of raising the right questions and identifying the important ideas relevant to their answers, have had more impact and influence on Western philosophy and Western educational theory than other writings in these fields. Plato's works offer, therefore, a natural beginning for our discussion of the questions great philosophers have asked and the answers they have proposed when they turned their attention to education."[6] It is in this same light that Rousseau's claimed that The Republic is the best educational treatise ever written is to be understood. By such a remark, Rousseau meant that the influence of The Republic was still being felt in the 18th century. The primary concern of Plato's educational philosophy is with the human ability to grasp Ideas and Forms through reason. Preoccupation with this question led Plato to elaborate the fundamental principles of education.

MEDIEVAL AND RENAISSANCE PAUSE

After Plato a long pause in the elaboration of systematic philosophical education ensued. Two reasons explain the pause. First, the immediate post-Plato era was that of refinement of Plato's educational philosophy by his disciples. Second, there was the rise of different interests in education other than a philosophical interest.

Plato's pupil, Aristotle (384-322 BC) gave theoretical attention to education, but in a limited rather than in the systematic way than did Plato. Aristotle treated education as part of his *Politics,* in which he contended that the theory of education should conform to the pattern of state. Local politics is *prescriptive* for education. Aristotle, therefore, elaborated a politics of education.

Other philosophers after Plato took education to different horizons. Thinkers of the Middle Ages were interested in *Christian philosophy of education.* Christian philosophy of education explores education in light of divine revelation. Hence, this educational theory emphasized the notion of God and human perfectibility. St Augustine (354-430 AD), for example, was interested in *synthetic education* – bringing together Greek thought and Scriptures. Philosophical knowledge was considered an adequate preparation for serious study of Scripture. Renaissance educational theory, while reacting to the medieval Christian philosophy of education, proposed *rhetorical education,* which emphasized educating the person as a citizen of the world. Thinkers found a good source in Quintillian, who postulated that the goal of education is to produce a good person skilled in speaking well. Renaissance intellectual culture was primarily literary and rhetorical not philosophical.

Christian philosophy of education or Christian humanism continued to be a major focus of education through many writers down to François de la Mothe Fénélon (1651-1715). A full treatment of the history of Christian philosophy is presented in Chapter IV. Rhetorical education was carried forward in the works of Peter Ramus (1515-1572). The epoch of rationalism and empiricism ushered in a new emphasis on education – *scientific education. Scientific education* appeared with René Descartes (1596-1650), who chose mathematics as the model of fundamental educational discipline. The emphasis was on clarity of thought and logical deductions, not on a search for ultimate meaning as in philosophy of education. Imagination, which plays a big role in philosophy of education, is considered by scientific education as a hindrance to knowledge. Francis Bacon's empiricism with its stress on factual information, practical relevance, and discovery method constituted another educational emphasis different from that of philosophy of education.

Rousseau and Later Development

Platonic educational philosophy emphasized the metaphysical and eternal realm. Medieval education shifted the emphasis from philosophy *simpliciter* to Christian philosophy of education with emphasis on God. Renaissance humanistic thinking shifted the emphasis of education from God to man by stressing the physical, material, and rhetorical. Scientific education stressed educational method. Despite these educational classics the next seminal educational work after *The Republic* of Plato is the *Emile* of Jean-Jacques Rousseau (1712-1778).

Educational Naturalism of Rousseau

Hellenistic educational philosophy and Christian humanism dominated the educational arena for centuries. Both philosophies claimed that the purpose of education is to preparation for life. Hellenistic philosophy claimed that education should prepare pupils for life in society. Christian humanism insisted that education should prepare pupils for afterlife, that is, life with God. Hence, both philosophies gave prominent place to 'useful knowledge' in school curriculum. Rousseau enters the scene and incites a revolution by indicting the previous philosophies for forcing precocity on children by being "indifferent to the natural needs and interests of children."[7] In the context of indifference to nature, Rousseau recommends a reform of the fundamental assumptions behind the aims and structure of education. Rousseau's reflections are found in his Emile published in 1762.

Rousseau's Emile

Emile is a treatise on the philosophy of teaching which will be the focus of educational thinking for the next two centuries.

The task of Rousseau's educational theorizing is social regeneration. Like Plato, Rousseau noticed that his society was corrupt and infested with injustices. According to Rousseau, society corrupts the state of nature (the world of the Noble Savage) in two ways: first, by creating laws of property. This constitutes the basis for inequality and restricts freedom. Second, society corrupts nature by creating unnatural desires like wealth, fame, position, and power. This idea of society as a source of degradation stands out in the opening sentence of Emile. "Everything is good as it comes from the hands of the Creator of things; everything degenerates in the hands of man."[8] Knowledge provided by society creates desires that one may not be able to fulfill and that can make one unhappy. For example, technology makes tools and machines that I cannot operate and this makes me dependent. From this observation Rousseau concludes that modern society is a conspiracy to prevent people from attaining their full human potential and maturity because it prevents them from getting full control of themselves. Modern society is the source of human problems. Existing conventional education has not addressed the situation because "the usual education of children is such as if children leaped, at one bounce, from the mother's breast to the age of reason."[9]

Rousseau's principal preoccupation with education was how to organize life purposefully and meaningfully in the changed world of the bourgeoisie. His central interest was countering the pernicious effects of society and putting in its place freedom and happiness for human beings. Rousseau found a purifying influence in nature since the current educational arrangement ran contrary to nature. To reshape society it is necessary to regain the goodness that nature gives. The goodness of nature are that nature makes us free, nature makes us independent, and natural man is not troubled by illusions. *Emile* is an educational directive that respects the native goodness of educands.

Rousseau's *Emile* gives priority to natural education in which the practice and content of instruction respects the natural process of the educand. Rousseau's developmental or progressive pedagogy moves through and respects the qualitative distinction of each stage of human development. Curriculum must be adapted to the developmental needs of the individual child. Rousseau finds the key to societal restoration in a thorough and continuing commitment to education. In light of *Emile* Rousseau is considered by many as the founder of progressive education that prevents children from the oppressive dictates of society.

Discontinuity with Classical Era

Crucial educational themes that emerged from Rousseau's educational philosophy are similar to those of the Classical Era. These include ideas of growth, nature, symbols, and society. However Rousseau takes another route when dealing with these issues thus inaugurating a new era of philosophy of education. This section outlines some of the novel educational twists present in Rousseau's Emile.

First, concerning nature and growth. Hellenistic educational philosophy viewed the pupil as a potential adult. According to Plato the basic aim of education is to assist the pupil in knowing the Forms. For Aristotle the major role of education is the development of happiness or virtue. Platonic and Aristotelian educational philosophies are interested only in the terminus ad quem of education. Education is a process of growth in which the finality alone is significant.

While acknowledging that education is a growth process, Rousseau criticizes the Hellenistic 'child as potential adult' view, which denied, "that childhood as such has any final cause of its own, apart from that of preparation for a later career."[10] Rousseau criticized Hellenistic educational androcentrism, that is, the view that holds a pupil as an undersized adult, thus depriving children of the joys of childhood. Rousseau insisted that education should be pedocentric because "nature wants children to be children before they are men."[11] Also, "nothing is useful and good for him (child) which is unbefitting for his age."[12] Childhood, according to Rousseau, is not a state of privation but has an actual nature of its own which education should pursue. Childhood has an intrinsic value of its own. Rousseau's insistence on the intrinsic goal of childhood has important ramification in the consideration of educational growth process.

Since the growth rate for human beings is explicitly discontinuous, the progress of education cannot follow a natural smooth curve.

Second, Rousseau departs from Greek consideration of the role of society in education. Like Aristotle, Rousseau acknowledges that society is a significant determinant of human habits. Rousseau's Emile is not a savage "to be banished to the desert; he is a savage who has to live in town."[13] However, unlike the Greeks who viewed society in a positive light, Rousseau abhorred society because it creates social necessities that distort or destroy the natural dignity of human beings. This dour view of society as a corrupter of the natural development of human beings comes out clearly in the botanical images by which Rousseau expresses this social comment: "cultivated fruit trees are stunted and deformed, compared to those in nature unaffected by contact with human societies."[14] For a child to develop naturally it is, therefore, important and imperative to protect that child from society.

Natural development is a cornerstone of Rousseau's educational philosophy. "The man", he writes, "is truly human who desires what he is able to perform, and does what he desires. This is my fundamental maxim. Apply it to childhood, and all the rules of education spring from it."[15] Rousseau advocates that education should occur through individual experience. "Nothing good enters into the human world except in and through the free activities of individual men and women. Educational practice must be shaped in accordance with the truth."[16]

The findings of anthropology today are at odds with Rousseau's account of the natural savage. Also, the use of textbooks to provide vicarious experience in education and the definition of education to include partnership with society, politics, and economics run contrary to Rousseau's negative view of society. However, Rousseau's educational philosophy still has some significance for today. Rousseau's insistence on the individual and his/her experiences highlights the preponderance of human nature in education. Rousseau's protest against society challenges educators and philosophers to think of the authentic and inauthentic roles of educational partners like politics. Rousseau's educational philosophy may not be implemented literally in educational practice today; but it can be a significant inspiration for educational theory from which later practice can be crafted.

Importance of Rousseau for philosophy of education

One area in which Rousseau is significant for philosophy of education is in developmental theory. Rousseau's contribution to educational philosophy is his concept of the stages of educational development corresponding to the periods of human development from infancy to adulthood. Rousseau classified human development into five stages – infancy, childhood, boyhood, adolescence, and adulthood – and insisted that each stage needed a peculiar pedagogical approach. For this reason Rousseau's battle cry was "not to manufacture adults from children" but to "let children be children". Gradation in the organization of education today may seem natural and normal. However, commonplace educational organization and gradation may be "it took a Rousseau to remind the pedagogues of his day of their importance."[17] Developmental theory is still important for education in that it affirms that the schedule for educational organization should come from inside a person, not from an external system. The notion of stages of development should be considered in terms of incremental improvements, which are child-centered and not system-centered.

A second influence of Rousseau is in the domain of educational purpose. Many critics of Rousseau have mistakenly criticized Rousseau's rejection of schooling and his advocacy of a return to natural education as "extravaganzas."[18] These critics hold that Rousseau was advocating an education with neither discipline nor instruction. Rousseau can only be understood from the background of the sources of education. According to Rousseau education "comes to us from nature, from man, or from things. The growth of our organs and faculties is the education from nature, the use we make of this growth is the education of men, what we gain by our experience of our surrounding is the education of things."[19] According to Rousseau public school arrangements and the work of teachers 'manufacture' little adults without letting the talents and skills of the pupils develop. What Rousseau was advocating was to give instruction from teachers a low profile while favoring personal development. By natural education Rousseau, therefore, was prizing personal education to social education. Rousseau is not opposed to educational instruction since without it "things would be worse, [for] mankind cannot be made by halves."[20] The importance of Rousseau for educational philosophy is his critic of the goal of education, namely, preparation for life, which has been taken for granted as the goal all education. By emphasizing the personal dimension of education as another possible goal, Rousseau raised the possibility of alternative goals in education. Rousseau, therefore, is important in the area of defining educational purpose.

Johann Friedrich Herbart

In the century following Rousseau it was Johann Friedrich Herbart (1776-1841) who gave systematic attention to educational problems. He was born in Oldenburg and died at Gottingen. Herbart was professor of philosophy at the University of Königsberg. Among his writings *The Science of Education* is his major work on educational philosophy. Herbart proposes a *scientific pedagogy* in order to redress the differences in instruction of his day. The overriding question that occupied his thought was how the behavior of children can be managed. He was interested in the objectives of education, method in education, and the possibility of education. Hence, like Rousseau, Herbart was interested in the philosophy of teaching. He was interested in the work of teachers and educational theory.

> The aim of all those who educate and demand education is determined by the range of thought they bring to the subject. The majority of those who teach have entirely neglected in the first instance to construct for themselves their own range of thought in view of this work; it opens out gradually as the work progresses and is formed partially by their own characteristics, partly by the individuality and the environment of the pupil.[21]

Assuming that education is not only teaching but also learning and practice, Herbart opened a school for teachers in Königsberg to be the mainstay for putting his educational philosophical theory into practice. With a commitment to shape educational policy, Herbart asserted that the mere acquisition of knowledge is not a legitimate end of education. Rather, "the one and the whole work of education may be summed up in the concept – morality."[22] Morality is the ultimate foundation of education. Morality will be used to determine the social ends of education. Five subordinate goals provide the conditions for moral education: inner freedom, perfection, justice, equity, and benevolence.

The elaboration of Herbart's educational philosophy is based on two principles: appreciation and interest. Appreciation is the act or process of assimilating, appropriating, and identifying objects, impressions, or ideas. All knowledge after the first percipient act is appreciation based on this perception. Education involves directing the process of appreciation by judicious selection of material that will constitute the experience of the pupil. Interest, the second aspect of Herbart's philosophy, stimulates voluntary attention to what is appreciated. In this light, Herbart's philosophy of education has a psychological component.

Herbart is valuable and stimulating for philosophy of education because of his invocation of rational principles, as opposed to mere empiricism, in education. Other points of interest include accentuating the value of interest, advocating ethical educational aims, manifesting faith in the potency of education, and enthusiastically putting into evidence the vocation of teachers.

MODERN DEVELOPMENT
Synthesizing Plato and Rousseau

Prior to the 20th century, systematic writers of educational philosophy were rare. The works of those few who wrote on this topic, like Plato and Rousseau, dominated extensive periods. After 1900 there was a proliferation of educational philosophies, perhaps due to the progress of science and increasing complexity in economics and politics. The only way to handle these numerous and diverse outbursts is to reduce them to comprehensive theories. Hence, the modern phase of the development of philosophy of education is characterized by explicit philosophies of education or schools of thought. Philosophy of education is not attributed to any one individual and his/her work but to a school of thought like Pragmatism, Existentialism, or Analytical Philosophy. Here it suffices to mention and summarize the salient features of some schools of thought that developed a formal educational philosophy. We shall take a tour of Progressive philosophy of education because it brings together Plato and Rousseau, both of whom have been studied already. Dewey (1859-1952) represents this school of thought. Like Plato and Rousseau before him, Dewey contended that education is an instrument of social reform. However, unlike Rousseau, he did not accept nature uncritically; nor did he, like Plato, seek his standard in some ideal realm behind and beyond nature.

Progressive Philosophy of Education

The quintessence of Progressive educational philosophy is that it senses the need to bring educational philosophy abreast with the times. Also called "the New Education," Progressive Education is a reaction against the rigidity and aridity of traditional education. The sources of Progressive Education go back before the 1850s. However the movement sprang into prominence both in Europe and the United States of America in late 19th and early 20th centuries.

European Progressivism

The European brand of Progressive educational philosophy, also called child-centered philosophy, reflects on the nature of individual people, the society, and the relationship of both. Sometimes progressivism will stress the need to respect diversity and to free individuals from the pressures of society that hinder their development. At other times progressivism stresses the need to provide a social environment that will develop human freedom. Progressivism, therefore, stresses the freedom of a child.

European progressivism found its inspiration in Rousseau, whose Emile and Social Contract linked social reforms and education. Like Rousseau who broke loose from 18th century educational theory European progressivism was anxious to abandon the conventional molds of 19th and 20th centuries. Major proponents of European progressivism are Stanley Hall (1844-1924), Sigmund Freud (1856-1939) who suggested that free self-expression is a way of avoiding neurosis caused by social repression, Ovide Decroly (1871-1932) in Belgium, Adolphe Ferreière (1879-1960) in Geneva, and Elizabeth Rotten in Germany.

1921 marked a significant development in the European progressivism. Beatrice Ensor, initiator of the magazine New Era for the exchange of ideas and experiences about the new education, organized a progressivist conference in Calais, France. About 150 pioneers from countries around Europe attended. At this conference the New Education fellowship was born to link pioneers of educational progressivism around the world. From 1921 Progressive Education promoted its interests in eleven European countries as well as in Australia, India, Pakistan, Egypt, New Zealand, South Africa, and South America. Until 1955 European progressivism maintained contacts with the American version, which was called American Education fellowship.

American Progressivism

Progressive education in the United States of America emerged in late 19th century as a pedagogical revolt in universities against the formalism of philosophy, psychology, and the social sciences. Before that, glimpses of progressivism were evident in the work of Francis Parker in the early 1870s.

John Dewey later attributed to Parker the title of the father of progressive education. Parker undertook a reform of the Quincy Schools in Massachusetts by attacking the prevailing rote learning and proposing in its place a new pedagogical technique that would make the study of subjects more meaningful. Success attracted national and worldwide attention to what became known as "the Quincy System."

American progressivism criticized traditional education for its narrowness and formalism, its aristocratic character, and its isolation from life. "The crux of progressive education was its universality and its closeness to life."[23] Dewey wanted schools to be 'embryonic social communities' permeated by the values of the surrounding community. "When the school introduces and trains each child of society into membership within such a little community, saturating him with the spirit of service, and providing him with the instruments of effective self-direction we shall have the deepest and best guarantee of a larger society which is worthy, lovely, and harmonious."[24] American progressivism is a development of a critical and socially engaged intelligence. Unlike European progressivism, which is child-centered, American progressivism is social reconstructionist.

The sources of American progressivism are many, but two of them are note-worthy. First, there was the influence of mainstream pedagogical reform coming from Europe. Second, the first half of the 1900s witnessed a rapid transformation of American society under the influence of industrialization (advancement in technical process) and a growing complexity of urban life due to large numbers of non-English-speaking immigrants. The two social factors above put pressure on American schools to assume educational responsibilities that were formerly borne by family and neighborhood.

Although many Americans were attracted to Progressive Education, John Dewey is singled out as its commanding figure. Dewey's educational outlook was influenced negatively and positively by the small town ethos of his birthplace, Burlington, Vermont. Negatively, Dewey contended that the traditional desk-bound education practiced in rural schools contained in it a recipe for disaster in a growing American economy that was rapidly transforming itself from a simple agricultural economy to an unprecedented industrialized economy characterized by immigration, population growth, and drastic social change.

> (The old education) was predominantly static in subject matter, authoritarian in methods, and mainly passive and receptive

from the side of the young… the imagination of educators did not go beyond provision of a fixed and rigid environment of subject matter, one drawn moreover from sources altogether too remote from the experiences of the pupils.[25]

Positively, Dewey was convinced that the ordinary contacts of daily community life (be it in the social, cultural, political or economic domain) each provided real and significant contextual learning situations.

> The school is primarily a social institution. Education being a social process, the school is simply the form of a community life in which all those agencies are concentrated that will be most effective in bringing the child to share in the inherited resources of the race, and to use his own powers for social ends… education, therefore, is a process of living and not a preparation for future living.[26]

To propagate his educational ideas Dewey founded a laboratory school whose purpose was twofold: first, to facilitate research and experimentation with regard to new principles and methods, and second, to allow children take experimental approaches to learning. As a prolific writer, Dewey articulated an educational philosophy that spans his entire collection. He synthesizes, criticizes, and expands the educational philosophies of Plato, Rousseau, and others. Starting with The School and Society (1899) and peaking with Democracy and Education (1916), Dewey's works epitomized "the close relationship between progressive education and the larger social transformation being wrought by science, democracy, and industrialism."[27] Dewey espoused a Darwinian theory of progress as open-ended. Leaning heavily on Dewey's The Influence of Darwin on Philosophy progressivism propounded the theory that the end of education is growth and the only end of growth is more growth. Education is a continuous reconstruction of experience not a commodity held passively in storage. The logical outcome from this kind of thinking concerning curriculum is that neither the truths nor the aims of education are final or fixed. Dewey's contribution to educational philosophy is enshrined in his pragmatism. Salient educational features of pragmatism include the following: education must be engaged with and enlarge experience; education must explore the nature of thinking and reflection in the learning process and the role of the educator;

education must consider interaction with environment as educational context; and the passion of education should be democratic aims.

1919 is an important landmark in American progressivism. In this year progressive education, which was only a revolt against pedagogical formalism, acquired an organizational status. Quickly it gained notoriety in the United States of America. Its membership rapidly grew from 5,000 in 1927 to 10,500 in 1938.

Progressive Education, whether of the European or American type, attracted severe criticism. Christian educators accused Progressive Education of materialism and general denial of supernatural spiritual values. Also, in 1930 the Essentialists levied criticism on Progressive Education for paying no attention to the need for disciplined study of systematic knowledge. Furthermore, humanists criticized the naturalistic and Rousseauean emphasis on freedom and interest. After World War II criticism against progressivism became strong as American society opted for the conservative approach. Unable to meet the challenges, Progressive Education was disbanded in 1955. In 1957 the journal Progressive Education ceased to publish. This was the death knell on progressive philosophical education.

SUMMARY

The history of educational philosophy is intermittent and its landmarks are important educational philosophical works. Basically educational philosophy has three phases: root, later development, and modern. The root phase is located in Classical Greek civilization. This phase is characterized by a metaphysical contemplation of education in Platonic-Aristotelian tradition and is concerned with knowledge necessary for social life (education and society). The second phase, later development, comes some 1500 years after the emergence of educational philosophy. The principal proponents of this phase are Rousseau and Herbart. The focus of this phase is the self-development of individuals without any consideration of society (education and individual). The modern phase of educational philosophy is different from the others in that it lacks a dominant philosophical orientation. It is a phase characterized by a proliferation of educational philosophies whose focus is the relationship among education, society, and the individual. Hence, this phase characterized by liberation or liberalization of philosophy of education. The importance of the historical approach to educational philosophy lies not only in the mention of its giants and their seminal works but also in the exposure of some themes that are of interest to philosophy of education.

[1] Ashley, B. M. (2003). *Philosophy of education.* In New Catholic Encyclopedia Vol. 5, pp. 88-92). (2nd Ed.). Detroit: Thomson Gale.

[2] Jowett, B. (1908) *The Republic of Plato* Vol. I. O.U.P. p. 473

[3] Brumbaugh, R. S. & Lawrence, N. M. (1986). *Philosophers of education. Six essays on the foundation of Western thought.* New York: University Press of America, p. 11.

[4] J. S. Br. *Philosophy of education.* In *Encyclopedia Britannica,* Vol. 7. Chicago, IL: William Benton Publishers, 1969, p. 1016.

[5] Power, E. J. (1995). *Educational Philosophy. A History of Ancient World to Modern America.* New York: Garland Publishing. p. 5.

[6] Brumbaugh & Lawrence, *op. cit.,,* p. 10.

[7] Powers, E. J. (1982). *Philosophy of education. Studies in philosophies, schools, and educational policies.* Englewood Cliffs, NJ: Prentice-Hall, p. 55.

[8] Rousseau, J. -J. (1938). *Emile. Trans. Barbara Foxley.* New York: E. P. Duton, p. 5.

[9] Rousseau, *op. cit.,,* p. 133.

[10] Brumbaugh & Lawrence, *op. cit.,,* p. 77.

[11] Rousseau, *op. cit.,,* p. 54.

[12] Rousseau, *op. cit.,,* p. 213.

[13] Rousseau, *op. cit.,,* p. 167.

[14] Brumbaugh & Lawrence, *op. cit.,,* p. 78.

[15] Rousseau, *op. cit.,,* p. 131.

[16] Nunn, T. P. (1945). *Education. Its data and first principles,* 3rd Ed. New York: E. Arnold, p. 12.

[17] Sahakian, M. L. & Sahakian, W. S. (1974). *Rousseau as educator.* New York: Twayne Publishers, p. 5.

[18] Compayré, G. (1907). *Jean-Jacques Rousseau and education from nature.* New York: Thomas Y. Crowell, p. 24.

[19] Rousseau, *op. cit.,,* p. 6.

[20] Rousseau, *op. cit.,,* p. 5.

[21] Rousseau, *op. cit.,,* p. 78.

[22] Herbart, J. F. *On the aesthetic revelation of the world as the chief work of education.* Trans by H. M. Felkin & E. Felkin. Washington, DC: University Publications of America 1977, p. 78.

[23] L.A.C (1969). *Progressive Education.* In *Encyclopedia Britannica* Vol. 18. pp. 606-608. Chicago: William Benton Publishers. p. 607.

[24] Dewey, J. (1889). *The school and society.* Chicago: The University of Chicago Press. p. 44.

[25] Flanagan, F. M. (1994). *John Dewey.* www.ul.ie/~philos/vol1/dewey. htm.

[26] Dewey, J. (1897). *My pedagogic creed.* www.pragmatism.org/genealogy/ dewey/My_pedagogic_creed.htm

[27] LAC. *Progressive education.* p. 607.

CHAPTER 4

CATHOLIC PHILOSOPHY OF EDUCATION

Catholic educational philosophy studies specific educational goals, proposes, values, and ideals drawn form Catholic philosophy. In other words, Catholic philosophy offers principles and norms that govern the entire scope of Catholic education. Catholic philosophy, therefore, constitutes the rational foundation of Catholic educational philosophy. Catholic philosophy of education is philosophical because it acknowledges and employs the truths of reason or natural way of thought. It is also Catholic because it is rooted in and constructed upon the Christian faith or supernatural way of life and thought.[1] This chapter will examine what Catholic philosophy is and its implication for Catholic education.

STRUGGLE FOR RECOGNITION

The legitimacy of the appellation Christian philosophy has agitated many minds for centuries. Many thinkers have asked the question: Is the expression a forced grafting? Is the expression a fact or fiction? Is there a philosophy undergirded by Christian principles and influences that it can be tagged Christian? Are there reflections in Christianity that are so rational that they can be called philosophy? Are Christian philosophers "counterfeit philosophers trying to pawn off a theological product under the guise of philosophy?"[2]

The philosopher Martin Heideggar describes Christian philosophy as "a round square and a misunderstanding."[3] Collin Brown expresses his uneasiness with the expression as follows:

> By no stretch of the imagination can the relationship between philosophy and the Christian faith be described as an ideal marriage. It is neither ideal, nor, strictly speaking a marriage. There are many Christians who regard an interest in philosophy as a dubious and dangerous flirtation. And perhaps the majority of professional philosophers today have serious doubts as to the intellectual respectability of counting religious beliefs. We are left with a tenuous liaison, sustained by sporadic, painful encounters. When the two parties come together the result seems all too often to be a string of bitter accusations from the philosophers or a series of lame attempts on the part of believers to patch things up. And even when the latter succeeds in convincing a few of the philosophers, they often seem to do so at the expense of compromising the faith.[4]

Other thinkers like Emile Bréhier have rejected the expression *Christian philosophy* outright while others like Etienne Gilson and Jacques Maritain accept it with restriction. In order to appreciate the dynamics of Christian philosophy of education it is imperative to understand the expressions Christian philosophy and Christian education. This section probes the genesis, problematic, refinement, and conclusion of the Catholic philosophy debate. The purpose is to survey what Christian philosophy meant in the history of ideas. At the end of the exercise conclusions pertinent to Christian education will be formulated.

Genesis of a Debate

The question of the relationship between faith and reason dates back to the Patristic era and the time of the Carthage-born lawyer, Tertullian (AD 160-225). Converted to Christianity in AD 197 Tertullian was later to become a Christian theologian with the ferocity of a crusader. It is his famous assertion 'Jerusalem has no need of Athens'[5] that started the faith-reason debate. Jerusalem and Athens are not literal designations but are used as metaphorical contrast between the locus of divine revelation and the domus of Greek philosophy, respectively. According to Tertullian faith and reason are antithetical, mutually exclusive, and contradictory. Tertullian reaches the conclusion of the irreconcilable nature of faith and reason from a conviction of belief. As Tertullian proclaimed, "God said it, I believe it, that settles it." The coherence of Scripture was compelling evidence to the truth it contains whereas the inconsistencies of heretical writings demonstrated the absurdity of human scholarship.

It is in the works of St. Augustine that the expression Christian philosophy occurs for the first time. St. Augustine started on the same side of the pendulum as Tertullian. St. Augustine describes in his Confessions how, as a youth, he sought that coherent philosophy that will guide him to the truth. Finding none he became a skeptic of the usefulness of philosophy. At age 33, he accepted the truth of the gospel. With this acceptance of the gospel, he realized that philosophy was incapable of bringing him salvation. However, philosophy did help him to distinguish truth from falsehood. Philosophy was at the base of his acceptance of Christ. Thus while acknowledging the priority of faith St. Augustine also acknowledged its incompleteness without the help of reason. As such, St. Augustine distinguishes himself from Tertullian by postulating an auxiliary role to philosophy in Christianity. According to St. Augustine philosophy has useful aspects (ideas and method) that can assist in an adequate elaboration and better understanding of revelation. Hence, philosophy is not an end in itself but an indispensable ancilla theologiae, a tool by which revelation can be better understood. Unlike Tertullian who drove a wedge between faith and reason St. Augustine championed the course of reasonable faith. Thus, St. Augustine's famous phrase 'Credo ut intelligam' meaning 'faith seeking understanding.' St. Augustine sees no contradiction between philosophy and the Christian faith. Philosophy is part and parcel of the believer's faith. St. Augustine's arguments can be summarized syllogistically as follows: Philosophy is the love of wisdom. God is absolute wisdom. Since faith encounters God revealed in the Bible, the philosophy of Scripture is true philosophy. It is in this light that the aphorism credo ut intelligam is to be understood.

Patristic Christian philosophy, epitomized by Tertullian and St. Augustine, emphasized a Scripture-centered or faith oriented education. According to these thinkers faith is knowledgeable dependence on God not gullibility – a blind acceptance of God or ignorant dependence. While affirming the importance of human reason in the process of understanding the Scriptures the eternal realm still takes center stage.

In the Medieval Age the pendulum of the faith-reason debate moved to another extreme with Thomas Aquinas. Starting with the doctrine of original sin Aquinas concluded that human beings lost the image of God in them. However, this loss of primeval status did not affect the intellect. Aquinas, therefore, argued that knowledge of God is still possible without any special revelation. "In regard to the validity of naturally grounded reasoning," writes Joseph Owens, "the Catholic teaching on original sin left human nature wounded yet, albeit with difficulty, able to function on its own proper level. Love of wisdom on the human plane could still be encouraged, and the results of its activity could always be appreciated and put to full use."[6] However, Aquinas was not ruling out the importance of Scripture and revelation. In his view, revelation can make use of its indispensable ancilla philosophiae, in order to reach a fuller explanation of what can be known about God through human wisdom. Hence, Aquinas' famous dictum "I understand in order to believe." Aquinas is, therefore, the reverse of St. Augustine as he emphasizes the priority of human reason and its incompleteness without the help of revelation. Aquinas found support for his stance on Christian philosophy from Aristotle whose philosophy affirmed the importance of the natural world to witness to the truth. Arguing from the fact that philosophy antedated Christianity, medieval philosophy concluded that the reciprocity of faith and reason is accidental and extrinsic. Joseph Owens summarizes the Scholastic perspective as follows:

> From this medieval viewpoint, one can readily deduce, the notion 'Christian' meant something extrinsic and accidental to purely philosophical reasoning. The considerations it denoted pertained intrinsically to revealed religion or to sacred theology. They were outside the content of unaided natural reason. They were only accidentally connected with philosophy, for they arose from the accidentally connected historical fact of divine revelation. Philosophy had existed in Greece centuries before the advent of Christianity. Christianity on its part had existed among ordinary people without a developed philosophy. From the viewpoint of precisely abstracted essence neither of them involved the other. In a word, Christianity was something both accidental to and extrinsic to philosophy."[7]

From the Patristic to the Medieval Era two trends are discerned in the faith-reason debate. The first trend elaborated by Tertullian can be characterized as that of *independence* of faith and reason from one another. Between the hammer and the anvil there is no peace. The second trend can be described as an *in-service-of* trend. In this category there are two diametrically opposed views by Augustine and Aquinas. Augustine attributes a central role to faith and a peripheral role to reason as evidenced by the unfolding of his life. Aquinas does just the opposite attributing centrality to reason and a peripheral role to faith boosting his argument from the effect of original sin and the natural philosophy of Aristotle. In Patristic and Scholastic thought there are no qualms accepting the expression *Christian philosophy* as it enjoyed an established and secured status. This complacency was jolted by Emile Bréhier thereby sparking a new interest in the expression.

Early 20ᵗʰ century Refinement of Debate: Renewed interest

The beginning of the 20ᵗʰ century saw a renewed interest in the meaning of Christian philosophy. Two events are responsible for this. The first, is the publication of the encyclical Aeterni Patris by Pope Leo XIII in 1879. This encyclical aimed at "the restoration of Christian philosophy in Catholic schools."[8] Restoration in this document points to "the use of philosophy to serve the Christian faith. This requires a choice of philosophical problems on the ground of their relation to revealed doctrines. It requires that the faith gives incentive and guidance to genuinely philosophical procedures in the solution of those problems."[9]

The second event is a series of three lectures by Emile Bréhier, a French historian of philosophy, in Brussels in 1928. These lectures, published in 1931, addressed the question: is there a Christian philosophy? In these lectures Bréhier claimed that philosophy and Christian revelation contradicted one another. The two notions Christian and philosophy "in Christian philosophy, taken as a notion, were contradictorily opposed to each other. Philosophy is based upon what is intrinsically evident, Christianity on what is mystery, what is authoritatively revealed without intrinsic evidence… Consequently the notion of 'Christian' cannot be a specifying differentia of philosophy."[10] Reactions to Bréhier brought division into two camps. The first group is made up of those who like Bréhier rejected the expression Christian philosophy. This group contends that the expression is self-destructive. The second group is made up of those who accept and promote the expression with reservations like Gilson and Maritain.

Emile Bréhier's lectures did not only separate thinkers according to their views of the expression Christian philosophy but it also refined the question. To the question what is Christian philosophy? Bréhier is clear that the question is not finding out if there is or was philosophy in Christian thought. This is self-evident for Bréhier who lauds the use of the philosophies of Plato and Aristotle by Augustine and Aquinas. Rather, when the question of Christian philosophy is asked Bréhier has in mind the quest: Can Christianity make a contribution to philosophy? Did Christian revelation play any positive role in the development of philosophy? This precision is important in order to understand the responses of Gilson and Maritain.

Endorsing the Notion Christian Philosophy

Etienne Gilson and Jacques Maritain saw promising hope in the expression if the definition of philosophy is further specified. They proposed that a distinction should be made between the substantive and modal uses of philosophy. The modal expression is a consideration of philosophy as a human activity in which persons bring to bear their background in the process of reflection. Defenders of the Christian philosophy contend that the expression is operative in the modal domain of philosophy. It is in the exercise of philosophy that Christian considerations bring about an intrinsic differentiation in philosophy.

Etienne Gilson (1884-1978) developed his arguments against Bréhier in his Gifford Lectures (1931-32) later published as The Spirit of Medieval Philosophy. Arguing that no one starts philosophizing as a tabula rasa but that each philosophy is shaped and determined by a priori truths Gilson concludes that Christianity "intrinsically affected the core of the philosophizing."[11] From the existence of a priori truths Gilson concludes, "this fact makes it hard for me to understand how a Christian can ever philosophize as if he were not a Christian."[12]

Gilson demonstrates the intrinsic relationship of Christian revelation and philosophy in his definition and condition for Christian philosophy. He defines Christian philosophy as follows:

> This effort of truth believed to transform itself into truth known, is truly the life of Christian wisdom, and the body of rational truths resulting from the effort is Christian philosophy itself. Thus the content of Christian philosophy is that body

of rational truths discovered, explored, or simply safeguarded, thanks to the help reason receives from revelation.[13]

As a condition for Christian philosophy Gilson states that:

> If it is to deserve the name [Christian philosophy] the supernatural must descend as a constitutive element not, of course, into the texture which would be a contradiction, but into the work of the construction. Thus I call Christian, every philosophy which, although keeping the two orders formally distinct nevertheless considers Christian revelation as an indispensable auxiliary to reason. Understood thus, this notion does not correspond to a simple essence that can be given an abstract definition; rather it corresponds to a concrete historical reality of which it indicates a description. It is but one of the species of the genus of philosophy and includes in its extension all those philosophical systems which were in fact what they were only because a Christian religion existed and because they were ready to submit to its influence. Insofar as they are concrete historical realities, these systems distinguish themselves one from another by their individual differences; insofar as they form one kind, they show common characteristics which justifies the grouping of them under one category.[14]

Gilson makes an important distinction between the 'texture' of philosophy and the 'work of construction'. The first is philosophy *simpliciter*, philosophy in its primary and substantive meaning. The second is philosophy *secundum quid*, philosophy in a restricted sense, the activity of philosophizing. In the primary sense Christian revelation and reason are separated. Only in the 'work of construction' can one entertain the possibility of a Christian philosophy. Christian revelation does not enter into the strictly philosophic content, it belongs to the philosophic process. Apart from the distinction that locates the level at which Christian philosophy is operative, valid, and reliable Gilson's definition also advances three important affirmations concerning the relationship of Christian faith/revelation and philosophy. First, in the formal sense faith and reason belong to separate and distinct domains. Second, the term

Christian philosophy does not designate an essence but a concrete historical reality. Hence, Christian philosophy is not a definition but a description of a precise activity. Third, Christian philosophy is the kind of philosophy that would not exist if there were no influence from Christianity.

The definition and condition of Christian philosophy evidenced some criteria of Christian philosophy that Gilson condenses in the following paragraph:

> In the first place, and this is perhaps the most apparent trait of his attitude, the Christian philosopher is a man who makes a choice among philosophical problems. By right, he is capable of applying himself to the totality of philosophical problems just as well as any other philosopher; in fact, he applies himself uniquely or especially to those problems the solution of which bears on the conduct of his religious life. The other problems, indifferent in themselves, become that which Saint Augustine, Saint Bernard, and Saint Bonaventure stigmatized with the name curiosity, *turpis curiositas*. Even Christian philosophers like Saint Thomas whose interest did extend to the whole of philosophy only did their creative work in a relatively restrained field. Nothing could be more natural. Because Christian revelation only teaches us about the truths that are necessary for salvation, its influence can only extend to the parts of philosophy that concern the existence of God, His nature, the origin of our soul, its nature, and its destiny. In a word, among all the Christian philosophers who really deserve the name, the faith exercises a simplifying influence such that their originality manifests itself especially in the area directly under the influence of the faith: the doctrine of God, of man, and of his relations to God.[15]

From the above description two criteria of Christian philosophy stand out. First, Christian philosophy is neither co-extensive with all the problems of philosophy nor with those of Christian revelation and faith. Christian philosophy is limited only to the problems of faith on which reason can reflect such as creation of the world, the existence of God, the immortality of the soul. In this light, one does not need to be a Christian to engage in Christian philosophy. Also, if a Christian engages in philosophical reflections on topics that do not pertain to faith that philosophy cannot be qualified as Christian. Hence, an element of faith is the first criteria of Christian philosophy. Second, Christian philosophy takes its cue from theology. "A Christian philosophy remains a distinctly philosophical venture, according to Gilson, but its order, structure, and set of problems is given by theology, not by independent philosophical considerations."[16] Theology, therefore, sets the philosophical pace.

Gilson explains three ways in which Christianity puts its stamp on philosophy. First, faith cautions the philosopher to rethink his/her conclusions in the light of the discoveries of religious truths. Second, Christian revelation offers reason an opportunity to have a depth perspective of philosophy. Third, Christian revelation contributes meaningfully to philosophy by presenting a content of faith to rational discovery for its investigation. Gilson, in fact, asks, "whether among those propositions which by faith he believes to be true, there are not a certain number which reason may know to be true."[17] According to Gilson, therefore, if among the truths of faith one finds among them "some that are capable of becoming objects of science he (Christian) becomes a philosopher, and if it is to the Christian faith that he owes this new philosophic insight, he becomes a Christian philosopher."[18] Christian revelation contributes to philosophy by setting the stage for Christian philosophizing. It does so by supplying Christian material for philosophical reflection which continues to use natural reason. Hence, one can infer that according to Gilson Christian revelation is at the same time intrinsic to philosophy by supplying material for reflection and extrinsic in the process of reflection. But this will only be a conceptual distinction not a division.

Jacques Maritain's (1882-1973) contribution to the fides et ratio debate is found in his two volumes Science and wisdom (1940) and Essay on Christian philosophy (1955). Like Gilson before him, Jacques Maritain starts his elaboration of Christian philosophy by distinguishing between substantive and modal philosophies. Substantive philosophy refers to "the nature of philosophy or what it is in itself."[19] Modal philosophy refers to "the state in which it exists in real fact, historically, in the human subject, and which pertains to its concrete conditioning of existence and exercise."[20] Christian philosophy does not operate at the level of the 'nature of philosophy'. At the substantive level

Table 1
Relationship of Faith and Reason

Philosopher and Major work	Description of Relationship	Elaboration
Tertullian: *The Prescription of Heretics*	Independent	Faith and reason are irreconcilable.
Augustine of Hippo *Confessions*	Subordinate	Reason is an auxiliary of faith.
Thomas Aquinas *Summa Theologica*	Subordinate	Faith is an auxiliary of reason.
Etienne Gilson: *The Spirit of Medieval Philosophy*	Independent/ Related	Faith and reason are distinct at primary level of philosophy but intrinsically related at operative level.
Jacques Maritain: *Science and Wisdom* & *Essay on Christian Philosophy*	Independent/ Related	Faith and reason are distinct at substantive level of philosophy and intrinsically related at modal level.
John-Paul II: *Fides et Ratio*	Related but with caution	Mutual fecundation of faith and reason in the process of intellectual inquiry.

philosophy is wholly rational: no reason issuing from faith finds its way into its inner fabric; it derives intrinsically from reason and rational criticism alone; and its soundness as a philosophy is based entirely on experimental or intellectual evidence and on logical proof. From these considerations it follows that since the specification of philosophy hinges entirely on its formal object, and since this object is wholly of a rational order, philosophy considered in itself – whether in a pagan or Christian mind – depends on some strictly natural or rational intrinsic criteria.[21]

Christian philosophy according to Maritain functions at the historical 'state' of philosophy or modal level.

> As soon as it is no longer a question of philosophy considered in itself but on the manner in which men philosophize, and of the diverse philosophies which the concrete course of history has brought into existence, the consideration of the essence of philosophy no longer suffices; that of its state must be undertaken. From this viewpoint of state, or the condition of exercise, it is manifest that before philosophy can attain its full normal development in the mind it will exact of the individual many emendations and purification, a disciplining not only of reason but of the heart as well. To philosophize man must put his whole soul into play in much the same manner that to run he must use his heart and lungs.[22]

In its historical state philosophy receives assistance "either from within in the form of inner strengthening or from without in the form of an offering of objective data."[23] Subjective reinforcements take the form of clarification and spiritualization both of which contribute to the philosophical habitus. Such inner strengthening come from "superior wisdoms, theological wisdom, and infused wisdom which rectify and purify in the soul the philosophical habitus with which they maintain a continuity not of essence but of movement and illumination, fortifying them in their proper order, and lifting them to higher life."[24] In its historical state philosophy also receives objective data from faith and revelation. Such data "deal primarily with revealed truths of the natural order. The highest of these have been regularly missed and misstated by the great pagan philosophers. Moreover, these objective data are also concerned with the repercussions of truths of the supernatural order on philosophical reflection."[25] Instances of such data proposed by revelation and faith for rational investigation include creation, human soul as object of salvation, God as substantial being, and so on.

Epilogue of a Debate

The expression *Christian philosophy* appears three times in the encyclical of John Paul II entitled *Fides et Ratio* published in 1998. In this encyclical the Roman pontiff approves the use of the term – not so much in the sense of recommending it but allowing its use – with certain qualifications. According to

John Paul II there are three legitimate ways in which philosophy and faith can stand. The first 'stance' is that "there is a philosophy completely independent of the Gospel's Revelation" (*Fides et Ratio §75*). The Pope postulates the independence of reason on the basis that it is possible for reason to function correctly and to open itself to transcendence without divine revelation. Examples of such independent philosophies will be that of Plato and Aristotle who developed their philosophies prior to the birth of Christianity. History, therefore, allows an entertainment of the independence of philosophy and by implication the autonomy of Christian revelation. But the Pontiff is quick to add that the affirmation of autonomy of reason is not synonymous to an affirmation of its self-sufficiency. Chapters 1 and 2 of *Fides et Ratio* demonstrate at length that reason can operate with full adequacy only within the framework of an "act of entrusting oneself to God" which "engages the whole person" and in which "the intellect and the will display their spiritual nature" (*Fides et Ratio §13*). The insufficiency or epistemic limitations of reason are founded in the doctrine of original sin and the inherent creatureliness of human beings capable of receiving only historical but not absolute revelation (*Fides et Ratio §§22, 42, 80, 81*).

The second 'stance' is that in which John Paul II endorses the Gilsonian description. "A second stance adopted by philosophy is often designated as Christian philosophy. In itself, the term is valid, but it should not be misunderstood: it in no way intends to suggest that there is an official philosophy of the Church, since the faith as such is not a philosophy. The term seeks rather to indicate a Christian way of philosophizing, a philosophical speculation conceived in dynamic union with faith. It does not, therefore, refer simply to a philosophy developed by Christian philosophers who have striven in their research not to contract the faith. The term Christian philosophy includes those important developments of philosophical thinking which would not have happened without the direct or indirect contribution of Christian faith" (*Fides et Ratio §76*). John Paul II endorses the legitimacy of the expression *Christian philosophy* but with caution. The term does not indicate the choice of any particular philosophy as the official philosophy of the Catholic Church. It refers to the mutual fecundation of faith and reason in the process of intellectual inquiry.

The third 'stance' is that in which philosophy is at the service of theology. According to the Supreme Pontiff philosophy prepares the groundwork on which theology should build if faith is to be intelligible. In this light, theologians who refuse the assistance of philosophy "would run the risk of doing philosophy unwittingly and locking themselves within thought structures poorly adapted to the understanding of the faith" *(Fides et Ratio §77)*. As such, the Pope affirms an intrinsic relationship between faith and philosophy. The Pope hesitates to call this approach a handmaid stance because it makes philosophy slavishly submissive to theology. The Pope's emphasis is, "theology needs philosophy as a partner in dialogue in order to confirm the intelligibility" of the faith*(Fides et Ratio §77)*. Philosophy is "noble and indispensable" not a servile contributor to the dialogue *(Fides et Ratio §77)*.

CATHOLIC PHILOSOPHY

What makes Christian philosophy stand apart from other philosophies has been treated in the historical section. The results are applicable to *Catholic philosophy* because *Catholic philosophy* is a species of Christian philosophy. Catholic philosophy, like other Christian philosophies, is characterized by a religious designation. However, some objections have been advanced against the label Catholic philosophy. One objection to the appellation stems from the fact that church hierarchy like Leo XIII's *Aeterni Patris* and John Paul II's *Fides et Ratio* use the expression Christian philosophy not Catholic philosophy. Another objection advances the point that what is designated as Catholic is not homogeneous. The Catholic religion in Africa, Europe, Asia, and America are not the same. Furthermore, some people object to Catholic philosophy out of fear that Catholic beliefs can be introduced in the philosophical thought process at the expense of rigorous philosophical method. The final objection comes from the fact that the expression has not been popularized by book titles and articles.

Foundations of Catholic philosophy

Founded on Revelation and Faith

Revelation, as recorded in the Bible, is a pillar of Catholic philosophy of education. The Bible is a pillar in that it does not only provide grounds for theoretical guidance and generalization concerning Catholic education but is also the integrating factor around which all other subjects are arranged. It also provides the ultimate criterion by which other subjects are judged. The Bible is central to Catholic philosophy of education in that "it is the basis by which all other channels of knowledge are evaluated and used. Through the Bible the inter-relatedness of all other subjects and truth is made possible... This is not to imply that the Bible is a textbook on anything and everything; but rather, that the Bible is to be the point of reference from which we can evaluate all other areas and sources of knowledge."[26] To understand how faith and revelation are quintessential to Catholic philosophy of education the distinction between subject curriculum and core curriculum must be made clear. Below are samples of Catholic school philosophies that affirm that the Bible is the foundation of their educational enterprise.

> Spiritual Goal: To educate students in the fundamentals of the spiritual life and provide opportunities for them to apply their learning, so that they may... adopt and apply Gospel-centered values even when these are counter-cultural.
>
> *(New York: Preston High School Handbook, p. 6)*[27]

> L'Ecole de Provence est un établissement catholique: sa mission s'inspire de l'Evangile selon les caractéristiques de l'éducation jésuite.
>
> *(France: Flyer of Ecole de Provence)*[28]

> Trans: Ecole de Provence is a Catholic School. Its mission is inspired by the Scriptures in accordance with the characteristics of Jesuit education.

Faith and revelation operate at the level of core curriculum by providing interconnectedness and focus in Catholic education.

> Without a common core, the school's curriculum has no focus; it lacks an integrated approach and the school cannot transcend the overwhelming problems that each of its general areas generates... A vision rooted in the agent within our schools.[29]

Faith is a presupposition of reason. That is, the justification of Catholic philosophy of education reposes on the fact of faith. The construction of a Catholic educational philosophy is, therefore, a transcendental argument (or backward argument) because the reasons offered for it try to show that faith is logically presupposed. Reasoning involves, *inter alia,* some philosophical techniques such as principled thinking, providing grounds, warrants, and backing for faith claims in education. Principled thinking is using logical criteria to make proper inferences and assess empirical evidence. It is also giving due weight to reasons and evidence, pondering and investigating the evidence to foster sympathetic understanding. Also, reasonable thinking includes providing *grounds* for faith claims, specifying particular facts in support of the claim that faith is the suppositum for Catholic education. Furthermore, faith has to provide the *warrant* for Catholic education. Warrant is establishing that it is legitimate or proper to accept the claim in terms of bridging the gap from grounds to claim. Finally, faith must provide the *backing* for the claim to Catholic education. A backing is a support for the warrant, validating the warrant.

Sacred/secular Structure

Catholic philosophy of education is the result of reflection on the religious experience of Christians. That experience is founded on the intimate relationship between God and humanity. This relation can also be expressed variously as that between body and soul, intellect and will, reason and feeling, in short between the sacred and secular.

Put philosophically, Catholic philosophy of education is supported by a theory of relative religious dualism. In general dualism refers to an interpretation of reality or an aspect of reality which postulates the existence of two principles, for example, God and human. It is a relative dualism because "one term is held to be subordinate to, derivative from, explicable by or in any manner dependent for its being upon the other; if neither term is held to be dependent in any such sense, then the dualism is absolute."[30] Here are some extracts from the philosophy of Catholic schools that underscore the dualism being elaborated here.

> Social Goals: To foster social responsibility, students are taught to create an atmosphere of respect for God, others, themselves, and the earth.
>
> *(New York: Preston High School Handbook, p. 6)*

> Success at school and in any community requires respect, both for the self and others. Respect flows from the appreciation of

God's gift for life, from thankfulness for one's own gifts, and appreciation of the goodness of all people.

(New York: Preston High School Handbook, p. 43)

In Catholic dualism God and the sacred aspect are dominant and the human and secular are dependent. In light of this dominance by the divine domain Catholic dualism is also described as religious dualism to distinguish it from metaphysical dualism like that of the matter-form of Aristotle, or the Cartesian epistemological dualism of *res cogitans* (mind) and *res extensa* (body). In the metaphysical and epistemological forms of dualism the two terms are heterogeneous and irreducible. This is dualism in the strict sense, absolute dualism. Religious dualism, for its part, is relative. It postulates an asymmetrical relationship not equality between the sacred and secular domains. On the basis of the relationship God and humans it may be more accurate to talk of an antithetical dualism.

Christian Anthropology

Underlying every educational enterprise is an understanding of the human (student) condition it hopes to modify. It is, therefore, appropriate within the context of Catholic philosophy of education to answer the question: what is the Christian understanding of the human person to be educated? What is the functioning anthropology of Catholic education? Thomas Groome asserts that an educator's "understanding of who people are and can become is fundamental to how they educate."[31] In a word, the educator's working anthropology has a preponderant influence on how they accomplish their role. An operative anthropology is necessary because it governs every educational choice that is proposed for teaching-learning, constitutes a principle for evaluating educational means, and is the hope that permeates the educational enterprise.

The modus operandi of Catholic education is shaped by a bifocal anthropology: human beings are created in the likeness and image of God (Gn 1: 27); this divine image in humans has been marred by sin (Rm 3: 23). Subsections in this anthropology will consider human being as created, sanctified, fallen, and redeemed. Christian anthropology is rooted in an understanding of the origin and destiny of human beings. The divine heritage of human beings is the raison d'être for their dignity and humanity. According to Christian anthropology any understanding of the human person is incomplete without thinking about God. Christian anthropology contemplates simultaneously the realities of human beings and divine realities. Christian anthropology has a theological and spiritual spin to it. Maintaining the unity of the divine and the human represents the challenge that Christian education is ultimately committed to promote.

Catholic education also has an ecclesial identity. This does not mean that Catholic educational institutions are churches *per se*. Rather, these institutions are ecclesial in the sense that they share in the mission of the church concerning education and formation. Christian humano-divine anthropology accounts for the adequacy of Catholic education and without it Christian education is nonexistent. Christian anthropology is a primary building block of Catholic education. An indissoluble bond, therefore, exists between Christian anthropology and education. It is also true of Catholic education.

CATHOLIC PHILOSOPHY OF EDUCATION

Educational Aims

Proposed Aims of Education

Catholic philosophy of education is guided by religious truths. Religion deals with the zone of a human being's relationship and response to God who is transtemporal, holy, and divine. When this relationship is institutionalized as in the case of Catholic Christianity, religion includes creeds, liturgies, and moral codes. Hence, religion is a question of experience, historical revelation, and dogma.[32] Catholic philosophy of education is religious in that religion, as defined above, reveals God to philosophy as the true goal of life, and by the same token the goal of all education. Philosophy of education is Catholic if its guiding principle is to put the educand into right relationship with God, the self, and society. Religion supplies and thereby solves the problem of aims and values in Catholic education. Religion is the driving force behind Catholic educational philosophy in that the elements of religion outlined above constitute the core around which the content, process, and theory of education are construed. They are the norm or touchstone for evaluating educational goals, aims, and ideals.

From the point of view of its goal Catholic philosophy of education is energized by religion. Religion spiritualizes and challenges the educative process. It does so by satisfying the higher aspirations of the educand. Each educand is beset by needs, wants, and goals. "Each is looking for fulfillment and growth in his own personal and spiritual life. Every learner starts with his own basic needs, thus the educator must seek to motivate the learner to discover and apply God's provisions to his life. In Christian education true learning comes as the learner experiences the wonders of God's truth applied to his life."[33]

Scope of Catholic Education

Catholic philosophy of education is catholic in a broader linguistic and etymological sense not in the narrow denominational sense.

Linguistically catholic means universal implying that the system for which Catholic philosophy provides inspiration and guidance is not limited to times, places, and influences. Catholic philosophy of education is universal in an Aristotelian sense of being worldwide and uniform. It is neither derived from nor devised for any particular culture, age, or political orientation. In its essence, it is the same today as it was five hundred years ago. Essentially it is the same in America, Africa, Europe, and Asia. This is the quantitative approach to catholicity.

Catholic philosophy of education is universal or catholic in the etymological sense of being open to the truth that is outside its own confines. Catholic comes from two Greek words κατα (kata) meaning every, including and όλος (holos) meaning whole (as in parts working together), everyone. καταλος (katholos) or catholic means welcoming everyone. Catholic, taken etymologically, stresses the qualitative aspect of Catholic educational philosophy. Joseph Marique makes the point of the universality of Catholic philosophy of education as follows: It is

> Catholic in the sense that it welcomes the truth and progress from wherever it may come, and it is catholic in the further sense that it embraces the whole man, both as an individual, and a member of the social organism, and therefore, embraces all phases of education.[34]

Thomas Groome also conceives catholic in terms of going beyond self-interest to inclusivity that is conscious of and caring for others. "Catholicity," writes Moore, "also entails an openness to truth wherever it can be found (regardless of its sources) and a willingness to learn from people whose perspectives on life and ways of making meaning are different from one's own."[35] Catholic educational philosophy is open to every influence because of the Christian principle of "taking the best and leaving the rest."[36] Catholic educational philosophy is nonsectarian and transcends parochialism because of its openness to every time, place, and philosophy. This stance underscores the fact that "Catholic educators share with all educators of good will the struggle for human dignity."[37]

The catholicity of Catholic educational philosophy is rooted in the universality of God's self-disclosure or revelation. Vatican II, in an ecumenical spirit stated that "the Catholic Church rejects nothing that is true and holy in other religious traditions because they often reflect a ray of the Truth which enlightens all people."[38] This is an echo of a biblical statement that God's wisdom "deploys herself from one end of the earth to another" (Wis. 8: 1). In these statements the Catholic Church affirms that it is not the unique proprietor of divine revelation. The implication of this affirmation for Catholic educational philosophy is universality as described above. Catholic philosophy of education is catholic because of its "willingness to learn from perspectives on life different from its own."[39]

The concept of catholicity has important implications for educational aim, style, and culture in Catholic educational institutions. Since Catholic education is opened to every influence and purports to be relevant to any and every instance it follows that one of the aims of Catholic education is to develop global consciousness. The catholicity of Catholic education invites all stakeholders "to appreciate diversity and be open to learn from other cultures and wisdoms; to cherish one's roots and yet to transcend parochialism."[40] Considering that global consciousness is an invitation to continuous learning Catholic education must enliven in learners the spirit of curiosity, a relentless interest in the limitless horizons of life. So, because of its catholicity Catholic education should aim at providing its learners with tools for continuous learning, making its learners lifelong learners. Furthermore, Catholic education must reflect catholicity in content and process. Concerning content catholicity is reflected by lending depth and breath to curriculum in Catholic institutions. This does not mean offering an encyclopedic knowledge to students. This means that teachers must develop expansive views of curriculum by pushing students beyond what they already know. Teachers must dispel the I-know-it-all attitude by insisting that there is always more to learn. Also, teachers must welcome diversity of views and perspectives concerning the topic under consideration. Concerning process catholicity is brought into play when teachers in Catholic institutions employ a variety of teaching methods so as to respect the different learning styles of the learners in Catholic institutions. Finally, catholicity of Catholic education can be reflected in a school's culture. Attention must be paid to the symbols of the Catholic institution so that they reflect its catholicity and foster its global view. School leadership must play a responsible stewardship role for the symbols.

Table 2
Foundation of Christian Philosophy

Nature of Christian philosophy	Sacred/secular structure, religious, catholic, and normative.
Source of knowledge	Faith and reason.
Nature of human	Created, supernatural destiny, sanctified, fallen, and redeemed.
Nature of value	Hierarchy of values: supernatural, spiritual, and eternal values are more important than natural, bodily, and temporal values respectively.

Catholic educational philosophy is an antithesis to static and closed-minded approaches to education. The catholicity of Catholic education is roots in its commitment to form partnerships and to fight division and discrimination. The hallmarks of Catholic philosophy of education are inclusion and outreach, care for the ultimate well-being of every person. Catholicity is usually presented in school handbooks in the form of nondiscriminatory policy like in the examples below.

> Preston High School welcomes diversity. It is committed to the advancement of intercultural understanding and respect, and the promotion of peaceful resolutions of differences. In accordance with these purposes and the Christian belief in the essential equality of all persons, *Preston does not discriminate in its policies towards persons of different races, color, national or ethnic origin, in the implementation of its admission policies or any academic and co-curricular policies and programs.* The energy of compassion is also directed outward to the global community as a natural extension of the social philosophy of the school.
>
> *(New York: Preston High School Handbook 2003-2004, p. 5)*

> Fordham University is an academic institution that, in
> compliance with federal state and local laws, does not
> discriminate on the basis of race, color, creed, religion, age,
> sex, gender, national origin, marital or parental status, sexual
> orientation, citizenship status, veteran status, disability or any
> other basis prohibited by law.
>
> *(Fordham University Graduate School of Education Bulletin 2002-2003, p. 54)*

Prescribes Standards for Education

From the point of view of its method Catholic philosophy of education is
normative. A God-centered Catholic curriculum underscores the sublime fact
that there can be no neutral curriculum as advocated by Paul Hirst and others.[41]
Every "curriculum reflects the order of interests in any given society. In a
theocentric society, first place will be given to religious studies; in a socialist
society, to social sciences; in a culture dominated by the veneration of antiquity,
to the ancient languages and literature, the increasing emphasis on the natural
sciences reflects the advance of technology."[42]

Catholic philosophy of education is normative in the sense that it is "the
application to education in all its phases of the Christian philosophy of life,
that is, of Christian beliefs and ideals… And it is explained in the light of
reason in all its fullness and implications by scholastic philosophy."[43] Catholic
philosophy of education undertakes the deductive, a priori method which looks
to authoritative Catholic sources for guidance. Examples of the normative
character of Catholic philosophy on Catholic education stand out clearly in the
mission statement of Preston High School.

> The mission of the school is educational in its broad sense,
> encompassing the intellectual, spiritual, physical, social, and
> emotional dimensions of growth and maturation. In keeping
> with the needs and opportunities of the times, the school
> provides a purposeful and challenging academic program
> within a Christian environment, where religious faith is a norm
> for conduct.
>
> *(New York: Preston High School Handbook 2003-2004, p. 4)*

Educational Curriculum

Curriculum is a comprehensive educational phenomenon whose constitutive elements include "all the learning of students which is planned by and directed by the school to attain its educational goals."[44] As an all encompassing term it takes into consideration[45] the organization of the content of education into subjects of instruction (subject curriculum), the means to educational goals (activity curriculum), targeted values and perspectives (core curriculum), impact of the environment on what is learned (hidden curriculum), what is taught by the teacher (taught curriculum), and program of studies (written curriculum). What cuts across all these types of curricula is that all have to do with educational content, educational objectives, and educational method. This section outlines the influence of Catholic philosophy in these three areas of curriculum development.

Nature of Catholic Student

The Catholic student is a supernature. Christian revelation, a statement of truth by God to humans, states that human beings are created and have a supernatural destiny which is union with God (Gn. 1, 27). The ultimate purpose of Catholic education is to assist the student to discover their God-oriented nature. True learning is achieved in Christian education only when learning leads the student to experience the wonder of God's truth in his/her life. In this light, the measure of educational growth in the Christian student is not determined by what the student hears but what the student does with what s/he hears. The important aspect of Christian learning is what is taking place inside the student – rejecting or accepting Catholic teaching. This view of learning imposes a methodology on the teacher. The teacher shall not impose knowledge on Christian students but guide and play a leadership role in the student's discovery of Christian truth.

The student's nature is also *fallen*, that is, marred by sin (Rm. 3, 23). Human beings have rejected God and one of the aims of Catholic education is restoration of humanity – teaching students their duties to God and neighbor.

Does this supernature of the student obliterate the natural in the student? The fact that the student is created means that the supernature does not repress but completes what is natural in the student. As a natural person the student has legitimate and immediate needs, wants, and goals. As natural beings each student is looking for personal growth and fulfillment. In Catholic education the student must be considered as an individual with personal worth, and as supernature revealed by God. Hence, the personal experiences of the student have important value for education.

Purpose of Catholic Curriculum

The goal of any educational enterprise answers the question: what should it be doing and why? This section answers the first part of the question.

Catholic education admits the presence of proximate and ultimate goals. Proximate goals are those here and now educational concerns which are situation and time bound, flexible, and changing in order to address daily questions. Such goals include intellectual goals (commitment to knowledge), affective goals (acquiring or strengthening attitudes and values), moral goals (formation of good person), and physical goals (development of skills). The ultimate goal of Catholic education, which is the interest of educational philosophy, is the stable, constant, and unchanging goal that is true and valid for all Catholic education irrespective of time, persons, and places.

Vatican II states that the ultimate goal, the reason for the existence of Catholic education is "to relate all human culture eventually to the news of salvation, so that the life of faith will illumine the knowledge which students gradually gain of the world, of life, and of humankind".[46] Accordingly, Catholic education should aim at integrating human and divine domains. Christian education should contemplate the historical, social, and cultural realities of humanity in conjunction with divine truths found in Sacred Scripture, Sacred Tradition, and the Magisterium. Writers, through time, have explicated this integration. Friedrich Schleiermacher defines integration as a "religious experience' which he defines as a human "sense and taste for the infinite" and a "feeling of absolute dependence."[47] Schleiermacher's characterization emphasizes human transcendence as part of the integration process. Harold Buetow describes integration as a "person's union with God."[48] Buetow's specification underscores the personal relationships that are quintessential in the integration. Roger Haight adds a dynamic element to the union by characterizing it as "personal encounter" which highlights the intersubjectivity and communicative facets of the integration.[49] Communication highlights the point that union between the human and the divine is neither an event nor an achievement but "an ongoing existential and experiential phenomenon."[50]

The goal of Catholic education is the mediation of transcendence. Elements of this mediation include: establishing unity between God and human beings, human transcendence, bringing about an experience of God as subject so that awareness of God is not knowledge about God as of an object but God experienced as personal. What makes Catholic education unique is the desire to go beyond the immediate and obvious world into the realm of the sacred. Preston High School acknowledges the mediation of transcendence by linking school success to the work of God.

> Success at school and in any community requires respect, both for self and others. Respect flows from the appreciation of God's gift of life, from thankfulness for one's own gift, and appreciation of the goodness of all people.
> *(New York: Preston High School Handbook 2003-2004, p. 43)*

Catholic philosophy of education can also be understood by contrasting its purpose with that of other philosophies of education. Naturalism, for example, considers the human person as a higher animal. Hence, the aim of naturalistic education is training to satisfy mental and physical needs and desires. Education is proffering of skills necessary to be a connoisseur. Humanism focuses on the moral penchant of humans. The aim of humanistic education is character formation, the acquisition of temperate civilization. Education aims at avoiding sub-rationality. Catholic philosophy of education, by contrast, is founded on a spiritual vision of education which directs the process of human development toward God. The compenetration of the supernatural and the natural domains, the supernatural destination of education constitute the specificity of Christian and, therefore, Catholic education. St. Augustine states this goal eloquently, "You have made us for yourself alone, and our hearts are restless till they rest in thee."[51] Such a goal is not only for the consumption of those who profess the Catholic faith. It can have an appeal to non-Christians who find no threats to their faith in such goals and who would, therefore, embrace the aim for their own reasons.

Content of Catholic Curriculum

Each educational institution has what can be called an 'Accrediting Formal Curriculum.' Essentially, this is a description of the standards, objectives, and content that must be mastered mandated by the accrediting office. However, the specificity of the demanding institution constitutes its Unique Formal Curriculum that makes it the type of school it is. In the case at hand we can call it a 'Catholic Formal Curriculum'. Catholic education proposes an integration of Accrediting Formal Curriculum and Catholic Formal Curriculum.

The Vatican Congregation for Catholic Education thinks in a similar vein when it states:

> In the Catholic school's educational project there is no separation between time for learning and time for formation, between acquiring notions and growing in wisdom. The various school subjects do not present only knowledge to be attained, but also values to be acquired and truths to be discovered.[52]

According to this document, the uniqueness of Catholic education lies in the fact that it proposes "knowledge set in the context of faith," and endeavors "to interweave reason and faith, which has become the heart of each individual subject, makes for unity, articulation and coordination, bringing forth within what is learnt in school a Christian vision for the world, of life, of culture, and of history."[53]

From the above, it follows that Catholic philosophy of curriculum is best captured by the concept of curriculum permeation. Curriculum permeation points to the fact that in Catholic education both the spiritual vision and core of Catholicism provides the connection between and among the subjects that would otherwise remain independent. It is, therefore, appropriate for Catholic educational philosophical thought to speak of both religious integration and religious permeation simultaneously.

Permeation comes from the Latin verb *permetere* which means to permeate. The concept implies a spread through the pores of an entity "like rain through sand."[54] Hence, "in the context of Catholic philosophy of education, permeation implies a diffusion of religion, values, and morals into all areas of school life."[55] The permeation of all school life by the spiritual core of Catholic religion indicates that this core holds together and permeates the totality of Catholic education. The spiritual core offers focus to the school curriculum. Also, permeation challenges educators and their associates to expand their lenses of educational elaboration, appreciation, and evaluation by incorporating Catholic philosophy as one plausible approach to education.

> Permeation causes us to think beyond what happens in the classroom or in any one subject and to consider all that happens in the life of a child within and out of school. All this naturally implies a holistic approach to education, one of

the basic premises of Catholic philosophy. No true philosophy of Catholic education will deny that the message of Jesus was meant to touch the whole person in a way that leads to the whole truth.[56]

Catholic philosophy that underlies curriculum is not limited to religion classes. Also, Catholic curriculum does not abrogate the accrediting curriculum but augments and embellishes it with a Catholic outlook. It is a curriculum that meets both the academic and social needs of students as well as their spiritual and faith needs.

Two examples will drive home the point. In Literature, for example, Catholic curriculum will not be limited to teaching only genres of writing like prose, drama, and poetry. The Catholic curriculum will expand its teaching of Literature by choosing material which not only emphasize the literary genres but also address the human condition, human nature and destiny, and human meaning and ethic. In Mathematics Catholic curriculum like any curriculum will aim at developing the ability to accurately measure and correlate things and time through the use of symbols, to reason logically and intuitively from what is known to figuring out unknown data and new possibilities. Catholic curriculum will employ such logical and intuitive reasoning to think about elements in its own agenda like God. This brief example demonstrates how Catholic curriculum integrates and permeates mathematics, literature, and faith.

A concrete example will drive home the point. Preston High School states its educational goals in four points. Its *intellectual goal* is to empower students, its *social goal* is to foster social responsibility among students, its *physical goal* is to offer an understanding of interrelationships, and its *spiritual goal* is to educate students in the fundamentals of the spiritual life. A first look at the goals will situate the first three in the rubric of Accrediting Curriculum and the fourth in the Catholic Curriculum. However, the Preston Handbook is quick to state that these goals are not realized in isolation or sequentially. Rather, permeation of the goals is stated in terms of holistic education.

> All dimensions of holistic growth and development, spiritual, intellectual, social, emotional, and physical are addressed by the academic and co-curricular programs. Learning takes place

within a Catholic community, where religious, human, and moral values are taught, and fostered through practice.

(New York: Preston High School Handbook 2003-2204, p. 5)

Permeation does not make the religious aspect of schools an appendix of the academic component or vice versa. Both are integral and constitutive elements of Catholic education. The philosophy of *Ecole de Provence* brings this out clearly.

La CULTURE RELIGIUESE n'est pas l'apanage de celui qui a la FOI. Elle se développe selon des axes linéraires, artistique, sociologiques, bref HUMAINS qui sous-tendent toute civilisation tributaire, comme la nôtre, de la Tradition Judéo-Chrétienne. Elle constitue une dimension inhérente à toute CULTURE HUMAINE digne de ce nom et à ce titre, ne saurait être négligée dans l'ensemble de l'enseignement.

(France: Flyer of Ecole de Provence)

Trans: Catholic philosophy of education is not a mere tinkering with the recommended education program of the State. Rather, it is a *planned* integration of what is *recommended* by State legislation (skills and knowledge to be acquired) and what Catholic educational agencies or providers of education consider as *important* (what is necessary for life) in education.

CATHOLIC CONCEPT OF TEACHER AND ADMINISTRATOR

The realization of Catholic philosophy of education is largely dependent on teachers, that is, administrators, faculty, and staff. Providers of Catholic education have always stressed the pivotal role of teachers in Catholic education.

The extent to which the Christian message is transmitted through education depends to a very great extent on the teachers. The integration of culture and faith is mediated by the other integration of faith and life in the person of the teacher.[57]

The concept of a Catholic teacher can be clearly presented in contrasts. The Catholic teacher is not one whose job is limited to dispensing knowledge but is an educator who helps in the formation of human beings. In pragmatism where the emphasis is on process the teacher is considered as a facilitator, resource person, change agent, and guide whose task is to look for challenging ways of bringing about critical thinking in students. In contrast to pragmatism Catholic education emphasizes content and considers the teacher as a spiritual and moral formator, a causal agent or mediator who transmits Catholic knowledge and values. In existentialism the teacher is a presenter of choices that take care of individual student's desires and needs. By contrast the Catholic teacher is an educator for human freedom and transcendence.

Within the context of Catholic education, therefore, a Catholic teacher is not one who *plays safe, hangs loose, or plays it cool*. A Catholic teacher is not one baptized into the Catholic faith and teaching in a Catholic School. Rather, what defines the Catholic teacher is commitment to the faith vision of Catholic education. Commitment here indicates that the teacher has both intellectual conviction and emotional passion for the faith vision, identifies with it, is loyal to it, and participates in it. Commitment to the Catholic educational vision is what makes teaching in Catholic institutions more than just a profession. In Catholic education there is an extension of self beyond mere profession. What is, therefore, necessary to be a Catholic teacher includes professional expertise, faith dimension to work, and personal growth and development in faith vision.

SUMMARY

Catholic philosophy of education does not teach the letter of the Bible but practices its spirit. It is a spiritual approach to education inspired by the depth structures of Catholic Christianity. Catholic philosophy of education is not a catechesis of the Catholic faith.

Table 3

Implication of Philosophy for Catholic Education

Aims of education	Ultimately to integrate human and divine; mediate transcendence.
Curriculum	Integration of Accrediting Formal Curriculum and Catholic Formal Curriculum.
Teacher	Commitment to school's vision; expert in human nature.
Student	Supernature, deprived and being restored, natural.

Through philosophy the Christian faith permeates the ethos and style of Catholic education. Catholic philosophy of education proposes a positive understanding of the human condition that at one and the same time gives a rationale for the work of educators and grounds their expectations. This understanding is one that considers students as essentially spiritual beings with a propensity to reach out to reality that is beyond themselves, is more than themselves, and which defines their being. Catholic religious dualism offers an understanding of salvation. This is a source of spiritual motivation for students trying to improve the quality of one's life and to prepare for eternal life. In other words, the dualism testifies to the conviction that human life is more meaningful when it is anchored (*re-ligare meaning religion*) in some experience and understanding of ultimate reality. Finally, through the concept of permeation Catholic philosophy of education reinforces the conviction that revelation and reason are partners, need each other, are gifts from God, and not essentially antagonistic.

[1] Redden, J. D. & Ryan, F. A. (1956). *A Catholic philosophy of education*. Milwaukee: WI: The Bruce Publishing Company, pp. vii-viii.

[2] Hart, C. A. (Ed.). (1936). *Christian philosophy and the social sciences*. Washington, DC: The Catholic University of America.

[3] Heidegger, M. (1961). *An introduction to metaphysics*. Trans. R. Mannheim. New York: Doubleday and Company.

[4] Brown, C. (1969). *Philosophy and Christian faith*. Chicago, IL: Inter-Varsity Press. p. 7.

[5] Tertullian, *The prescription of heretics*. p. 7.

[6] Owens, J. (1990). *Towards a Christian philosophy*. Washington, DC: The Catholic University of America Press, p. 2.

[7] Owens, J. *op. cit.,,* p. 4.

[8] Owens, J. *op. cit.,, p.* 63.

[9] Owens, J. *op. cit.,,* p. 73.

[10] Bréhier, E. (1931). *Y a-t-il une philosophie chrétienne? Revue de métaphysique et de morale* 38, pp. 6-7.

[11] Owens, J. *op. cit.,,* p. 10.

[12] Gilson, E. (1940). *The spirit of Medieval philosophy*. Trans. A. H. C. Downes. New York: Scribner's Sons, p. 5.

[13] Gilson, E. *op. cit.,,* p. 35.

[14] Gilson, E. *op. cit.,,* p. 37.

[15] Gilson, E. *op. cit.,,* p. 38.

[16] Baldner, S. *Christian philosophy, Etienne Gilson, and Fides et ration*. www.nd.edu/departments/maritain/ti99/baldner.htm.

[17] Gilson, E. *op. cit.,,* p. 36.

[18] Gilson, E. *op. cit.,,* p. 36.

[19] Maritain, J. (1955). *An essay on Christian philosophy*. Trans E. H. Flannery. New York: Philosophical library, p. 11.

[20] Maritain, J. *op. cit.,,* p. 11-12.

[21] Maritain, J. *op. cit.,,* p. 15.

[22] Maritain, J. *op. cit.,,* p. 17.

[23] Maritain, J. *op. cit.,,* p. 18.

[24] Maritain, J. (1940). *Science and wisdom*. Trans. B. Wall. London: Centenary Press, p. 80.

[25] Maritain, J. (1940). *Science and wisdom*. p. 80.

[26] Cates, P. W. *A Christian philosophy of education*. [on-line] www.faithchristianmin.org/articles/cpe.htm.

[27] New York: Preston High School is an all girls Catholic High School in the Bronx, New York, founded in 1947 by the Sisters of Divine Compassion (RDC) who are still in charge to date.

[28] Ecole de Provence is an all boys Catholic High School in Marseille, France, founded by the Jesuits who are still in charge to date.

[29] Trafford, L. (1991). *Transforming Catholic education. Transforming our world.* Ottawa: Novalis, St. Paul University Press. p. 50.

[30] M. E. (1969). *Dualism. In Encyclopedia Britannica,* Vol. 7. pp. 717-718 p. 717.

[31] Groome, T. (1998). *Educators for life. A spiritual vision for every teacher and parent.* Allen, TX: Thomas More p. 72.

[32] Donohue, J. (1973). *Catholicism and education.* New York: Harper & Row. p. 42.

[33] Cates, P. W. A *Christian philosophy of education.* [on-line].www.faithchristianmin. org/articles/cpe.htm. p. 3.

[34] Marique, P. J. (1970). *The philosophy of Christian education.* Westport, CT: Greenwood, p. 29.

[35] Groome, T. *op. cit.,,* p. 396.

[36] Buetow, H. A. (1988). *The Catholic school. It's roots, identity, and future.* New York: Crossroad, p. 50.

[37] Wagner, D. *Total education. A faith inspired Catholic philosophy.* [on-line] www. saskschools.ca/-cathcurr/articles/totaleducation.html p. 3.

[38] Vatican II, Declaration on non-Christian religions #2.

[39] Groome, T. *op. cit.,,* p. 405.

[40] Groome, T. *op. cit.,* p. 415.

[41] Hirst, P. H. (1976). *Knowledge and the curriculum.* London: Routledge & Kegan Paul.

[42] Perry, R. B. (1966). *Education and the science of education.* In I. Scheffler, (Ed.). *Philosophy of education. Modern readings.* 2nd Ed. pp. 17-38. Boston: Allyn and Bacon, Inc. p. 23.

[43] Marique, *op. cit.,,* p. 28.

[44] Tyler, R. W. (1980). *The curriculum. Then and now.* In Tanner. E. & Tanner, L. N. *Curriculum development. Theory into practice.* New York: Macmillan Publishing Co. p. 16.

[45] Smith, B. O., Stanley, W. O., & Shores, J. H. (1957). *Fundamentals of curriculum development.* New York: World Book Company. p. 80.

[46] Vatican II, *Declaration on Christian education,* §8

[47] Schleiermacher, F. (1928). *The Christian faith.* Edinburg: T. & T. Clark. P. 75.

[48] Buetow, H. A. (1988). *The Catholic school. Its roots, identity, and future.* New York: Crossroads, p. 98.

[49] Haight, R. (1990). *Dynamics of Theology.* New York: Mahwah, p. 71.

[50] Haight, R. *op. cit.,* p. 81.

[51] St. Augustine, *Confessions,* Book 1 §1.

[52] *Congregation for Catholic Education,* (Dec. 28th, 1997). The Catholic school on the threshold of the Third Millennium. §14 www.fargodiocese.org/cef/catholicschools/theory/csttm.html.

[53] *Congregation for Catholic Education,* (Dec. 28th, 1997). The Catholic school on the threshold of the Third Millennium. §14 www.fargodiocese.org/cef/catholicschools/theory/csttm.html.

[54] Buetow, *op. cit.,,* p. 109.

[55] Wagner, *op. cit.,,* p, 8.

[56] Wagner, *op. cit.,,* p. 8

[57] *Sacred Congregation for Catholic Education* (1975). Catholic schools #4. In A. Flannery (ed). Vatican II:. *The Counciliar and Post Counciliar Documents* Vol. II. Northport, NY: Costello.

CHAPTER 5

FEMINISM AND EDUCATIONAL PHILOSOPHY

Feminism is not a monolithic phenomenon but an umbrella term regrouping many feminisms with different rationales. Sonya Andermahr et al. short list some variations: Black Feminism, Cultural Feminism, Lesbian Feminism, Liberal Feminism, Marxist Feminism, Radical Feminism, and Socialist Feminism[1]. Barbara Houston corroborates the wide application of feminism when she writes, "In fact, toward the end of the twentieth century there are such differing political perspectives encompassed by the term feminism that it is common to speak of feminisms"[2]. Barbara Houston advances the idea of hyphenated feminisms to describe the different emphases and shades of feminism. Some writers have probed feminism as a political movement, others as a methodology, and still others as philosophy. This chapter will study feminism and its educational import under these three approaches.

FEMINIST THEORY

Feminism as Advocacy Movement

Feminism is a political movement that struggles for women's suffrage. It aims at emancipating women since it claims that wielders of power systematically marginalize women and other 'minorities'. Sonya Andermahr et al. define politics "as that branch of moral philosophy dealing with the state or social organism as a whole"[3]. As such, politics deals with public life as concerns the common good and social relationships.

Feminism is a political movement because it is concerned with the public life of women. Feminism is committed to exposing the gendered nature of public life by raising awareness to different expectations and biases that govern views and attitudes concerning the abilities of males and females. Feminism, therefore, advocates the transformation of public life expectations and relationships. "Feminist theory," writes Stomquist, "has always been committed to corrective work, that is, altering individual perceptions and actions and modifying institutions".[4]

Hester Eisenstien notes that there has been a remarkable shift in feminist theory. It "has moved from an emphasis on the elimination of difference to a celebration of that difference as a source of moral values."[5] Brenda Alamond is among the feminist writers who acknowledge that gender difference is morally significant. "I want to suggest that whatever anthropological and economic truths are embodied in these and similar statements," writes Almond, "the fact is that there are indeed certain systematic differences in the lives of women and men, and that this fundamental contrast in life experience does indeed account for and to some extent also justify a difference in their moral outlook and assumptions."[6] Almond postulates that beyond the overt physical biological differences between males and females there "is a much deeper and more significant fact" which generates their self-identity and self-concepts.[7] However, Almond remarks, "the ethical perspective of women has evolved within a framework of powerlessness to affect external events."[8] A change in the self-conception of women and the perception of women by others is morally significant. Feminism is no tinkering at the edge of ethical questions. Feminism is an advocacy movement for reconstructing and redefining "the methods and subject mater of philosophy in ways that value women's experiences and enable women to move from a position of object to positions of subjects, of knower, and of agent."[9]

Mary Midgley offers a concrete orientation for feminist self-reconception. Arguing that the present 'oppression' of women is socially rather than biologically determined Midgley indicates vistas in which assumptions underlying social thinking about women can be revisited. First, sexual differences should not be thought of in hierarchical terms. "Difference does not mean worse or better, it means difference."[10] Otherness rather than hierarchy should guide ethical thinking about the sexes. Mary Midgley's second principle is "equality does not mean standardization."[11] Equality between males and females is not equated to a symmetry of the sexes that calls for same ethical standards for both. Sexual equality is not likeness. Equality is acknowledgement of similarities and differences at one and the same time. According to Midgley it is important to start taking cognizance of differences in ethical thinking rather than seek to establish standards always. "The pursuit of standardization – the failure to value a difference – here goes beyond a mere passing mistake and becomes actively pernicious."[12] Equality of males and females should be understood in terms of equal opportunity, possibility, freedom, and range of choices not in terms of pre-established standards to be pursued.

The axiological challenge of the feminist movement is cast in terms of ethics and gender. Are ethical ideals for males and females similar or different? If the ideals are different can the difference be explained by gender difference alone? On the flip side, are differences in male and female ethical perceptions dependent on sex? Ought there to be different ethical codes for males and females? Brenda Almond summaries the ethical challenge inherent in the feminist movement as a question thus, "must we, in other words, accept an ultimate sexual apartheid as far as ethical values are concerned?"[13] The feminist movement is a critique of traditional stereotypes that denigrate the value of women's experience. It raises consciousness concerning the necessity to redefine and reinterpret the assumptions on which ethical ideals are generated or justified. Feminism advocates moral pluralism that valorizes the thinking of women and men. It searches for alternative rationale for explaining social relationships between males and females.

One such alternative is feminism's endorsement of a shift from prevailing Kantian ethical paradigm to a virtue ethical paradigm. Kantian ethics is founded on obedience to universal moral principles "derivable from (the practical side of) pure reason and. . . exerting a more or less conscious influence on morally decent individuals in all the circumstance of their lives."[14] Feminism advocates virtue ethics because it is concerned with the sort of person women are, what makes their life worthy, and their place in the universe. Nel Noddings and Michael Slote define virtue ethics as "a moral domain that recognizes both a moral obligation to develop one's character and personal potential."[15] Feminism is a movement that encourages the adoption of alternative views of morality.

In brief, feminism is a socio-political movement characterized by activism and commitment to progress concerning gender relationships. Gender is a strategy for the empowerment of women and feminism a movement for social justice and respect for gender diversity.

Feminism as Philosophy

Today, the expression "feminist philosophy" is current currency. However, its reception has brought about mixed feelings. There are skeptics who prefer to talk about radical feminism rather than feminist philosophy. There are others who endorse the legitimacy of the expression. Philosophy itself seems not to give hope for feminism. According to Ellen DuBois et al. "philosophy purports to be a search for universal truths unhampered by such incidental matters as sex differences, this discipline seemed at first to provide few footholds from which the study of women or the growth of feminist perspectives could begin."[16] This section probes the relationship between feminism and philosophy. How can philosophy be a locus of feminist inquiry? Is feminist philosophy possible? What is the philosophical genre of feminism? What are the philosophical contours of feminism?

Premise for feminist philosophy

According to Nancy Bauer there are two groups of skeptics. Skeptical feminists contend, "Philosophy – with its emphasis on passionless thinking, reason, objectivity, universality, essences, and so forth – apotheosizes a way encountering the world that is inherently and hopelessly tailored to serve the interest of men and thwart those of women."[17] Skeptical philosophers, on the other hand, argue, "philosophy's unimpeachable commitment to open inquiry is incompatible with feminist "theory", which, in their view is by definition constrained by a political bottom line."[18]

On what grounds can feminist philosophy be legitimized? What is its logical premise? Andrea Nye prefaces her argument for the legitimacy of feminist philosophy with an expression of exasperation. She is disappointed that feminist works of the caliber of Trinh Minh-ha, Patricia Hills Collins, Gloria Anzaldúa, Regina Harrison, María Lugones, and Elizabeth Spellman that have proven their worth in women's studies and other interdisciplinary studies continue to be shrugged off by men and women philosophers from being included as philosophy texts in courses on the pretext that "it's not philosophy."[19] Andrea Nye makes the argument for the possibility of feminist philosophy from a historical controversy and the possibility of expanding the contours of philosophy. The controversy over the philosophical status of feminist philosophy dovetails with that of other philosophies when they were "in the process of redefinition."[20] Andrea Nye likens the present rejection of feminist philosophy to the rejection of upstart Descartes by Aristotelians in Medieval universities. She also compares the rejection of feminism to the rejection of the Vienna Circle's logical positivism by German academics. Even "philosophy's very origin could be said to be rooted in controversial self-questioning and self-renewals, as Socrates substituted for the Sophist's claim to 'know' a more humble 'love of knowledge.'"[21] The historical import of Socrates is that his questioning gave an opportunity to redefine the Sophist philosophical paradigm. Feminism, according to Andrea Nye, has brought about an intellectual challenge. The challenge is not to use feminism as a criterion for classifying philosophy and non-philosophy. Rather, feminism's challenge is to redefine the canon of philosophy. "Philosophy, through its long, diverse, and contested history, has concerned itself with the basic themes of human life: the identity of the self, nature of reality, the possibility of knowledge. Changes in philosophical paradigms often signal or reflect radical change in the way the human and the real are conceived. At the present moment, virtual realities, possible worlds, and artificial intelligence exercise analytic philosophers to revise and expand their logical and scientific assumptions. . . what is to be human, what it is to think, what it is to know reality can no longer be defined according to one dominant cultural code. A Babel of tongues and ideas can no longer be dismissed as 'barbarian.'"[22] Assuming that the boundaries of philosophy qua philosophy are not rigid Andrea Nye postulates feminism is a challenge to redefine the confines of philosophy.

The nature of feminist philosophy

What is the scope of feminist philosophy? It is a truism that there are women philosophers and philosophical works written by women. The fact, therefore, of feminist philosophy is undeniable. The question of *how it exists* is the subject matter of this section. Advocates of feminist philosophy critique philosophy on its own premise as well as entertain the possibility of mutual fecundation of feminism and philosophy. Nancy Bauer, paraphrasing Simone de Beauvoir, remarks that feminism is both a problem *for* and *of* philosophy.

> To say that it is a problem for philosophy is to propose that insofar as philosophy fails to take account of the being of

women it cannot lay claim to the universality to which, by its own lights, it must strive; it lacks the standards, one might say, by which to interpret its own use of the term "men" in the absence of an account of woman. To say that it is a problem of philosophy is to propose that insofar as one fails to explore the bearing of philosophy on the being of woman, one will not be able to give an adequate account of what kind of a problem being a woman poses and, therefore, may close off certain possibilities for addressing this problem."[23]

Bauer outlines four ways in which feminism and philosophy relate as a means of understanding the nature of feminist philosophy.

♦ Feminist philosophy can be understood as applied philosophy in the sense that feminism uses the tools of philosophy to elucidate its stance.

♦ Corrective stance: feminism exposes the limitations or pitfalls of philosophies that exclude feminist theory.

♦ Standpoint stance: Feminism proposes unique and typically women orientation to philosophical questions.

♦ Difference stance: Approach that celebrates the differences between men and women as a positive note of philosophy.

Feminist philosophy is *applied philosophy*. Feminism uses the works of established philosophers to guide its thinking, and to explain and evaluate its practice concerning the female condition. Jeffery Gauthier makes the point clearly in a consideration of Hegel,

> The link that I develop between Hegel's thought and feminism finds its origin in the broad areas of shared concern in these likewise diverse endeavors. In the first place, Hegel combined a traditional moral and political concern for the justification of actions and institutions respectively with a historical account of the emergence of self-consciousness through social and political practice. Such a project has obvious relevance for those

who are concerned with the normative implications of the emergence of a history of ethical and political 'invisibility.'[24]

Simone de Beauvoir and Sandra Harding are also doing applied feminist philosophy when they use Hegel's master-slave dialectic as an informative paradigm for understanding male-female relationship. Carol Galligan uses Kantian ethics as example of antithetical ethics to feminism. Catharine MacKinnon engages applied philosophy when she uses Marx's social stratification to compare women to a social class. "Sexuality," writes MacKinnon, "is to feminism what work is to Marxism."[25] Feminism is interested in philosophical theories that are of immediate importance to women. As an applied philosophy feminism is an interdisciplinary and integrative discipline. Its transdisciplinary interest is evident when it compares, contrasts, and juxtaposes feminist theory with theories from other disciplines in order to bridge the gap that separates these disciplines from feminist theory.

Feminist philosophy is a critique in that it takes a corrective posture. Feminist philosophy is a critique of specific themes of traditional philosophy. It criticizes philosophies that in one way or the other deny the personhood of women, excessively relies on hierarchical dualism (male/female dichotomy) for its theorizing. The aim of the critique is to pinpoint the contingent nature of hierarchical dualism and its malleability. Another term that feminism criticizes is philosophy's use of universalism that excludes women. Feminism is a critique of any philosophy in which the exclusion of women "is inscribed as a logical necessity."[26]

Let us take the example of Kimberly Hutchings to extensively illustrate the point that feminism is critical philosophy. Kimberly Hutchings, drawing inspiration from Hegelian philosophy, defines feminist philosophy as "thinking differently," envisaging how "to escape the conceptual binary oppositions. . . which have associated women with the denigrated term and prescribed the exclusion of women from the practices of both philosophy and politics. As I expound it, feminist philosophy can be defined as a project to think the world differently, but one which is forever prey to the tendency to lapse back into the terms it is seeking to transcend."[27] Feminism, according to Kimberly Hutchings, endorses any mode of thought that avoids the one-sidedness and exclusivity of either masculinism or feminism. Feminist philosophy also resists modernism's transcendence that reifies gender differences. Feminist philosophy historicizes gender and is "largely preoccupied with developing framework for thought which do not repeat the hierarchical binaries of the tradition."[28] The specificity of feminist philosophy, therefore, gravitates around the question of how the categories of sex and gender are to be understood. The task of feminist philosophy is comprehension.

Kimberly Hutchings grounds the possibility of this kind of thought in the conclusions of post-kantian philosophy. This philosophy holds that in the creation or acquisition of knowledge "reason as a capacity is seen as having nothing to do with concrete aspects of the knower's identity (state of mind) or their identity with others (social existence)."[29] Feminist philosophy is out to demonstrate the baselessness of gender stereotypes in philosophy. Feminist philosophy argues that reason is asexual, has no gender. Mary Woolstonecraft makes the point for genderless reason, "reason is, consequently, the simple power of improvement. . . of discerning the truth. Every individual is in this respect a world in itself. . . The nature of reason must be the same in all, if it be an emanation of divinity, the tie that connects the creature with the creator."[30] Feminist philosophy is out to establish a truism that thinking transcends physical existence. It wants to establish faith in the rationality of women and belief in the ontological identity of reasoning faculty in women and men. It does so by questioning the history and assumptions on which previous practice was grounded.

Feminism does not simply criticize how traditional philosophy has devaluated or dismissed the experience of women. It also provides an enriched philosophical conception which will impact feminist philosophy. For example, Allison Jaggar criticizes the way emotions are treated in Western Philosophy.

> Although Jaggar's critique of 'rationalist epistemology' is not specifically directed toward normative theories of justification, the points that she develops parallels those raised by critiques of moral rationalism. Jaggar focuses her criticisms on positivist accounts that conceive of emotion on a purely involuntary sensation or even a behavior associated with a particular feeling.[31]

Jaggar advances the argument that emotions are not simply episodic and sensual. They are 'dispositional' and so have a cognitive value. Every emotion has sensual and cognitive value simultaneously. Jaggar hopes this enriched perspective is significant for feminist theory since it will "explain the perceptual aptitude of certain emotions, that is, how certain emotions have the capacity to provide new and liberating views of the world" to oppressed women.[32] The importance of feminist advanced critique of traditional philosophy is that the critique provides a positive accounting for feminist action. Also, it provides a rationale for taking feminist philosophical points of view seriously. As a critique feminism defines the being of woman not as a lack or privation. It answers the questions: What can be learned about women from feminism? How can feminism alter or respond in important ways to the challenges in the discipline?

Feminism is a standpoint philosophy. Standpoint philosophy is an engagement to cultivate an explicitly woman-centered perspective on issues that are up for discussion. It purports to create its own way of seeing. Standpoint feminist philosophy is a theory building enterprise that addresses the complex reality of women's experience and situation. The assumption underlying this approach is that philosophy must account for the truth about women and validate the theories about women. Feminism is a moral philosophy that operates on the assumption that albeit women's experiences have not been explicitly excluded from moral theories "their exclusion is implicit in that the moral concerns and activities that make up the initial sphere of morality are typically not central - and can even be quite alien – for the moral world of many women."[33] The purpose of feminist standpoint philosophy is to proffer the argument that women have the capacity for full moral agency. In its analysis of interrelationships it develops rules, principles, and beliefs that justify this stance. A glaring example of standpoint philosophy is found in Nel Nodding's ethic of care.[34]

The philosophical import of feminist standpoint is its contribution to the development of feminist epistemology. Epistemology, the theory of knowledge, addresses the following questions: Who can know? What can be known? How is knowledge validated? What is the nature of the relationship between the knower and the known? Feminist standpoint explores the possibility of 'feminist knowledge.' The importance of feminist standpoint is that it reveals or uncovers dominant ideology that has been systematically ignored or denied in society. Two trends developed as a result – a philosophical trend prominent in the works of Nancy Hartsock[35] and a sociological trend prominent in the works of Dorothy Smith.[36]

Using a feminist materialist approach, Hartsock argues that women's experiences of their daily lives gives them privileged access to understanding the relationships of ruling. The work of Hartsock is viewed as arguing for a feminist standpoint that will in consequence justify distinctive forms of feminist knowledge and methodologies. In her focus on everyday life Smith explores the social meanings that can be derived from how women talk about their experiences. Smith is concerned to stress that her position is not to argue for a feminist standpoint that in consequence will justify feminist knowledge. Rather, she is arguing for attention to be paid to women's standpoint. By this she means that the actualities of women's lives are sites through which 'concepts and theories are examined for how they are activated in organizing social relationships.[37]

Some epistemological principles emerge from standpoint philosophy. Firstly, there is nothing like knowledge from nowhere. All knowledge is situation specific. The position of the knower is crucial to feminist epistemology. Human experience structures and sets limits to knowledge. The present situation of women – marginalized, oppressed, and devalued – is the vantage point from which feminist epistemology must unfold. Feminist epistemology does not admit of a purely rationalistic account of knowledge. Secondly, by proposing alternative views of male-female relationship standpoint philosophy attests that knowledge is not static or a finished product. It spirals in a never-ending process. Hence, feminist epistemology is always in process. Finally, standpoint renounces the adequation theory of knowledge as perfect mirroring of reality divorced from human experience. It adopts Dewey's approach. According to standpoint "knowledge is the result not of perfect mirroring, but of a method of experimental inquiry in which people investigate the problems with which they are confronted in order to develop possible solutions to them that are then tested in experience to see if the desired results occur."[38] Standpoint philosophy's emphasis on experience runs aground as a justificatory strategy. Issues of relativity of knowledge present in Empiricist epistemology can also be directed toward feminism. Also, in this philosophy sex is located at the causal level. Can this be adequately proven? Despite these setbacks should standpoint philosophy be abandoned?

Feminism is a philosophy of difference. Feminism is an articulation of difference between males and females, and among females. Feminism wants to know if the differences are significant or only incidental. The preoccupation of this approach to feminist philosophy is "how feminist method can accommodate difference."[39] It is a method that purports to theorize on difference that will not lose sight of gender difference. Feminist philosophy of difference is a theory of the self-worth of women and affirms that, "there really are extreme personality and skill differences between the genders."[40] Differences, whether they are innate or socialized, are so much a part of the identities of men and women and cannot be changed. People's identities are neither ephemeral nor do they change whenever it is expedient. Identities are essentially relational; hence one's relation to their gender is quintessential to their personal identity. To be an authentic woman women must strive to be and remain women. Feminist philosophy of difference has moved through different phases. Nancy Hartsock notes that

> in the first stage of feminist reform efforts, which I date roughly from the founding of the National Organization for Women up to the beginnings of the Women's Liberation Movement (1964-1968), feminist implicitly held that the differences between women and men were not a sufficient base on which to construct Difference, that is, that differences of gender were superficial and insufficient grounds on which to construct radical alterity, or 'Otherness.' Thus efforts to overcome discrimination against women took the forms of attempts to create what could only be a false universality and a concomitant refusal to recognize the economic and social underpinnings of power differences.[41]

Sub-themes in the philosophy of difference include domination, importance of difference, and the nature of change. Its foundational quest is to find out whether difference can be used as ground or justification for human relationships. Feminist philosophy of difference is a philosophical method that wants to shift feminist theory to a new paradigm that incorporates the advantages of gender analysis.

Philosophical feminism is a thought pattern that developed alongside studies on topics like the problems of minorities, civil rights and liberties, and legislation for change. Feminist philosophical inquiry developed two trends. One trend is critical and focuses on "the assumptions of the discipline (philosophy) itself, including the assumption of neutrality, and began to reveal male biases deeply hidden in the methods and substance of traditional philosophical theory."[42] The other trend is applied because it creates "a place for the study of subjects of particular relevance to women by turning the normative fields of ethics and social philosophy away from more abstract metatheory and toward the application of ideas to particular social problems... So feminist philosophy has been part of a larger resurgence of interest in applied social philosophy."[43] Feminist philosophy challenges the traditional view that philosophical issues should be examined only for their abstract and universal nature. It calls for rethinking philosophical definitions.

Feminism as Method

The present section defines feminism as a method proposing consciousness-raising as its technique, experience as one of its principles, and traditional philosophy and feminist movements as its sources.

Definition of method

From the point of view of its task three usages of methods are distinguishable: technique, principle, and resources.

Method is conceived as acceptable specific procedures that are used in a given science to inquire into that science. Method, as technique, calls for right ways and wrong ways of proceeding or good and bad ways of proceeding. The technique of a science is its *modus operandi*, which for compelling reasons is considered acceptable. The concern of method is with generality.

Method is also a principle. Principles are the perspectives and doctrines that play a significant though indirect influence on the conduct of inquiry and the formation and acceptance of hypothesis. Method, as principle, is concerned with the logic of analysis, the logic of description, and the possibility to predict.

Method is also about resources. In this case method answers the question, "What elements does the science employ?" In brief, method helps in an understanding of processes. It increases awareness about what is being done.

Consciousness-raising

Feminist method has been considered as a defining characteristic of feminism. Two methods – consciousness-raising and method of difference – facilitate the understanding of feminist theory. Only consciousness-raising shall be treated fully here. Method of difference is interspersed in the whole chapter.

Catherine MacKinnon defines feminist method as "consciousness-raising" which she says signifies "the major technique of analysis, structure of organization, method of practice, and theory of social change of women's movement."[44] Feminist theory contends that although male consciousness is palpable in most thought processes and practices it is often masqueraded as natural, normal, and inevitable. Consciousness-raising is a mode of analysis in that it emphasizes an examination and understanding of women's experiences and patriarchy and connecting these to the structures that define social relationships. Consciousness-raising is an analysis, which aims at unveiling and manifesting the effects of male-oriented thinking. It heightens awareness to a previously ignored and surreptitious male domination. Consciousness-raising is an analysis, which purports to expose male domination, which before now has been hidden from public view.

Consciousness-raising is a theory of women's point of view apropos of the female condition. It is not a female therapy but a strategy for constructing a sympathetic internal female experience. "Through consciousness-raising women grasp the collective reality of women's condition from within the perspective of that experience, not from outside it."[45] Consciousness-raising lays claim to women's perspective as a claim to truth. It connects women's experiences in ways that transcend their personal experiences. Radical feminists developed consciousness-raising in the 1960s. Alix Kates Shulman, one of the participants, describes consciousness-raising as a technique:

> Consciousness-raising sessions were really gathering sessions, research sessions on our feelings. We wanted to get the truth about how women felt, how we viewed our lives, what was done to us, and how we function in the world. Not how we were supposed to feel but how we really did feel. The knowledge, gained through honest examination of our own personal experience, we will pool to help us figure out how to change the situation of woman.[46]

Consciousness-raising is, therefore, a method organized around the experience of women.

What are the methods that consciousness-raising employs? First, it encourages women to develop an understanding of the issues that are important to them. This calls for analysis of their personal experiences.[47] Second, it eschews a moral point of view in which the evaluation of any phenomena is in terms of its effect on women. "We take the women's side in anything. We ask not if something is 'reformist', 'revolutionary', or 'moral'. We ask, is it good for women or bad for women?"[48] Third, the understanding of the issues and their evaluation leads to the development of alternative practices in wake of current circumstances.

Consciousness-raising is rooted in two assumptions. First, it is assumed that, "What women had to say about the details of their lives, about their personal experiences, and histories, mattered; it had significance, and above all, it had validity."[49] The above assumption authenticates the authority of the experience of women. It affirms that the being (life and experience) of women is a source of legitimacy, authority, and validity of feminist methodology. Something is true about women not because it is supposed or expected to be so by others but because it stems from the lived experience of women. The validity of the above assumption is proven by the corroboration of shared experiences of women.

The second assumption that underlies consciousness-raising is that there is a "commonality underlying the diversity of women's experience."[50] This assumption underscores what is often referred to as the female condition or the consciousness of women as a sex-class that cuts across women of all races, creeds, and orientation. The assumption entertains the supposition that it is possible to bring women to understand that they belong to a category called 'all women' from which they cannot escape. The assumption reveals a salient truth, namely, that there is nothing like an exceptional woman meaning a woman who thinks like a man. The female condition is ahistorical.

Consciousness-raising is a critique of commonly held accounts of societal relationships based on gender. It is an extended and developed analysis of the working of patriarchy with the aim of eliminating a sex-class system, which considers women as inferior. It does so by proffering and sharing reliable information about the experiences of women. Consciousness-raising is a method of creating a sense of connection among women, of creating space in which women's experiences count and have authority. It is a redefinition of identity in which the woman's sense of self is re-adjusted. In brief, consciousness-raising hopes to transform people's thought about women by opening new vistas in which the positive value and richness of women's experiences can be appropriated. Consciousness-raising is, therefore, not a naïve dissemination of information about women and social institutions but an active engagement to change social relationships. Consciousness-raising is not a simple complaint by women about social injustices. Rather, it is a critique that sharpens the perspectives and perceptions of women to unapologetically examine their plight in greater detail.

Principles of feminist method

Feminism is founded on principles that provide it with an explanatory framework. One principle is the *centrality of experience*. The foundational element of feminist analysis is women's experience. Experience is also the starting point of feminist epistemology. The centrality of experience in feminist theory has been captured in Mackinnon's summary sentence, "the personal is the political" which she says,

> Means the women's distinctive experience as women occurs within that sphere that has been socially lived as the personal – private, emotional, interiorized, particular, individuated, intimate – so that what it is to know the politics of women's situation is to know women's personal lives... To say that the personal is political means that gender as a division of power is discoverable and verifiable through women's intimate experience of sexual objectification, which is definitive of and synonymous with women's lives as gender female. Thus, to feminism, the personal is epistemologically the political, and its epistemology is its politics.[51]

The importance of experience stands out clearly in consciousness-raising. Feminism claims uniqueness to women's experience. What is important is that feminism does not take experience in the sense of a metaphysical category. Feminism is interested in the substantive concerns of experience: coherence (do women have a common experience?), validity (how unique are women's experiences?), and relation to theory (how can a valid theory of feminist experience be constructed?).

Sources of feminist philosophy

Ann Garry and Marilyn Pearsall designate two sources of feminist philosophy. According to both authors feminist philosophy builds on the achievement of feminist movements. "The feminist movement," note both authors, "has opened our eyes to the deep and varied ways in which the ideals and institutions of our culture oppress women. In addition to providing a devastating critique of male-dominated society, feminists have affirmed the positive value of women's experience. Academic feminist philosophers build upon and contribute to the insights and work of the women's movement. Feminist philosophers examine and criticize the assumptions and presuppositions of the ideals and institutions our culture."[52]

The second source of feminist philosophy designated by Garry and Pearsall is traditional academic philosophy.

> Although traditional philosophy has been shaped by men who have taken their experiences, their values, and their views of the world as the standard for all human beings, it is in the philosophical traditions of these men that academic feminists were educated.[53]

According to feminist philosophical paradigm of Ann Garry and Marilyn Pearsall philosophical themes that interests feminist philosophy are topics like "value-hierarchical thinking" and "normative dualism."[54] Value-hierarchical thinking refers to the thought process that considers difference or diversity only in terms of greater or lesser value. Feminist philosophy is an antidote to arguments that use this kind of thinking to perpetrate women's subordination. Normative dualism or binary opposition that feminism criticizes is an either-or thought process that excludes any idea of complementarities.

FEMINIST PHILOSOPHY OF EDUCATION

Down the centuries feminist educational thought has undergone significant shifts of emphases. Prior to the 19th century feminist education was shaped by traditional gender expectations and social assumptions. After the 19th century the emphasis shifted to a demand for equal educational opportunity for males and females. There was a demand to open school doors to girls. It was, therefore, imperative at this time to develop a philosophy of co-education. In North America the demand for equal educational opportunity peaked in the 1980s when Jane Roland Martin began to report on her findings to two fundamental questions: What is the place of women in education? What happens to educational thought when women are brought in? Jane Martin developed her answers in thirteen essays in which she outlines avenues in which educational philosophy can "be redefined to include women's experiences, women's values, activities, and social responsibility."[55] From the 20th century to date feminist educational thought has shifted from asking educational doors to be opened to challenging educational practice taking place behind the doors. Feminism in education is not disinterested or a simple academic problem. It is a real question that touches not only the foundations of educational policy and arrangement but also the lives of persons.

Aims of Education

Feminism is committed to an ideal that engages social change or perspective transformation. What is the nature of this ideal when translated into educational aims and assumptions? Feminist philosophy of education is a search for viable strategies of change. It purports to revise the vision of education.

Education for healing

According to Magda Lewis who wrote the forward to Becky Ropers-Huilman's *Feminist teaching in theory and practice*, one of the aims of feminist education is healing:

> Students and faculty (both men and women) whose commitment
> to teaching and learning for purposes of healing and mending
> a scarred world cannot be bought off by promises of academic
> prestige and advancement.

Two important remarks about feminist educational aims standout here, namely, what education is for and what education is not for. Feminist education is not for career advancement. Rather, it is a quest to render satisfactory accounts about the moral agency of women and by so doing counter popular culture concerning women. Feminist education must address the problematic relations and identity of women and the structural sexist, ontological, or epistemological framework that premises their exclusion or misrepresentations. Hence, feminist education aims at seeking alternative interpretations and symbolism of women that will constitute the foundation for change and growth in the consideration of women.

Positively, feminist education aims at healing. The hurt that feminist education must heal is one of omission. The hurt is that of misrepresentation. Healing the misrepresentation of the nature and ideal of women through theories that present them otherwise than they really are. How will feminist education achieve this goal? It must develop multi-disciplinary research, theory, and scholarship. It must contribute to progressive policy-making in the field of gender equality and social change. It must give serious thought to values such as empowerment and inclusion. It must engage in liberating experiences by teaching about self-realization and return to wholeness as it assists students to know who they are and what their purpose in life is.

Re-reading the canon

Nancy Tuana, in the Preface to Feminist interpretations of Dewey edited by Charlene Siegfried, notes that the concepts of philosophy are generally "associated with traits historically identified with masculinity... [and] the realm of rationality will be reserved for men, with grudging entrance to those few women who are capable of transcending their feminity."[56] From this observation Tuana concludes that there has been a general neglect in the consideration that philosophical texts are neither gender-neutral nor do they offer a universal perspective of human nature. She, therefore, suggests "to be fully aware of the impact of gender biases, it is imperative that we re-read the canon with attention to the ways in which philosophers' assumptions concerning gender are embedded within their theories."[57] One goal of feminist educational philosophy is to reevaluate the assumptions that undergird education. Feminist educational philosophy has as its mission to decipher what is included and not included in educational texts and why. It must analyze the impact of gender ideology in educational activity, uncover the history of women therein, and recover any neglected or lost meaning. In so doing feminist educational philosophy will carefully examine the reasons for the treatment of women in them.

The purpose of re-reading the canon of education is to make a case for inclusion and the valorization of the experience of women. Feminism suggests inclusion as a legitimate alternative educational ideal to the current practice of exclusion. Feminism's argument for inclusion is based on the assumption of universality, namely, that "no viewpoint should be systematically excluded from our conversations; no groups or individuals should be rendered invisible or silent by either our practices or our theories."[58] Another assumption underlying the case for inclusion is that education is a cultural representation that can be contested and renewed. In making their case for inclusion philosophers of education must answer questions like: Is inclusion an educational value? The exclusion of women from educational activities has been attributed to what can be called epistemic weakness. Is inclusion an epistemic or moral virtue? Is inclusion a question of truth or a question of justice?

Feminism and Curriculum

Transforming the curriculum

How has feminism permeated educational theory with respect to content? What are the reasons for this transformation?

Feminism contends that curriculum in most, if not all, educational institutions is male-centered. As such only half the human experience is represented in such programs. Elizabeth MacNabb *et al.* make the point that

> the overt curriculum of all levels of education has been criticized by feminist for being too androcentric (male-centered) and Eurocentric... In textbooks, readers, and biographies they found a world in which females were virtually invisible... Feminist research in education has contributed to the transformation of K-12 curriculum materials by making people much more sensitive to the overt sexism contained in textbooks. Increasingly, children are using textbooks and literature that reflect positive images of girls and women from all races and generations. Nonetheless, there is still much work to be done in creating gender-balanced textbooks.[59]

Feminist critique of curriculum is less about making women the pivotal concern of curriculum and educational research. Rather, the concern of feminism is the transformation of existing curriculum from within or developing an alternative philosophy of curriculum that integrates the experiences of women and men. "A feminist perspective," write Langland and Gove, "whether it is present in women's studies courses or in scholarly essays such as those in this volume, seeks to correct the biases present in our academic disciplines by uncovering and questioning the hidden assumptions about men and women that have shaped and informed standard academic subjects."[60] The assumptions that curriculum developers deal with include assumptions about the nature of learners and teachers, the purposes of schools, the kind of knowledge that is appropriate for a learned person, and the world in which learners live and want to live in. These assumptions guide and govern the selection of educational texts.

Feminist argument for a transformation of curriculum is an argument from the relevance of curriculum. The argument is based on a two-tiers distinction concerning curriculum. There is the discipline per se, that is, the theories, methods, concepts, laws, and the like that govern the discipline. Also, there is the educational consideration of the curriculum that considers the "skills to be acquired, techniques to be mastered, activities to be learned, attitudes to be developed, convictions to be encouraged, ways of acting to be promoted."[61] Feminist educators are against curriculum that studies only the discipline per se, this is, learning about the discipline, taking a spectator stance vis-à-vis the discipline. Feminists advocate the inclusion of consideration about human conduct in the elaborating curriculum. The disciplines illumine human conduct. It is, therefore, imperative for curriculum elaborators to consider how the choice of 'curriculum discipline' influences the conduct of males and females. Feminism is not simply advocating an enrichment of or enlarging of curriculum. Rather, it is proposing a radical study of the implication of gender for curriculum. According to Jane Roland Martin "the study of gender is as germane to the reconstruction of curriculum as to its deconstruction."[62]

What role is reserved for feminist philosophers of education? These philosopher-educators must engage in a genetic analysis of educational texts in order to trace and understand their treatment of males and females. This approach is undertaken by Nel Noddings in her Philosophy of Education. Her interest in this volume is "to introduce readers to the content of philosophy when it is relevant to problems of education."[63] One of such relevant content is the history of the education of women in the texts established by philosophers like Socrates, Rousseau, Herbart, and Dewey. The purpose of this analysis is not simply to clarify, enhance, or reject existing theories and concepts about women in education. The purpose according to Nel Noddings is to create new curriculum theories or fudge alternative visions. Noddings, however, remarks that, "whether this work is properly called philosophy is part of an exciting contemporary debate."[64] Feminist philosophers must also engage in textual analysis. Textual examination is a close reading of gender concepts like man, woman, and human to determine if they are problematic and why. Another task for feminist philosophers is logical analysis. Logical inquiry tests the effects of subject curriculum on students' self-esteem, for example. Finally, feminist philosopher-educators must engage in hypothetical analysis. Hypothetical investigation addresses philosophical questions like: should the differences between males and females be exalted or denied? Should schools change or sustain the sexual mix? What role should schools play in explaining any understanding or tolerance of the male-female equation? What values are at stake in the feminine discourse?

The task of the feminist philosopher-educator is summarized in philosophical analysis. The feminist analyst is not looking for the unifying factor of curriculum. The analyst is concerned with the question: what does this curriculum aspect mean? The feminist is engaged in clarifying educational concepts by pointing out the beliefs that underlie the choices or detect inconsistencies in educational theories and practices. The clarification process can include uncovering neglected meaning in current expressions, clear pseudo-questions and problems, explore alternative dimensions of educational terminology, and expose the inconsistencies of current theory.

Women's studies curriculum

Feminism has moved from the struggle for women's access to education to a recognition of women's studies as a critical discipline in educational curriculum. However, women's studies has experienced a mixed reception. Some educational institutions have admitted it as a discipline with departmental status. Others have challenged it and looked upon it with apathy because it trivializes curriculum. Still, others granted it legitimacy reluctantly as part of the academic curriculum. "Women's studies is not simply the study of women; it is the study of women which places women's own experience in the center of the process. It examines the world and human beings who inhabit it with questions, analyses, and theories built directly as women's experience."[65] Women's studies is an interdisciplinary discipline whose richness and fascination comes from its interconnections with other disciplines, theories, and sciences. Theoretically, it calls for knowledge beyond individual disciplines and takes a critical look at each discipline. It is also a practical discipline. The founders of the program in the State University of New York, Buffalo stated that "the education (women's studies) will not be an academic exercise; it will be an ongoing process to change the ways in which women think and behave. It must be part of the struggle to build a new and more complete society."[66]

Women's studies has already taken root in curriculum in the United States of America and India as well as in the writings on education elsewhere. In the United States women's studies developed within the background of the struggle for women's rights and flourished in the 1970s. The following statistics bespeak the point.

> In 1970 when scholar-activists established the first program at San Diego State University, no one could have predicted just how successful women's studies would be. Just three decades later, women's studies now occupies a prominent place within the academy. There are approximately 615 programs in the United Sates, and women's studies enrolls the largest number of students of any interdisciplinary field. The Department of Education has estimated that 12 percent of all undergraduate students receive credit for courses in women's studies. Although only a handful of universities offer doctoral degrees specifically in women's studies, graduate students have carved out a sizable niche for themselves with the discipline. Between 1978, when women's studies first appeared as an indexing category in *Dissertation Abstract International*, and 1985, the total number of dissertations recorded under the heading was more than thirteen thousand. Far from being a fad, as many detractors had gibed, women's studies has become an integral part of higher education.

Florence Howe also reports the inception and subsequent expansion of women's studies program in her report to the National Advisory Council on Women's Educational Program. In 1976 there were 270 programs and 15,000 courses in women's studies in 1500 institutions. Also, there were 850 teachers designing interdisciplinary curriculum that included women's studies. In 1981 the programs had increased to 350.[67]

In India the emergence of women's studies is also intricately tied to women's movements. However, it is thought for the most part to be an off-shoot of the process of development in India.

> The Education Commission (1964-66), popularly known as Kothari Commission, which examined in depth the roles and goals of education in the process of national development toward secular, socialist, and democratic society, endorsed the view of the Hans Mehta and the Durgabai Deshmukh Committees, and observed: 'In the modern world, the role of women goes beyond the home and the bringing up of children. She is now adopting a career of her own and sharing equally with men the responsibility for the development of society in all its aspects. This is the direction in which we shall have to move.'[68]

After about two decades of research, data collection, and data analysis women's studies was legitimized in India.

The 1980s symbolized the peak of the struggle for legitimizing women's studies with a dual agenda: (a) to transform dominant ideologies and mindsets that consciously or unconsciously remain resistant to gender equality, and (b) to expand the social concern against injustice, marginilization, and oppression of women by harnessing the services of the educational system. The National Conference on Women's Studies held in 1981 in Bombay sought to stimulate/ initiate the process by generating a wider awareness of the problem of women as well as by demonstrating the capacity of women's studies as a critical instrument of change.[69]

Some authors are also showing how women's studies is transforming individual disciplines. Elizabeth MacNabb et al. edited Transforming the disciplines. A woman's studies premier, which is a collection of thirty field-by-field essays ranging from anthropology, economics, physics, to library science. The purpose of the collection is "to describe exactly how feminism relates to various academic disciplines and, thereby, to explain what the field known as women's studies is. Without going into great detail or attempting to include fine nuances of scholarship, the essays spell out, in basic terms and concepts, exactly how the feminist approach has transformed (or how it could transform) each of the scholarly disciplines."[70] The same approach is taken by A feminist perspective in the academy edited by Elizabeth Langland and Walter Gove. Both editors come to the conclusion "that feminist analyses have begun to alter scholarship, but women's studies has yet to have substantial influence on traditional curriculum, principally because such analyses challenge fundamental assumptions in each discipline."[71]

[1] Andermahr, S., Lovell, T., & Wolkowitz, C. (1997). *A concise glossary of feminist theory.* London: Arnold. p. 77. Also see Hutchings, K. (2003). *Hegel and feminist philosophy.* Malden, MA: Blackwell Publishing Inc. p. 2.

[2] Houston, B. (1996). *Feminism.* In J. J. Chambliss (Ed.). *Philosophy of education. An encyclopedia.* New York: Garland Publication. p. 25.

[3] Andermahr, et al. *op. cit.,,* p. 164.

[4] Stomquist, N. P. (2002). *Contributions and challenges of feminist theory to comparative education research and methodology.* In J. Schriewer (Ed.) *Discourse formation in comparative education.* New York: Peter Lang.

[5] Eisenstein, H. (1984). *Contemporary feminist thought.* London: Allen & Unwin. p. xviii.

[6] Almond, B. (1988). *Women's rights. Reflecting on ethics and gender.* In M. Griffiths & M. Whiteford (Eds.). *Feminist perspectives in philosophy.* Bloomington, IN: Indiana University Press. p. 53.

[7] Almond, *op. cit.,,* p. 53.

[8] Almond, *op. cit.,,* p. 55.

[9] Garry, A. & Pearsall, M. (Eds.). (1992). *Women, knowledge, and reality. Explorations in feminist philosophy.* New York: Routledge. p. xii.

[10] Midgley, M. (1988). *On not being afraid of natural sex differences.* In M. Griffiths & M. Whiteford (Eds.). *Feminist perspectives in philosophy.* Bloomington, IN: Indiana University Press. p. 37.

[11] Midgley, *op. cit.,,* p. 37.

[12] Midgley, *op. cit.,,* p. 36.

[13] Almond, *op. cit.,,* p. 42.

[14] Noddings, N. & Slote, M. (2003). *Changing notions of moral education.* In N. Blake, P. Smeyers, R. Smith, & P. Standish (Eds.). *The Blackwell guide to the philosophy of education.* Malden, MA: Blackwell Publishers Inc.. p. 342.

[15] Noddings & Slote, *op. cit.,,* p. 343.

[16] DuBois, E. et al. (1985). *Feminist scholarship. Kindling in the groves of academe.* Chicago, IL: University of Illinois Press, p. 29.

[17] Bauer, N. (2003). *Simone de Beauvoir, philosophy, and feminism.* New York: University of Columbia Pres. p. 19.

[18] Bauer, *op. cit.,,* p. 19.

[19] Nye, A. (2000). *It's not philosophy.* In U. Narayan and S. Harding (Eds.) *Decentering the center. Philosophy for a multicultural, postcolonial, and feminist world.* Bloomington, IN: Indiana University Press. p. 101.

[20] Nye, A. *op. cit.,,* p. 102.

[21] Nye, A. *op. cit.,,* p. 102.

[22] Nye, A. *op. cit.,,* pp. 102-3.

[23] Bauer, *op. cit.,,* p. 1.

[24] Gauthier, J. A. (1997). *Hegel and feminist social criticism. Justice, recognition, and the feminine.* New York: State University of New York., p. xiii.

[25] MacKinnon, C. (1982). *Feminism, Marxism, method, and the State.* N. O. Kechane, M. Z. Rosaldo, B. C. Gelpi, (Eds.). *Feminist theory.* Brighton, MA: The Harvester Press, p. 1.

[26] Holland, N. J. (1990). *Is women philosophy possible?* Savage, MD: Rowman & Littlefield Publishers Inc., p. 4.

[27] Hutchings, K. (2003). *Hegel and feminist philosophy.* Malden, MA: Blackwell Publishing Inc. p. 2.

[28] Hutchings, K. *op. cit.,,* p. 2.

[29] Hutchings, K. *op. cit.,,* p. 17.

[30] Wollstonecraft, M. (1975). *A vindication of the rights of women.* Baltimore: Penguin. p. 142.

[31] Gauthier, *op. cit.,,* p. 101.

[32] Gauthier, *op. cit.,,* p. 102.

[33] Gardener, *op. cit.,,* p. 6.

[34] Nodding, N. (1995). *Philosophy of education.* Boulder, CO: Westview Press.

[35] Hartsock, N. (1998). *The feminist standpoint revisited and other essays.* Boulder, CO: Westview Press.

[36] Smith, D. (1988). *The everyday world as problematic. A feminist sociology.* Milton Keynes: Open University Press.

[37] Hughes, C. (2002). *Key concepts in feminist theory and research.* London: Sage Publication, p. 153.

[38] Seigfried, C. H. (2002). *Feminist interpretations of John Dewey.* University Park, PA: The Pennsylvania State University, p. 219.

[39] Heckman, S. (1999). *The future of differences. Truth and method of feminist theory.* Malden, MA: Blackwell Publishers Inc. p. 52.

[40] Garry & Pearsall, *op. cit.,,* p. 96.

[41] Hartsock, *op. cit.,,* p. 59.

[42] DuBois, *op. cit.,,* p. 29.

[43] DuBois, *op. cit.,,* p. 29.

[44] MacKinnon, *op. cit.,,* p. 22.

[45] Mackinnon, *op. cit.,,* p. 22.

[46] Eisenstein, H. (1983). *Contemporary feminist thought.* Bodon, MA: G. K. Hall and Co. p. 37.

[47] Gauthier , *op. cit.,,* p. 61.

[48] Morgan, R. (1970). *Goodbye to all that.* In L. B. Tanner (Ed.). *Voices from women's liberation.* New York: Signet, p. 580.

[49] Eisenstein, *op. cit.,,* p. 37.

[50] Eisenstein, *op. cit.,,* p. 38.

[51] Mackinnon, *op. cit.,,* pp. 73-74.

[52] Garry & Pearsall, *op. cit.,,* p. xi.

[53] Garry & Pearsall, *op. cit.,,* p. xi

[54] Garry & Pearsall, *op. cit.,,* p. xii

[55] Houston, B. (1996) *Feminism.* In J. J. Chambliss (Ed.) *Philosophy of education. An encyclopedia.* New York: Garland Publication. p. 219.

[56] Seigfried, *op. cit.,,* p. ix.

[57] Seigfried, *op. cit.,,* p. x.

[58] Siegel, H. *What price inclusion?* http://www.ed.uiuc.edu/EPS/PES-Yearbook/95_docs/siegel.html, p. 2.

[59] MacNabb, E., Cherry, M., Popham, S., & Prys, R. (Eds.). (2001). *Transforming the disciplines. A women's studies premier.* New York: The Haworth Press. p. 21.

[60] Langland, E. & Gove, W. (1983). *A feminist perspective in the academy. The difference it makes.* Chicago, Il: The University of Chicago press. p. 3.

[61] Martin, *op. cit.,,* p. 143.

[62] Martin, *op. cit.,,* p. 241.

[63] Noddings, N. (1995). *Philosophy of education.* Boulder, CO: Westview Press. p. 2.

[64] Noddings, *op. cit.,,* p. 2.

[65] Hunter College Women's Studies Collective, (1983). *Women's realities, women's choices. An introduction to women's studies.* New York: Oxford University Press. p. 3.

[66] Howe, F. (Ed.). (2000). *The politics of women's studies.* New York: City University of New York. p. xxv.

[67] Howe, F. *Women and the power of education.* American Association for Higher Education Bulletin. 33(1981) 13-14.

[68] Jain, d. & Rajput, P. (2003). *Narratives from Women's Studies Family.* New Delhi: Sage Publication. p. 51.

[69] Jain & Rajput, *op. cit.,,* p. 57.

[70] MacNabb et al. *op. cit.,*, p. 5.
[71] Langland & Gove, *op. cit.,*, p. 1.

CHAPTER 6

IDEALISM AND EDUCATION

PHILOSOPHICAL FOUNDATION

Sketch Of Historical Development Of Idealism

The term idealism was first used philosophically by Gottfried Leibniz to characterize the thought of Plato, while at the same time contrasting it with the materialism of Epicurus. Idealism is a collective designation of those philosophies that regard the mind as the principle of explanation of all activities and all the universe. For idealists only ideas constitute true reality. Hence, the principal concern of idealism is the search for eternal and perfect truth, which cannot be found in the changing world of things. A preliminary delimitation of idealism states that

> ultimate reality is of the same substance as ideas... Behind the phenomenal world is an infinite Spirit that is both substructure and creator of the cosmos... The existence of God is made necessary by certain factors of selfhood... The self is the prime reality... Man as a thinking being is a part of God... By examining his own ideas and testing their consistency man can achieve truth... The self reads meaning and unity into the objective world.[1]

What stands out in this definition and what constitutes salient aspects of idealism are individuality, perception, and God as Infinite Spirit. Idealism is a philosophy in which only mental and spiritual values are real and fundamental. The spiritual aspect in idealism is not to be equated with religion. Rather, the spiritual refers to an ontological view of the universe. However, it should be noted that idealism has strong affinities with religion since most of its cadre were pastors or deeply religious.

Idealism emerged as a reaction against naturalism, the philosophical stance that the mind and spiritual values emerged from and are reducible to material things and processes. Idealism also rejected realism as a philosophy that held the view that material things exist independently of being perceived. In an attempt, therefore, to answer the question concerning the relationship between thinking and being, and between spirit and nature, idealism asserts the primacy of spirit over nature. The primacy is not according to time, though idealism emerged earlier in time than realism. Rather, primacy is to be understood in statutory terms of the mind and the spiritual as fundamental and basic elements of existence. Whereas naturalism and realism believe in the universality of matter as the basic reality, idealism believes that the key to reality is to be found in the final, immutable, and eternal mind. Naturalism and realism are philosophies of this-worldly experience and idealism is a philosophy of spiritual existence and otherworldly perfection.

Various types of idealistic philosophy are distinguished following the facet that the exponents of this philosophy want to emphasize. Plato's Platonic idealism postulated a separation of the world of ideas (forms) which is eternal and unchanging from the fleeting world of matter. According to Plato material objects are imperfect embodiments of ideas. Material things serve only as reminders of absolute ideas. For Plato the pursuit of truth must be a pursuit of the ideas or forms that are perfect and eternal. Plato, therefore, proposed an education, especially for rulers, which will bring them closer to the ideas. So unlike his predecessors, the physicists who centered their attention on the forces of nature, Plato (through elaboration of the forms in the allegory of the cave) "indicates the primacy for him of mind and reason in the experience of man… For him the life of reason was the focus from which all else stems. This is the spirit of idealism."[2] In the dialogues of Plato one finds the roots and direction in the formulation of the philosophy of idealism.

St. Augustine (354-480) in his The City of God developed his own version of the Platonic dichotomy in terms of the City of God and the City of Man.

His educational philosophy, contained in his De Magistro, is patterned after the Platonic tradition. Augustine upholds the position that "worldly knowledge gained through the senses was full of error but that reason could lead toward understanding, and he held that, ultimately it was necessary to transcend reason through faith. Only through faith, or intuition, can one enter the realm of true ideas."[3] People do not create knowledge. God created knowledge. People can discover knowledge progressively in their search for God.

Table 4
Types of Idealism

Type	Proponent/work	Explanation
Immaterialism	Berkeley: *Principles of human Knowledge*	There is no such thing as material substance; *esse est percipi.*
Religious	Augustine: *The City of God*	Knowledge to be accepted by faith is demanded by the church.
Critical	Kant: *Critique of Pure Reason*	Spatiotemporal context and categories of understanding necessary for knowing
Absolute	Hegel: *Encyclopedia*	The finite is not genuinely real

In modern times idealism found a voice in the French philosopher René Descartes (1596-1650) and his Discourse on Method. From his launching platform of the methodic doubt Descartes doubted everything, even his own existence. Only one thing was certain to Descartes, namely, the fact that he cannot doubt that he is doubting or thinking. Hence, the Cartesian principle: 'cogito ergo sum' meaning 'I think, therefore, I am.' The importance of this principle is that it puts the mind and thinking at the center of Descartes' thought about the nature of human beings.

The Irish born George Berkeley (1685-1753) came up with a brand new version of idealism called subjective idealism or immaterialism. In his Principles of human knowledge (1710) Berkeley contended that nothing can exist without a mind perceiving it. If they are not perceived by the human mind, at least they are perceived by the mind of God. Hence, Berkeley's principle 'esse est percipi' meaning 'to be is to be perceived.' Nothing can exist independently of the perceiving mind. The motivation behind Berkeley's adoption of idealist metaphysics is his defense of the Christian faith. As minister of the Episcopalian Church in Ireland, idealism and its emphasis on the spiritual presented a more plausible avenue for thinking about God than realism.

The idealist, Immanuel Kant (1724-1804) was born in Königsberg, Germany. He was called a destroyer because he propounded a critical philosophy that undermined realism and any form of "a mystical tendency."[4] He also criticized the rationalistic idealism of Descartes and the empirical idealism of Berkeley as deficient.

Kant was very influential in the establishment of the primacy of reason and expounding idealist moral principles. In his Critique of Pure Reason (1781) Kant, after thorough examination of conscious reason, concluded that reason is the unifying center of the world. The world by itself has no unity of its own. Experience of the sun, a table, and a window, for example, are fragmented experiences at the sensory level. Only reason can construct connections among them through its operations on what is received through space and time so that the mind can come to understand them. Kant is, therefore, credited with proposing reason as a principle of cosmic unity. Kant's moral thoughts are found in his Metaphysics of Morals (1785), Critique of Practical Reason (1788), and Critique of Judgment (1790). Among the salient points of Kant's moral theory are the following: universal moral laws exist and people have an obligation to obey them (the categorical imperative). However, people also have the power not to obey these laws. The knowledge of these laws is not the result of some ethical intuition but that of reflective practical reason. Kant also advanced a theory about the immortality of the soul that suggested that we must presume the soul to be immortal even if we cannot prove it, for otherwise the moral law would be without sanction. Finally, Kant also suggested that one must postulate the existence of God even if it can never be proven.

Other influential idealists whose contributions have set the limits and direction of idealism and who will be mentioned include Arthur Schopenhaur (1788-1860), Giovanni Gentile (1875-1944), William Harris (1835-1909), Herman Harrell Horne (1774-1946), Michael Demiashkevitch (1891-1938), Boris Basil Bogolovsky (1890-1966), and Donald Butler (b. 1908).

Synopsis Of Foundation Of Idealism

Philosophy answers three fundamental questions: what is real? What is true? What is good or beautiful? According to idealism what is real is what is in a person's mind, truth is found in the consistency of ideas, and goodness is an ideal state to strive after. This section highlights the basic structure of philosophical idealism and those idealistic themes that have a significance for this tradition's educational thought.

Anthropology of Idealism

René Descartes' *cogito* established the fact that what is irreducible in human experience is the experience of consciousness. One can doubt everything but not that one exists. One certainty for Descartes, therefore, is that because he thinks, he must exist. Hence, the primary and ultimate implication of any thinking experience is that the really real is guaranteed by mind and consciousness. As a philosophical system, idealism

> is the elaboration and systematization of this basic proposition that mind is the primary and irreducible fact of human experience. One part of the basic thesis of all idealism is that mind is prior; that when we seek for that which is ultimate in the world, when we push back behind the veil of immediate sense experience we find that that which is ultimate in the whole universe is of the nature of mind or spirit… just as it is the mind that is ultimate in the inner world of personal experience.[5]

Idealism, therefore, considers the reality of human beings chiefly in terms of mental activity. A human being is an individual mind, an individual entity, and a spiritual being. The mind is essential to the description of humans in idealism because it is the mind that thinks, raises questions, and seeks solutions to problems. It is the mind that inquires and evaluates. It is the mind that observes and interprets the world of phenomena. According to idealism nothing can be observed unless there is a mind to observe it. Idealism's stress on the mind and self-awareness lead to a conception and formulation of the central tenet of its philosophy as the principle of the priority of consciousness. Priority of consciousness states that it is the mind (individual or Universal) that brings about the unity of the coherent reality that is experienced. From this central principle certain inferences can be made concerning the character of ultimate reality that are important to the tradition of idealism.

Consciousness associates the mind with certain powers, abilities, or capacities, three of which are thought, free will, and prerogative for immortality. Experience shows that conscious beings are capable of rational thought and knowledge. Thought is the most important power of the mind. Here we recall Descartes' cogito. According to idealism it is the mind that thinks and knows, not the body. Hence, it follows that one of the characteristics of ultimate reality is reason – one's power of cognition and logical thought. This tenet is very important in that any activity that is worthy to be classified under education must be associated with the mental powers rather than with the biological functions of the educand. A second power of the mind is free will. Idealistic analysis of self-realization underscores the point that individual development is not auto-determined but is self-directed by the choices that one makes. Freedom of choice is a sine qua non for human development. Human existence is unthinkable without the possibility of choice. A third attribute of reality is the will. This viewpoint is important in that education will be considered as a process of development rather than in terms of hereditary determinism. As a spiritual entity, the mind is indestructible and imperishable. Experience also reveals to idealists the fact that human beings are endowed with the powers of ongoing creation of the self, "the urge to self-realization – the drive not only to preserve, but also to realize ourselves."[6] This creative dynamic activity for self-realization is what we described above as the propensity for immortality. A conclusion that follows from this conception is that death is not the end of existence. This mode of thought has important ramifications for the formulation of the educational goals of idealism.

Apart from these powers the mind has other characteristics, which for convenience we call its nature. The mind is not matter but spirit. As spirit the mind is without weight or dimension, and does not occupy space. Also, the mind is a microcosm (miniature version) of the entire macrocosm or universe. Each individual is a miniature of the cosmos or Universal Mind. Most idealist equate this Universal Mind with God. According to idealistic metaphysics human beings are a reflection of God. In brief, idealism is a philosophy that stresses the pre-eminence of the mind, soul, and spirit. Human beings are part of the purposeful universe, hence are intelligent and purposeful beings.

Epistemology Of Idealism

Epistemology answers the question: how do we know? What is the legitimate avenue of knowledge? Since idealism is a philosophy rooted in mental activity, it must recognize a mode of knowing predominantly associated with the mind. As a philosophy that emphasizes the mind, it goes without saying that epistemology should be the nerve center of idealism.

Prior to Descartes, idealism had a religious flavor because most of its themes like spirit and God as Universal Mind found resonance in Judeo-Christian beliefs. Christian idealists like St. Augustine capitalized on idealism and propounded the theory of true knowledge as knowledge taught by the church and accepted in faith. Only a fine line divided religious idealism and philosophy of religion. The mutuality of idealism and religion led to the definition of education as teachings accepted as truth because the church puts them forward.

The cogito of Descartes took idealism to the horizon of experience and reason as foundations of knowledge. Starting with doubt as the only way to truth Descartes arrived at one self-evident truth, namely, the reality and primacy of the self. Any thought process must begin with the firsthand experience of the self. The cogito did not end at the level of experience. Descartes also realized that in his doubting there was thinking still going on. He was a thinker in process. Hence, rational thinking or reason is a way of knowing.

George Berkeley's brand of modern idealism postulates "that all of man's knowledge is derived from the ideas of sense experience and cannot reach to anything different from ideas, apart from minds in which ideas exist."[7] Things exist because of the thinking mind. For Berkeley, the independent existence of material things is unconceivable. That is, the evidence of any material thing is dependent on the experiencing subject. Knowledge, in this context, is characterized by a one-way dependence. The existence of material things without human perception is attributed to God's mind.

Table 5
Philosophical Principles of Idealism

Nature of person	Mind endowed with reason, ability to choose, and self-creation
Nature of reality	Only spiritual reality exists
Source of knowledge	Reason, experience, faith, and intuition
Nature of value	Moral laws constitute code of conduct

Immanuel Kant's (1724-1804) version of idealism is called critical idealism because of his criticism of Descartes' rationalism and of Berkeley's acosmic idealism as sources of knowledge. Kant dismissed Descartes rationalism as problematic because it doubted the existence of objects outside the thinking subject. Kant faulted Berkeley's view as dogmatic because it considered things in space as mere imagination. Kant's critique of Descartes and Berkeley carries his idealism beyond both. For this reason it is also described as transcendental. Kant affirms that knowledge of the world is not possible through reason or rational thought only. On the other hand, sense experience alone cannot be a source of knowledge for without interpretation sense experience will remain a chaotic process. Kant, therefore, advances the argument that unless sense perceptions are arranged within the matrix of pure *a priori* intuitions of space and time, and in terms of rational principles knowledge of the objective world is impossible. *A priori* intuitions of space and time and rational categories of understanding are conditions for the possibility of any experience. Without them sense experience will be fleeting. What is of importance here is the fact that Kant advances a third modality of knowing in idealism, namely, intuition.

Idealism recognizes reason as the primary way of acquiring knowledge. However, it also acknowledges experience, intuition, and faith as other legitimate avenues of knowledge.

Axiology of Idealism

Idealism's theory of value is rooted in three principles: values are rooted in existence, individuals possess values, and values are concretized when parts and wholes are related. Three kinds of value are distinguished in idealism:

ethical, aesthetic, and social. The educational import of idealist axiology will be evident in the curriculum and aims of education.

Principles

According to most idealists, values are neither ephemeral nor fleeting but constitutive of human existence. Values are not what they are simply because of their capacity to arouse human emotions and sentiments. Values have their own existence independent of their causal ability. Wilbur M. Urban, one of the guiding spirits of idealism, describes the inseparability of value and existence thus:

> I hold that there can be no existence without value and no value without existence. Reality is neither material nor mental, but a realm in which thought and thing, fact and value, are inseparable.[8]

The second principle of idealism's axiology states that values are not what they are because of what is intrinsic to them but because of the one who possesses and enjoys them. Urban again states that

> Values are real only in and for selves that feel them. There are really no such entities or subsistents as Truth or Beauty or Goodness, and the like. There are concrete truths, things felt to be beautiful, satisfying goods for themselves. Individuality is both the locus and measure of value.[9]

The point of this principle is twofold: first, to support the first that there is no value *per se* in the abstract and second, to highlight the uniqueness of individuals since idealism is a champion of individuality.

> The third principle postulates that effort is needed for value to be concretized. According to Mary W. Calkins, idealist values are found in relationships and "the ultimate real relations are those of whole and part, of including and being included."[10]

Ethical Values

Ethical values are those ultimate goals that are considered to be the end for which all life is lived. In a way, idealistic ethics will be the same for perfectionism.

Kant advanced persons and the moral imperative as two moral values in idealism. According to the metaphysics of idealism, what gives human beings higher quality and ultimate worth is the fact that they are individual minds and unique personalities. As such, humans cannot be treated as mere means to someone else's ends but should always be treated as ends in themselves. Kant states the categorical imperative in this way: "act so that in your own person as well as in the person of every other you are treating mankind also as an end, never merely as a means."[11] In dealing with one another, therefore, human beings shall treat one another as ends, not merely as means. Also, according to Kant's moral imperative, the propensity to do good is innate, inextricably woven in the fabric of each person. Each one is bound to do good. Hence, idealists consider "duty as the guide to conduct."[12] Moral corollaries from these two basic principles are the existence of a universal moral law, society as a society of ends, and the presence in everyone of good will to obey innate nature.

Idealistic ethics assumes the existence of inherent cosmic laws, and participation in these laws amounts to moral goodness. However, there is no authoritarianism that obliges participation since, according to some idealists "the law of duty… requires the assumption of sufficient freedom to carry out its commands."[13]

Aesthetic Values

Art, be it in the form of architecture, poetry, movies, or any other form of expression, is of vital importance to idealism. For Arthur Schopenhaur, the problem with the idealist principle of individuality is that it marks individual minds off from the Universal Mind, union with which is the goal of idealism. The value of art, therefore, lies in the fact that its perception brings about transcendence and a temporal loss of individuality.[14] According to Kant people "enjoy a disinterested pleasure in objects of beauty which enables them to forget their limited and warped perceptions, thus they glimpse together, momentarily, their common and eternal unity."[15] An artwork occasions a "transfigured Nature."[16] That is, in contemplating individual art, the mind also glimpses their spiritual universality and perfection, reaches their common and eternal value, and idealizes them. Through spiritual imagination the mind shatters "the shapes of things which marks him off as an individual" and that person is thereby "released from this squirrel cage of individuality."[17] An example of aesthetic value is transcending from the love of a particular pet to love the idea of the pet class.

Social Value

One criticism levied against idealism is that it lacks a theory of social responsibility because of its emphasis on individuality. Also, because of the importance of the spiritual pattern of explaining the world, idealism has been pejoratively described as an ivory tower. Despite these accusations, idealism has a social theory that emphasizes the value of participation by individuals in the affairs of society. According to idealist theory, society is not an aggregation of individuals but an organism in which one's self-realization is actualized through participation. Idealistic social theory is couched in three principles: representation, coordination, and planning.

The principle of representation states that "every part of society or community should have opportunity to participate in the deliberations as well as in the activities of the whole."[18] The ethical import of society for idealism, therefore, involves providing members with a genuine opportunity to participate in the deliberations and activities of society. Society optimizes its value when and only when individuals achieve their self-realization in society.

The principle of coordination states that "in the deliberations of community organized representatively direct attention should be given to relating individuals, groups, and services so that each segment of the community will have some consciousness of the function fulfilled by every other; that there will be no duplication or competition between services; and that no area of real community need will be neglected."[19] According to this theory the value of society lies in the fact that it provides a medium for interconnections, thus welding individuals together. Another value in society is its representativeness.

The principle of planning states that "communities need not remain devoid of deliberation, blindly allowing social processes to go on as they will, but that communities can muster powers of deliberation, formulate some objectives, and guide social processes at least partially in the direction of fulfilling these objectives."[20] The value of society involved in this principle is that society provides a consciousness concerning goals to be fulfilled and a raison d'être for existence.

EDUCATIONAL PHILOSOPHY OF IDEALISM

Idealism is a philosophical system that prizes ideas to the detriment of the material world. By devaluing material existence, idealism seems to close the door to education, in a way, since the accumulation of information about material existence will be a waste of time and effort. This makes one wonder about an idealist philosophy of education. This section is concerned with idealist educational theory and offers only broad strokes and dominant characteristics of idealist education.

Scope of Education

Schools exist for the twin purpose of individual and societal betterment. The achievement of these aims overlaps with the work of home, church, and other educational agencies. The specificity of schools according to the idealist Thomas Greene is

> the preservation, dissemination, and extension of man's knowledge of himself and his total environment... The school is the only institution whose primary responsibility are scholarship and education, the pursuit of knowledge, and the cultivation of the mind.[21]

This does not mean that idealism falls prey to some narrow intellectualism that overlooks the fact that the educand has other abilities like the senses, imagination, will, and emotion. Rather, what idealism is advocating is that these other abilities cannot take center stage in education. They must remain peripheral in relation to mind or intellectual cultivation.

Idealism is, therefore, in agreement with other views concerning the rationale of education. But idealism goes further to state that the cultivation of the mind should not be an end-in-itself. The purpose of cultivating the mind is not for human culture alone but must also provide the individual with a basis for making inferences about the Ultimate or God. For idealists the cultivation of the mind and other social aims of education constitute the penultimate aim of education whereas union with God constitutes the ultimate aim.

Idealist education is a serious and orderly initiation into the intellectual, imaginative, moral, and emotional inheritance of the system. It is, therefore, an engagement that calls for effort and study. The idealist school is concerned with a conscious orientation of learners' attention ultimately toward God. The scope of idealistic education is theocentric. Although union with God may not be overtly and consciously manifested in the daily running of idealistic schools it is the invisible center that suffuses the whole educational enterprise. Union with God is that center which arranges everything that revolves around education as well as unifies every educational thought.

Student to be Educated

Every educational philosophy must start with the person to be educated. It is important to know what idealism says about the human capacity before elaborating its educational purpose. In the consideration of the idealistic pupil, the Italian idealist Giovanni Gentile warns that it is not enough to look at the external perceptible phenomenal side; one must also "enter into the very mind of the child where his life is gathered and centered."[22] From this internal forum idealism notes that a pupil is a developing self.

The idealist pupil is a self. Descartes considers pupils as individuals endowed with the fundamental conviction of the reality of their personality and spirituality of their minds. The pupils are conscious that their personality is founded not on their body but on a profound spiritual reality, the thinking mind. The pupil thus described has powers of thought and choice. The motivation to learn comes from the perception of self as a way to guarantee the perpetuation of freedom. This suggests that the 'self' of the pupil is something deeper than the physical and that it is superior to the physical. This perspective of the nature of student is very important for the classroom teacher. The idealist teacher will not look at students only as physical bodies. Rather, that teacher must go beneath what is perceived to see a deeper, spiritual, and real person. Also, the conception of a pupil as essentially mind is of vital import for the definition of learning. Logically, learning according to idealism is the self-development of mind as spiritual substance. The educational approach that is appropriate for the development of mind is that which emphasizes the training of the faculties – ability to remember, to reason logically, and to know the permanent value of things.

The pupil is in the process of becoming. Idealism admits a gap between one's actual existence and one's ultimate existence, which is grounded in Ultimate Mind. This gap is not just one of time and eternity. It is a moral separation. Herman Horne characterizes the pupil "as a finite personality growing into the likeness of an infinite ideal."[23] Idealism, in this way, calls attention to the purposeful nature of pupils in particular and to the cosmos as a whole. Education is considered one of those formative opportunities needed to close the gap. According to idealism pupils are not born good or bad but neutral. "Bad characters," writes Horne, "are not born they are made."[24] Education plays a vital role in the process of becoming through which self-realization is achieved. The commission that idealists assign to education is to assist individuals to act correctly and to avoid the expediency of evil. It is imperative for education to offer opportunities for living a genuine life. Given the moral situatedness of pupils, it is important for idealistic education "to lay the foundation for moral and intellectual discipline, a foundation on which genuine human life must always stand."[25] Idealism embraces a theory of spiritual evolution of individual mind to Universal Mind and rejects an evolutionary materialism in which pupils evolve from lower forms of life. Idealism admits the idea of human perfection in the spiritual realm and not in the material.

Educational Process

Idealism has no predilection for one teaching method. According to Herman Horne, the maturity and interest of the students, class size, the subject matter, and the purpose of the lesson will determine the method for any one lesson. The only criterion for judging a good method is the extent to which it assists in cultivating the students' mental powers. This is what Horne means in his axiom "Teach pupils, not subjects."[26]

However, idealists are concerned with the role of the teacher in the educational process. Idealists recognize that self-realization by students cannot be achieved through the solitary effort of pupils. Unaided discovery of knowledge is superior learning. But experience shows that teachers are still essential in the educative process.

The following characteristics of an idealistic teacher run through the writings of idealist philosophers and educators.[27] First, the idealist teacher must be an expert in human nature. An effective teacher must understand the nature of the educand. Knowledge that the becoming mind is the center and quintessence of pupils is a sine qua non for useful teaching. This knowledge assists teachers to articulate a developmental vision for pupils. Also, the teacher must be broadly educated. The teacher must be professionally trained, and must master and communicate the subject matter adequately. This is important if the teacher is to be an appropriate mediator between the pupil-learner and the subject matter. Furthermore, the idealist teacher must be morally sensitive. By this is meant that the teacher must personify the ideas and ideals after which idealism strives. The teacher must be worthy of admiration by pupils as role model and source of inspiration for the cultivation of the mind through ongoing learning. Finally, the teacher must be an excellent pedagogue.

Educational Content

Given that the cultivation of the mind is the purpose of the idealist education, what should teachers teach and what should students learn? Curriculum is of strategic importance to idealism because it determines the direction of the mental development of pupils and society.

As a general principle of constructing curriculum Horne advises that "the ideal character of man and the characteristics of an ideal society" should first be elaborated.[28] After that "experiences, activities, and life situations and studies that, according to one's best judgment, best contribute to these ideal ends" should be selected.[29] The objective of any chosen subject in the curriculum should provide pupils with the facts and opinions they need to feel and act as they should. The language of Horne concerning curriculum objectives suggests that education should provide the pupil with the ability for environmental adjustment. From this it follows that education should bring about habits of conservation and survival in pupils. Horne[30] propounds three principles that should determine the content of curriculum: the abilities and needs of learners, the requirements of society, and the nature of the universe in which we live. In accordance with human nature that thinks, feels, and acts, curriculum should be subdivided into three groups. This means teaching subjects that engage human intellect (physics, chemistry, mathematics, sociology, astronomy) because the knowledge they produce is organized and verifiable. Concerning subjects that take care of the emotional nature of pupils Herman Horne mentions music, literature, painting, and architecture. These subjects educate the discriminating sense of pupils. Among the subjects that will manifest the pupil's nature as an active agent with a will to change and improve conditions are politics, trades, industrial arts, and so on. According to Greene the regimen of curriculum should include formal subjects (studies of correct thinking like logic, mathematics, and language), factual subjects (natural, social, and behavioral sciences), normative subjects (morals, fine arts, religion), and synoptic subjects (disciplines that unify all the pupil's knowledge and experiences like history, theology, and philosophy). The specific subjects suggested by Horne and Greene are to be spread out through the years of formal learning and adjusted to meet the abilities of pupils at varying levels.

It is important to note that the idealist subject curriculum is not immediately useful as a preparation for citizenship or social efficacy. Rather, their primary aim is the betterment of the individual. Also, a cursory look at the curriculum displays the preponderant role of the intellectual disciplines. Even the normative disciplines are approached as cognitive activities.

Educational Evaluation

Although idealism is concerned with the mental progress of students, it does not consider education only as knowledge of subject matter. Such objective evaluation does not do justice to the pupil's mental functions, which include the ability to organize, logical consistency, and deductive powers. True or false questions and one word answers offer only piecemeal knowledge and do not express rational wholes or connections, which constitute intellectual or mental activity. Objective questions never reach the heart of true mental powers. Hence, idealists endorse questions of the type as discuss, evaluate, or explain. These types of questions call for an exercise of the mental abilities in the form of expression, organization, clarity, and profundity. The primary concern of idealist evaluation is to determine the mental development of the educand.

Aims of Education

Idealism considers education as a means not an end in itself. Giovanni Gentile, an Italian idealist, proposed self-realization as the ultimate aim of education. Bogoslovsky[31] envisaged twin goals for his ideal school, namely, the preparation of specialists in concepts and the attainment of a superior life. Bogoslovsky is seconded in his proposal by Horne,[32] for whom the supreme task of education is the attainment of the spiritual ideal of truth and a progressive realization of the hierarchical values of beauty and goodness. If considered from the backdrop of the foundation of idealism, these aims of idealist education can be condensed into three points: self-realization (a metaphysical aim), search for truth (an epistemological aim), and moral development (an axiological aim).

Self-realization

Idealist anthropology emphasizes selfhood. This is conspicuously evident in Descartes' cogito and Berkeley's esse. However, idealists realize that the self is not what it should be. Thus, idealism postulates an Ultimate Mind that the self can become through progressive identification with this supreme spiritual reality. The purpose of idealist education, therefore, is to assist the human spirit to apprehend and be identified with the Ultimate. Self-realization is then the goal of idealist education.

Self-realization is a fulfillment of one's nature, the development of the pupil's immanent potentialities of character and intelligence by identifying the mind imaginatively with the spirit of the best (Ultimate Mind) that is considered to exist. Learning does not end with the self. The individual knows the self better only by achieving and assimilating new insights concerning its relationship with Ultimate Being, God. Self-realization comes about when the individual progressively acquiesces in the spirituality of Ultimate Being. According to the idealist-educator Butler James, the task of education will be incomplete no matter how well it establishes human relationships if it does not open the pupil to the possibility of becoming related to the Ultimate. The task of idealist education is to give the individual a superior life through expanded knowledge and self-identification with the Ultimate. Education fulfils an adjusting role insofar as it mediates between the individual mind and Ultimate Mind.

At this point it is fitting to let some idealists speak for themselves. Horne, an American idealist, says this concerning the aim of education: "Education is the eternal process of superior adjustment of a physically and mentally developed, free, and conscious human being to God, as manifested in the intellectual, emotional, and volitional environment."[33] Ozmon and Craver, commenting on the educational aims of the American idealist Harris, wrote that he "proposed that education should lead people to what he called 'a third level of enlightenment."[34] This involves the individual becoming aware of the spiritual union with God and personal immortality.

Despite the inevitable emphasis on the individual in the process of becoming, self-realization is not to be understood only in subjective terms.

Moral development

Among idealist philosophers there is considerable agreement concerning the primacy of value. In the educational sphere it is very evident because one of the salient attributes of an idealist teacher is to be a moral agent. Also, metaphysically the pupil is considered by idealism as a spiritual unity of mind and free will. Hence, any development of the intellect invariably constitutes a moral development as well. Still, for idealists human beings are following unchanging moral laws and are trying to be in harmony with them as they conduct their lives.

Inasmuch as idealist schools exist to cultivate the intellect they are, by the same token, responsible for assisting pupils in apprehending and incorporating value in their lives. The school is, therefore, simultaneously an intellectual and a moral enterprise. "The school as curator of the great intellectual heritage of mankind is thereby a potent force in the moral life of men, for the school preserves and transmits the great literary heritage whose very essence is ethical."[35] Moral development is constitutive of intellectual development.

But, when it comes down to the specifics of moral development, the idealists have their specific emphases. Kant is a ferocious advocate that moral development be the center of education. According to him education must aim at six dispositions[36]: nurture, discipline, cultivate and make human beings prudent, moralize, and give guidance. From this enumeration one can distinguish the intellectual skill (nurture, discipline, cultivate, and make prudent) and moral dispositions (moralize and give guidance) that education should aim at. A few quotes will highlight Kant's moral thrust. He writes: "Education… must see to the moralization of man. He is to acquire not merely skills needed for all sorts of ends, but also the disposition to choose only good ends."[37] Kant goes on, "practical or moral education is that through which a man is so formed as to be able to live as a free being… It is education for personality, education of the free being who is able to maintain himself and to be a member of society while keeping a sense of his own personal value."[38]

According to Kant, the greatest and most important task to which people should devote themselves is education. The goal of education should be intellectual and moral enlightenment. Morally, education should teach pupils how to think according to principles – moral laws, moral ideals, and moral imperatives. Education should enable students to experience and grow in their ability to distinguish standards of right and wrong and progressively incorporate them in their personal and social life. The bottom line for education as a moral enterprise is the liberation of the will. This freedom to act and choose will enable pupils to build their own personality.

Unlike Immanuel Kant, for whom moral development meant enlightenment to make better choices, Giovanni Gentile viewed moral development as education for political loyalty. As a staunch supporter of Benito Mussolini and Fascism, Gentile considered human beings from the point of view of statehood. According to him the destiny of individuals and state are commensurate. Moral education, therefore, should dispose the pupil to greater loyalty to the state. "Proper character education," commented Ozmon and Craver about Gentile, "would thus develop the attribute of loyalty because an individual without loyalty would be incomplete. When the teacher acts according to the interests of the state, the true interest of students are being met."[39]

Intellectual training

Idealism is a thought system that emphasizes the mind or spiritual reality as a preeminent principle of explanation. It is a philosophy that discards material things because they are changing and ephemeral. Idealism is a search for the enduring substance or ideas, transcendental universals or ideals that are the true object of knowledge. Idealist education is concerned with ideas, not with matter. Idealists want to give students a broad understanding of the world in which they live. For idealism the concept of chair, for example, is what is important and must be taught to students. A particular chair can be destroyed but the concept of chair cannot. The concept of chair is the real, eternal, intelligible, and explanatory principle of all chairs. Hence the idea of chair is the ultimate truth that education must strive to put across.

Table 6
Principles of Idealist Educational Philosophy

Educational objectives	Development of talent, moral formation, fulfillment of nature, cultural conservation
Nature of student	Self that is in the process of becoming
Role of teacher	Expert in human nature, broadly educated, moral agent
Curriculum	Humanism to teach wisdom, sciences to sharpen intellect, normative subjects for practical living
Scope of education	Individual and societal betterment

Furthermore, idealism is a philosophy of life that begins first with an understanding of the self then moves outwards to understand the cosmos. The purpose of education is to assist the self-development of the mind as a spiritual reality. As such the curriculum should emphasize the training of intellectual faculties that can account for self-creation.

Cultural conservation

The American idealist, Michael Demiashkevitch, states that the purpose of education is social progress.[40] Social advancement is a double-edged phenomenon that Demiashkevitch designates as "mobility-aspect" and "equilibrium-aspect" respectively. By social mobility is meant that schools must enable pupils to change their society for the better by developing them as creative spirits. By social equilibrium is meant that the school must conserve and teach the social heritage of the 'group' to younger generations. William Hocking[41] follows a similar pattern to that of Demiashkevitch but with a different emphasis. Demiashkevitch's "equilibrium-aspect" and "mobility-aspect" correspond to Hocking's "communication of type" and provision of growth beyond type, respectively. By "communication of type", Hocking understands the transmission of group heritage to younger generations. The importance of this is that cultural learning fulfills what would otherwise have been a knowledge vacuum in a generation. Education, therefore, is a social transmission process in the sense of passing on the learning, culture, habits, traditions, arts, and so on commonly accepted or used by a group to succeeding generations. Education aims at the reproduction of a cultural type and the adjustment of pupils to society through inculcation of cultural facts and knowledge. Education through social transmission guarantees continuity and forestalls the need to always begin again. According to Hocking, safeguarding societal heritage is not advocating conservatism or opposing change.

The second aspect of education, which must be concomitant with and complementary of the first, is that education must lead to the emergence of new social characteristics. Learning about societal heritage is, therefore, recommended by Hocking as the starting point for societal accretion and maturation. In brief, the principle that holds together the social objectives of education are permanence and change taken simultaneously. Education is a means of cultural reinforcement and a guide to change a culture progressively toward perfection. Cultural conservation in education is achieved through emphasis of the humanities in curriculum design, educational structures and practices.

Both the personal and social aims of education highlight a character of idealist education that is dynamic rather than static. However, this dynamic conception underscores the recognition of creativeness and highlights discovery of the universal and invariant realities. Education is made necessary in idealism by a pupil's need to develop and be identified with Mind. In this light, education is a means of intellectual birth that we have variously called self-creation or self-realization. Also, education is made necessary by pupil's need for culture. So education becomes a means of cultural birth or reproduction. Finally, education is a value-transmitting institution because its purpose is "to educate children in the respect and preservation of fundamental social values."[42]

DECLINE OF IDEALISM

Until the 20th century America remained the last bastion of idealism. The idealistic cause continued to be champion by educational philosophers like Ralph Waldo Emerson (1803-1882), William Harris (1835-1909), Josiah Royce (1855-1916), Herman Horne (1874-1946), Michael Demiashkeritch (1891-1938), Boris Basil Bogoslovsky (1890-1966), Robert Ulich (1890-1977), and Donald Butler (b. 1908). With such a roll of distinguished expositors one has to look elsewhere for the reasons of the decline of idealism other than to attribute that decline to a lack of quality exponents.

One reason for the collapse of idealism is the changing temper of Americans. Idealism is a philosophy that emphasizes the spiritual, albeit without any explicit affiliation to one denomination. This is very evident in its treatment of humans as extensions of the divine mind. However, without any disdain for religion Americans allowed the quasi-religious foundation of their thought and life to be superceded by other centers like materialism. With materialism becoming a dominant attitude in this part of the world the religious attitude in idealism began to lose its grip as the mainstay of life. Materialism, therefore, ushered in an era of metaphysical skepticism that brought about the decline of idealism.

Also, idealism's emphasis on the mind and education as only a mental process began to be challenged seriously by the end of the 19th century. By this time the teaching of Darwinian evolution gave people greater awareness of their physical nature, a view downplayed by idealism. The psychology of this period also popularized the mind-body relationship to the detriment of idealism's emphasis on pupils as minds without bodies. The rise of new sciences and the popularization of their thought patterns constituted a serious challenge to idealism. Despite its intellectual rigor idealism was becoming a hurdle because it lacked a practical component that was now being supplied by other sciences.

Another reason for the decline of idealism, which is also valid for any other systematic philosophy, is the contemporary loss of interest in philosophical system building. Systematic philosophies are interested in designing rounded modes of thought. Contemporary philosophy and educational philosophy are not interested in system building but in the analysis and criticism of particular educational problems and issues.

[1] Bramel, T. (1955). *Philosophies of education in cultural perspective.* New York: The Dryden Press. p. 207.

[2] Butler, J. D. (1968). *Four philosophies and their practice in education and religion.* 3rd Ed. New York: Harper & Row, Publishers.

[3] Ozmon, H. & Craver, S. (1999). *Philosophical foundations of education.* 6th Ed. Columbus, OH: Merrill. p. 19.

[4] Acton, H. B. (1967). *Idealism.* In P. Edwards (Ed.). *The encyclopedia of philosophy.* Vol. 4.New York: The Macmillan Company & The Free Press. p. 114.

[5] Wingo, G. M. (1965). *The philosophy of American education.* Lexington, MA: Heath.

[6] Wingo, *op. cit.,,* p. 127.

[7] Peifer, J. F. (2002). *Idealism.* In B. C. Marthaler et al. (Eds.) *The New Catholic Encyclopedia.* 2nd Ed. Washington, DC: The Catholic University of America. p. 297.

[8] Urban, W. M. (1930). *Metaphysics and value.* In G. P. Adams & W. P. Montague (eds.). *Contemporary American philosophy.* Vol. II. New York: The Macmillan Company. p. 375.

[9] Urban, *op. cit.,* p. 155.

[10] Calkins, M. W. (1917). *The persistent problems of philosophy.* 4th Ed. New York: The Macmillan Company. pp. 210-211.

[11] Kant, I. (1938). *The fundamental principles of the metaphysics of ethics.* Trans. O. Manthey-Zorn. New York: Century-Crofts, p. 47.

[12] Butler, *op. cit.,* p. 178.

[13] Bramel, *op. cit.,* p. 228.

[14] Butler, *op. cit.,* pp. 179-180.

[15] Bramel, *op. cit.,* p. 230.

[16] Butler, *op. cit.,* p. 181.

[17] Butler, *op. cit.,* p. 180.

[18] Butler, *op. cit.,* p. 185.

[19] Butler, *op. cit.,* p. 185.

[20] Butler, *op. cit.,* p. 186.

[21] Greene, T. M. (1955). *A liberal Christian idealist philosophy of education.* In N. B. Henry (Ed.). *The Forty-fifth Yearbook of the National Society for Study of Education.* Part I. Chicago, IL: The University of Chicago Press. p. 116.

[22] Gentile, G. (1922). *The reform of education.* Trans. D. Bigongiari. New York: Harcourt, Brace, & World. p. 148.

[23] Horne, H. H. (1954). *An idealist philosophy of education.* In J. S. Brubacher et al. (Eds.). The Forty-first yearbook of the National Society for the Study of Education. Part I. Chicago, IL: The University of Chicago press. p. 154.

[24] Horne, H. H. (1931). *The new education.* Nashville: Abingdon Press. p. 178.

[25] Power, E. J. (1982). *Philosophy of education. Studies in philosophies, schooling, and educational policies.* Englewood Cliffs, NJ: Prentice-Hall. p. 83.

[26] Horne, H. H. *An idealistic philosophy.* p. 172.

[27] Thompson, M. M. (1934). *The educational philosophy of Giovanni Gentile.* Los Angeles, CA: University of Southern California press. Horne, H. H. (1927). *Philosophy of education.* New York: The Macmillan Company. Horne, H. H. (1931). *This new education.* Nashville: Abingdon Press.

[28] Horne, *The new education.* p. 90.

[29] Horne, *The new education.* p. 90.

[30] Horne, *An idealist philosophy of education.* p. 161.

[31] Bogoslovsky, B. B. (1936). *The ideal school.* New York: The Macmillan Company. p. 132.

[32] Horne, H. H. (1927). *Philosophy of education.* New York: The Macmillan Company. p. 102.

[33] Horne, H. H. (1908). *The psychological principle of education.* New York: The Macmillan Company, p. 37.

[34] Ozmon, H. A. & Craver S. M. (1999). *Philosophical foundations of education.* Upper Saddle River, NJ: Merrill. p. 32.

[35] Wingo, *op. cit.,* p. 160.

[36] Kant, I. (1960). *Education.* Trans. A. Churton. Ann Arbor: University of Michigan Press. pp. 7-8.

[37] Kant, *op. cit.,,* p. 20.

[38] Kant, *op. cit.,,* p. 30.

[39] Ozmon & Craver, *op. cit.,,* p. 33.

[40] Demiashkevitch, M. (1935). *An introduction to philosophy of education.* New York: American Book Company. pp. 339-342.

[41] Hocking, W. E. (1918). *Human nature and its remaking.* New Haven: Yale University Press. p. 278.

[42] Demiashkevitch, M. *op. cit.,,* p. 348.

CHAPTER 7

EXISTENTIALISM AND EDUCATION

EXISTENTIALISM AS PHILOSOPHY

Historical Background

The French philosopher Gabriel Marcel (1889-1973) was the first to use the expression existentialism after World War II. Although traces of this philosophy can be found in the writings of St. Augustine, René Descartes, and Blaise Pascal contemporary existentialism is generally attributed to the Danish Lutheran pastor Søren Kierkegaard (1813-55). Kierkegaard's preoccupation was personal, namely, how to become a Christian. According to Kierkegaard his native Lutherans had a false notion of what it meant to be Christian. Kierkegaard observed two approaches to Christianity. First, there are those who considered Christianity solely as a body of doctrines to be grasped intellectually and understood speculatively. Those who fall in this category consider religion as a head-trip only. Kierkegaard rejected this speculative, abstract, impersonal, and dispassionate approach to Christianity. A second approach is the one that considers "Christianity as a way of life, a mode of living that consists in appropriating and assimilating the message of Christ into one's own existence. If one wanted to call Christianity a body of doctrine then that person should understand that it is a doctrine that proposes guidelines to be realized in existence; that the true way of understanding the doctrine of Christianity is to understand its task as one of existing in a doctrine not of speculating on it."[1] The purpose of Kierkegaard's critique of Christianity was to revitalize it from within.

Existentialist philosophy is a unique case in that it is not a philosophical system but a family of philosophies whose prime focus is to interpret human existence in the world. What, therefore, makes it possible for the different interpretations to be grouped under existentialism? The thread that unites existentialist philosophers cannot be found in their formal allegiances that are so diverse. They came from different countries or cultural backgrounds, lived in different epochs, and professed different faiths as presented in the tables below.

Table 7
Origin of Existentialists

Country of origin	Philosophers
Germany	Martin Heidegger, Karl Jaspers
France	Gabriel Marcel, Jean-Paul Satre, Albert Camus, Simone Weil, Simone de Beauvoir
Russia	Vladimir Solovev, Nikolai Berdyeav, Paternack
Spain	Miguel de Unamonon, José Ortega y Gasset
USA	William Barrett, Paul Tillich, Reinhold Niebuhr
Switzerland	Karl Barth, Brunner
Israel	Martin Buber

Table 8
Epoch and Religion of Existentialists

Epoch	Theists	Atheists	Agnostics
19th Century	Søren Kierkegaard	Friedrich Nietzsche	
20th Century	Gabriel Marcel, Karl Jaspers, Martin Buber, Paul Tillich, Karl Barth	Jean-Paul Satre, Albert Camus, Simone de Beauvoir	Martin Heidegger

What ties existentialists together is their common opposition to academic speculation. Existentialism defies conventions and system building. It neither beseeches absolutes nor does it invoke (apostrophize) any form of abstraction. Rather, the primary concern of existentialism is with the concrete as opposed to Platonic Forms. Existentialism stresses human subjectivity (passionate individual action) with particular emphasis on individuality and uniqueness. John Wild makes it quite clear that existentialists neither feign issues nor invest in impractical interpretations. "They are interested rather in concrete data of immediate experience and in describing these data so far as possible exactly as they are given."[2] Fredrick Mayer further illustrates the specificity of existentialism by contrasting it with speculative philosophy.

> The academic view of philosophy stresses the study of great ideas; the existential concept of philosophy leads to self-exploration. Academic philosophy is concerned with correctness; existential thinking cherishes suggestiveness. Academic philosophy is aware of the significance of great authorities; existentialism regards the worship of authority as a primary obstacle in man's search for enlightenment. Academic philosophy stresses the need for definitions; existentialism views definitions as intellectual exercises. Academic philosophy is concerned with the past; existentialism dwells in the uncertainty of the present. Academic philosophy distrusts paradoxes; existential philosophy makes paradoxes the center of life.[3]

Although existentialists have peculiar stresses they propound certain notions that permit generalization concerning existentialist theory. It encourages people to actualize their potentials. It exhorts people to take up their freedom and exercise it responsibly.

Salient Themes in Existentialism

Metaphysics: Moral Individualism and Systems

Existentialism, like many other philosophies, is interested in existence. However, its contribution is in the domain of individual human existence.

The human existence, which is the predilection of existentialism, is neither physical, chemical, nor biological, but moral existence.

Existentialism is concerned with that which makes human beings who they are as individuals and what makes them live genuinely as humans (possibility of choice). Thus, this philosophy focuses on what makes human beings different from other beings in the universe. Existentialism, for example, is involved with the fundamental concerns of humans such as making sense out of life and death, their cares and desires. These become central to existentialism's philosophizing. From the above, it stands out clearly that Kierkegaard's "what does it mean to be authentically Christian" is translated by existentialists into "what does it mean to be authentically human." According to existentialism human beings are not primarily knowers but persons with fundamental needs to be satisfied.

Existentialism is busy with individual existence. Existentialism neither absorbs human beings into a wider essence nor does it consider them as pale reflections of an absolute. Existentialist philosophy emphasizes the uniqueness and isolation of each person. Hence only individuals have a purpose. There is no such thing as universal purpose. "Existentialism is more interested in particulars that universals. It is more interested in trying to fathom the import of a single human life than to come to some grand theory which allegedly explains the 'All' and the 'One'."[4] Among the reasons for existentialist contempt for universals and abstractions in favor of individuals are that the former do not do justice to human individuality. Abstractions and universals take away that which is peculiar to each human being. Also, existentialists are suspicious of abstractions and universals because they drop any interest in human freedom which is the backbone of existentialism. According to existentialists human beings are not detached observers of the world. They are in the world. Human beings have a special existence that other objects do not have. The essence of other objects is determined and they cannot act differently. On the contrary, human existence has no special or fixed essence. Human beings make themselves by their choices in life (Kierkegaard) or by their choices of actions (Satre). Abstractions and universals compromise the contingency and indetermination of human freedom which existentialism is not ready to trade off.

The individual human existence which interests existentialists is moral existence. Mayer states, "philosophy, in an existential sense, becomes an intensely personal matter by which choices are illuminated and by which depth perceptions are achieved; education becomes a creative encounter between men and wisdom which ends in profound paradoxes; morality becomes an awareness of the infinite sources of self-deceit, of the immense distance between ideal and creativity."[5] Existentialism is a moral philosophy inasmuch as it exhorts humans to develop a genuine concern for life, to be committed to a way of life. Since existentialism does not believe in system building it develops no systematic ethics in the sense of rules and values. Rather, it presents a matrix for viewing choices and actions. This matrix is not prescriptive but lays bare the fact that there are right and wrong choices. One reason why Kierkegaard rejected philosophical systems, which he equated with Hegelianism, is because they consider human beings as outsiders or spectators. They explain away individuality from which action and choices can be explained. Fyodor Dostoyevsky notes that universals do not make sense and that in them are no discernible rational patterns.

Existentialists, therefore, are united in their rejection of abstractions and concepts (rationalism) as deceptive masks. In this rejection existentialists implicitly propound a theory of the limitations of reason.

Epistemology: Freedom and Choice

The central tenet of existentialism without which this philosophy will not exist is the possibility of choice. Two sub-themes that emerge from choice are consciousness and freedom.

According to existentialist philosophy choice is implicit or explicit in every human action. In acting if people do not explicitly decide on a choice that choice is implied in some other choice that was made or thought about. Choices are made on the bases of some criteria that are themselves chosen. It is in light of this possibility to choose that the other existentialist maxim existence precedes essence is to be understood. Basically, this means that human beings have no fixed nature that determines the kind of persons they are or will be. Rather, it is their choices that create their nature. Through choice they continue to define their essence. It is in light of this that Jean-Paul Satre affirms that existentialism is nothing but an affirmation that human beings are who they make themselves.[6] The possibility of choice constitutes the specific difference of human beings in comparison with other objects whose natures are determined. As such, existentialism, as a moral philosophy concerned with choice, considers the individual as a conscious self and a responsible agent. According to the existentialist dictum existence precedes essence it follows that an individual is not born with a ready-made nature. Human beings have no predetermined nature. Jean-Paul Satre explains the point.

> What is meant here by saying that existence precedes essence? It means that, first of all, man exists, turns up, appears on the scene and, only afterwards defines himself. If man, as the existentialist sees him, is indefinable, it is because at first he is nothing. Only afterwards will he be something and he himself will have made what he will be… Not only is man what he conceives himself to be, but he is also what he wills himself to be after this thrust toward existence. Man is nothing else than what he creates himself.[7]

For existentialists, therefore, each one creates his/her own nature. Human beings are nature makers. But to do this one must be free.

Freedom in existentialist thinking does not mean noninterference but a state of mind. It is for this reason that freedom is defined in relation to consciousness. This position rejects all traditional definitions of human beings as rational animals or spiritual beings. It also rejects the view that human beings are the products of society. Rather, for existentialists the individual is a product of his/her choices. Freedom and choice also distinguish existentialist from traditional metaphysics and skepticism. According to traditional metaphysics the real is what is yonder whereas for existentialists the real is lived reality, "what is in the human condition."[8] Against the skeptics who affirm that nothing can be known with certainty and that human experience is deceptive existentialism affirms the possibility of discovering the truth of one's own existence.

The first sub-theme from choice is consciousness. According to Merleau Ponty human existence is a self-conscious movement. That is, lived experience begins with an experience of one's own body. "CONSCIOUSNESS and FREEDOM are central themes in all existentialist thought. Man becomes truly existent only when he lives an intensely conscious life in which he is vividly aware of all the exigencies, decisions, and problems of human living. The existentialist demands that men should become conscious of themselves as reflective beings whose existence must be interpenetrated with thought. He insists that they become fully alive to the richness inherent in every experience; that they live a life that is vibrantly alert to all the anguish, burden, and care of existence."[9] Choice, according to existentialism, goes beyond a mere selection among alternatives. To make a choice invariably means that the chooser believes in the choice, accepts it as true. Choice involves a knowledgeable judgment. Hence, for existentialists choice does not only have a moral significance but also an epistemological import. In every personal appropriation there is knowing and vice versa. Choice, as a conscious act is different from perception. Perception is consciousness of things outside the knower. Existential self-consciousness is presence to the self. It is immediate. Since consciousnesses of the self and of its deeds are not mediated knowledge of them is intuitive. It is in light of the above that the statement about knowledge of the truth being an existential choice is to be understood.

It is in defense of consciousness that Martin Heidegger abhorred crowd followers because they lacked personal judgment. According to Heidegger the existentialist person must be a person capable of personal decision-making, self-thinking, and free. Hence, to be authentically human that person should be conscious of his/her freedom and its dangers. Inauthentic existence, which is a threat to human existence, consists of not acknowledging one's freedom. The exercise of freedom is possible only when the individual has a passionate interest, which calls for a conscious decision for and commitment to that passion rather than its alternatives. Hence, in its elaboration of freedom existentialism continues to endorse its clarion call of radical entrustment to life or existence.

What do the existentialists themselves say? Kierkegaard views choice as a decision between ways of life that are fundamentally different (Christian versus non-Christian lifestyles). For Satre choice is ubiquitous, omnipresent in every human action. Individuals are thus arbiters of value. Heidegger employs the term consciousness in conjunction with choice to bring out the difference between humans who are free beings and other beings that are determined.

Axiology: Dread and Absurdity

Existentialist emphasis on human beings as individuals in concrete situations leads to a consideration of these human beings as isolated, solitudinarians, and shut-in from others. From the moral standpoint existentialism has no objective ethical standards. Each individual is left on his/her own. This brings out a sense of human abandonment. This is what Heidegger meant when he wrote that human beings are thrown into the world. For Albert Camus human beings are strangers in the world. They find themselves in specific situations with limited choices. In brief, individual human beings live an alienated existence. Morally, human beings live at cross-purposes with others. This life can be characterized as fragile instability. According to existentialists the alienated and fragile status of humans brings about a bewildered, anxious, and frustrated life. This leads Heidegger to qualify human existence as a movement toward nothingness. Jean-Paul Satre groans that human existence is a useless passion. For existentialists human existence always confronts a void.

Existential awareness of a void in human life occasions a sense of anxiety. Anxiety is not fear. Fear has a particular object. One is always afraid of something or someone known. Anxiety is a consequence of the human condition that can neither explain its origin nor the development of society. Human existence is a given, and only a partial understanding of it is possible. However, "anxiety may be negative and may merely lead to a sense of alienation. We may feel that society is beyond hope, that institutions are corrupt, that time has passed us by and that life is a bad joke. Thus Ecclesiastes speaks of the vanity of existence… But there can be another reaction to a realization of man's anguish. We can look for a tower beyond uncertainty; we can search for a cause that can give meaning. Existential theologians have usually found this cause in God and, like St. Augustine, they have pointed to man's nothingness without God."[10]

Another key theme in existentialism is absurdity. Existentialists believe that it is impossible to conceptualize being because something of being always evades human understanding. Absurdity is, therefore, used to characterize that which escapes human comprehension. For Kierkegaard, for example, Christ is absurd because no one can explain why God decided to take human form in Christ. This is grasped only by a leap of faith. In the atheism of Satre the absence of God in the world means that there is no rational explanation for the existence of things. Since no reason can be given for the existence of things (other than stating the fact of their existence) Satre concludes that things are absurd.

Conclusion

Existentialism is a protest philosophy against traditional philosophies. It puts up resistance against standards externally imposed or inherited as tradition. The development of the individual enjoys a place of predilection in existentialism. Existentialism also puts its premium on individual choice and personal freedom.

Table 9
Basic Tenets of Existentialism

♦ Emphasizes individual responsibility, individual personality, and individual existence.

♦ Emphasizes the uniqueness and freedom of the individual person.

♦ Against the herd, the crowd, and mass mentality.

♦ Thrust is the quest for the meaning of life, death, and love.

♦ Not a uniform system of thought.

♦ Basic themes include human consciousness, anxiety, absurdity, nothingness, alienation, and death.

Existentialism is not concerned with the nature, origin, and destiny of the universe, which it considers the office of science not philosophy. The task of existentialism is individual human beings as choosing, valuing, living, and dying beings. The specific angle from which the existentialist studies human beings is "not man as an object of study by psychologists or biologists but man as a free agent involved in that most serious process, existing. Consequently, ethics and aesthetics constitute the two major areas of philosophic concern for existentialists."[11] As a philosophy that throws its whole weight in grounding and affirming the individual existentialist discusses few if not no social questions. George Knight echoes this when he writes, "existentialism has focused mainly on philosophical issues and has not been too explicit on educational practices. Its relative silence on education has also undoubtedly been influenced by its concern for the individual rather than on social group."[12] Mitchell Bedford is blunt about Kierkegaard on this point. "In the educational endeavor the works of Kierkegaard have hardly dented the surface. In the first place, Kierkegaard did not concern himself with the problems of education, not even theological education."[13] What prospects of education can, therefore, come out of such a philosophy without a social component? Did this book not define education as a social instantiation in Chapter 1?

EXISTENTIALISM AS AN EDUCATIONAL PHILOSOPHY

The neglect of educational topics by 19th century existentialists begins to interest exponents in the second half of the 20th century. The major names that readily come to the fore are Martin Buber, Maxime Greene, George Kneller, and Van Cleve Morris. Existentialism began to make its way into the International Index of Periodicals and Readers Guide to Periodical Literature only in 1945 and 1947 respectively. But articles contained no educational material. It was not until April 1952 that a group of graduate students under the leadership of Theodore Brameld researched and published their findings on the educational implication of existentialism in Educational Theory.[14] One of their findings was that existentialist education will be child-centered, not curriculum centered, because its parent philosophy rejects any system that submerges individuals into an impersonal social world. This section will continue the search for the educational implications of existentialism in the areas of educational aims and processes, curriculum, and role of teacher and student.

Aims of Existential Education

Existentialist education, like its philosophical parent, is a renaissance of human interest in the individual self after the 'depersonalizing' effects of systemic philosophies like idealism. Existentialist education is a lofty venture whose aim is to free the student from societal dominance. The freedom that education aims at is bifocal: freedom from societal dogmatism and freedom for selfhood. First, the goal of education is to free the students from social fetters. Education aims at waking the individual from dogmatic slumbers. Second, the goal of education is to free the students for greater awareness of their freedom. Education aims at assisting each student to become a fully authentic self. Resistance and selfhood, therefore, constitute the aims or learning expectations of existentialist education. Ralph Harper captures the double-edged purpose of existentialist education as follows, "Every existentialist philosopher is a doctor and a missionary."[15]

Fighting Social Conformism

The negative purpose of education is to oppose the idols of the masses, herd mentality, and groupthink in order to liberate the individual freedom of the students. Education must lead students to understand that each one of them is not bound to think and act as the others. Education must liberate the student. Existentialist education neither aims at social conformity since its focus is on the individual student nor does it envisage the acquisition of professional competence since this will limit freedom too. As such, existentialist education diverges from conventional education, which is always considered as a social phenomenon. Existentialism repudiates educational dogmatism by rejecting so-called educational standards and educational authorities, which it considers as drawbacks or stumbling blocks in the quest for self-enlightenment and fulfillment.

Table 10
Existentialist Education

Purpose of education	Become authentic, encourage selfhood, resist social standard, self-fulfillment.
Curricular emphasis	Affective, individual, self-development, no generally prescribed curriculum.
Role of teacher	Fellow searcher, questioner, facilitator, non-interfering provocateur.
Role of student	Curious, active, developing, chooser.
Method of instruction	Individual exploration, Socratic questioning.
Value of education	Personal value, choice.

Existentialism is a bitter critic of speculative education. It rejects any search for objective truth but endorses the search for subjective ideals as the proper goal of education. "In society which is concerned with the externals of education," writes Mayer, "… which is other directed in its consciousness, existentialism fills a desperate need. It calls for strenuous self-examination so that life may not be wasted with triviality and superficiality and so that the authentic individual can emerge both with a sense of limitation and a sense of unfulfilled possibilities."[16] Existentialist educational philosophy advocates a shift from an educational stance that has a global outlook, advocates groupthink credentials, and fosters national purpose to one that fosters an individual life approach. Existentialist education is, therefore, a crusade against traditional education because it violates fundamental existentialist principles of individuality and personal freedom. Existentialist educational philosophy is not what it is only because of what it rejects. The case it makes for itself as an educational philosophy is based on what it positively offers.

Searching the Self

The positive aim of existentialist education is the development of free or authentic individuals. That is, education must lead students to acknowledge their freedom and accept the responsibility that goes with it. Education must bring about subjectivity, a development of a personal perspective, or an individual's understanding of his/her situation in the world. Becoming an authentic self is grounded in the possibility of moral choice as a way to self-definition. "An education which grasps a child by his moral coat collars and lifts him up to see over the crowd to the task of taking personal responsibility for being human – that education can be called existentialist."[17] Authenticity, understood in terms of choice and self-definition, suggests two specific aims of education, namely, development of attitude and fulfillment of personal goals. Existentialist education emphasizes a passionate individual action of the student in search of the truth. The student must be an individual agent in the search for truth.

Since existentialist philosophy is concerned with openness to the choices of life exploration of those choices suggests itself as a possible attitude for education to foster. Exploration takes into account other attitudes such as involvement and creativity. Exploration, according to existentialists, is an inquiry that awakens the individual to an awareness of responsibility. "Let education be the discovery of responsibility. Let learning be the sharp and vivid awakening of the learner to the sense of being personally answerable for his own life."[18] Jean-Paul Satre endorses exploration as the goal of education so that everyone should be without excuse for his or her acts.[19] Traditional education, which takes the form of lecture or transfer of pre-certified knowledge, insulates learners from being personally involved in the educational process because teaching is always presented in the third person. As such learners are detached, passive, and irresponsible in the learning process.

The 'discovery of responsibility' that existentialist education aims at calls for an educational curriculum that prioritizes the personal involvement of the learner. Educational involvement here is not taken in the traditional sense of relating to others (group dynamics) in the learning process. In existentialism involvement is affective (personal and emotional) in nature. "In education it (involvement) means the learner's experience of getting personally implicated in his subject matter and in the situation around him. It means being aroused by question of good and bad, right and wrong, pro and con, yes and no. In short, it means awakening to the normative quality of experience in books, in a teacher's remark, in a classroom situation."[20] Involvement, as an educational aim, is not a soulless process of quantitative acquisition of knowledge. It is not mere cognition. Existentialist involvement is an emotional encounter with knowledge. It is in this light that Kneller, paraphrasing the existentialist definition of philosophy, writes, "Existentialists reject the traditional view that philosophy should be calm and detached above all. Philosophy, they (existentialists) say, should be reason informed by passion because it is the passion, in states of heightened feeling, that ultimate reality is disclosed. Passionate reason is not unreason but the reason of the whole man. It is reason at grips with those fundamental realities of freedom, death, and other people with which human beings must contend. It is the opposite of dispassionate calculation which manipulates abstractions and ignores the human predicament."[21] It is an encounter with knowledge in such a way that such knowledge transforms the life of the student. Hence, the aim of existentialist education is to make students active participants not passive receptors in the learning process.

The 'discovery of freedom' also calls for creativity. "Real education leads to creative life."[22] According to Jean-Paul Satre one of the aims of existentialist philosophy is to create dissatisfaction with the present. In light of this, existentialist exploration of possible choices depends largely on the imagination of the individual students. It is only when the imagination gives new significance to facts that further possibilities about them can be explored. Hence, existentialist education is a ceaseless quest for the subjective ideal because insight is never exhausted. Creativity is constitutive of exploration in the sense that it is a positive and critical attitude toward education and the possibility opened to the student. Successful education should lead to creativity; that is, a development of imagination which offers the possibility to explore new existential possibilities. Creative education leads to different viewpoints and lays the foundation for educational pluralism.

The aim of existentialist education is neither the acquisition of historical knowledge nor is it to foster the duplication of successful people. As an egocentric educational philosophy it does not seek objective truth but a subjective ideal. Hence, constructions of experience, critical awareness, being responsible, and confronting the self with the self constitute the goal of education. Existentialist education is not about the acquisition of knowledge that has been endorsed. It is a soul-searching process. It is an education that leads to authentic existence, that is, taking responsibility for one's commitment and choices.

Existentialist education is a reversal of what has been taken as commonplace in education, namely, that education is a social undertaking. Instead of the analytical approach that is passionless and external, existentialism takes the self-awareness, life, and interior approach. In place of probing an objective certainty as the goal of education existentialism seeks freedom of choice and responsibility as the platform for launching education. Instead of formal teaching as the means to educational goals, existentialism endorses *discovery* as the path to educational goals. The goal of existentialist education is not to prepare students for life. Rather, it is an education that encourages students to greater autonomy in 'creating themselves' according to their desires and interests as well as heighten their sense of responsibility for such creations. Existentialist education aims at molding and shaping the inner freedom of students so that they become concerned creators of their lives rather than critics who speak from outside. In brief, the aim of education is to assist individual students to become aware of their freedom to create themselves and to promote a successful commitment to a significant and meaningful existence. Education should enable students to explore and reconstruct their individual history. This goal can be detailed as follows:

♦ To develop individual awareness
♦ To provide opportunity for free ethical choices
♦ To encourage the development of self-knowledge
♦ To develop a sense of self-responsibility
♦ To awaken a sense of individual commitment.

The Student and the Teacher

Existentialists reject the view that students are born with an innate program of development, an inborn power that automatically takes care of their growth process. According to existentialists students are self-conscious individuals challenged to take responsibility for their lives. This means that the students are challenged to question the meaning of their biological and existential life. In light of the above, existentialism defines the student as an individual in quest of the meaning of the self and life. Existentialism also rejects the notion that a student is a social animal. Rather it considers the student as a unique subject.

Existentialist education emphasizes the role of the student as an individual moral agent capable of choosing freely and responsibly. Within the matrix of such an anthropology "the existentialist teacher will not demand adjustments, rather he will fight against adjustments. In avoiding indoctrination like a deadly sin, he will encourage rebellion and opposition as bases of progress. He will not be concerned with externals and instead will dwell upon the need for inwardness both in his own life and in the existence of his students."[23] In light of the nature of the student existentialist teachers cannot exercise their profession as traditional teachers. They shall neither lecture nor consider themselves as omniscient. In their teaching the teachers will not present cures or expediencies that violate the autonomy of students.

Table 11
Don'ts and Dos of Teachers

DON'TS	DOS
Must not impose wishes and curriculum on students	Have close personal relationship with student without dominating student or discouraging student's free thought.
Must not impose personality on students	Encourage student creativity, discovery, and inventiveness.
Must not direct students	Act as a resource person.
	Possess strong personal beliefs and commitments.

Rather, the teacher will first of all fulfill the role of a 'detective' who identifies the needs and concerns of students. According to Kierkegaard a teacher must start out as a learner not an information-giver. Teaching must begin by finding out where the students stand in their needs and concerns.[24] Empathy is the starting point of teaching. The teacher will not treat students as a homogenous group but consider each one as a unique individual. The teacher will respect the intrinsic diversity of each student and provide experiences in which students can express themselves freely as individuals. The teacher must respect the pluralistic attitudes in the classroom. In this light, the teachers should consider themselves as facilitators who help each student to become autonomous and self-reliant. According to George Knight, "the existentialist teacher will seek to relate to every student in what Martin Buber refers to as an 'I-Thou,' rather than an 'I-It,' relationship. That is, such teachers will treat the student as an individual with whom they can personally identify, rather than an 'It' that needs to be externally directed and filled with knowledge."[25] As facilitator the main concern of the teacher shall not be a transfer of knowledge to the student. On the contrary, the teacher should be concerned that the student has become aware of his/her responsibility; that the student has broken loose from societal injunctions; that the student has become genuinely creative and a participant in the search for knowledge.

Educational Process

Educational process describes content – what should be taught in schools – and method – how it should be taught. This section deals with existentialist curriculum and method.

Existentialist Curriculum

Concerning what should be taught, it is important to know some of the principles of existentialist curriculum. With its emphasis on the individual one would expect that the first principle of the curriculum should be the primacy of the individual over the subject matter. This is evident in Kneller's comment "that school subjects are only tools for the realization of subjectivity."[26] Existentialist curriculum is viewed from the point of view of the learner, not the material to be covered. In light of this, existentialism is amorphous concerning the content of curriculum "because it is seen as important only when it is personally meaningful. It is an individualized curriculum designed for the individual's search for personhood. The existential curriculum is based upon personal needs."[27] According to existentialist education, therefore, curriculum content is of lesser importance. What is more important and determining for existentialists curriculum is whether such a curriculum offers the possibility for the individual student to develop relevance and meaning out of it.

Existentialist curriculum, unlike modern curriculum, is not prescriptive nor is it a body of knowledge to be mastered. Curriculum has an encyclopedic character, a sort of storage vault from which the learner has to choose the knowledge that is meaningful and significant. It is not the curriculum that determines the learner but the learner who determines the curriculum by actively choosing what is necessary for authentic existence. "The curriculum of the Existentialist school is intended to be merely available, to be there for the asking, the choosing, the appropriating."[28] Curriculum exists only as possible knowledge awaiting the choice of the student.

Since existentialist curriculum is student-centered it offers only guidelines and no specific curriculum. Every curriculum is an ad hoc curriculum because it takes into consideration the lived experience of the learner. It constructs its curriculum with a view of the student-in-situation. However, existentialism has a heavy penchant for the humanities "because they deal with the essential aspects of human existence, such as the relationships between people, the tragic as well as the happy side of human life, and the absurdities as well as the meaningful aspects of life. In short, existentialists want to see humankind in its totality – the perverted as well as the exalted, the mundane as well as the glorious, the despairing as well as the hopeful – and they believe that humanities and the arts do this better than the social sciences."[29] Existentialist choice for humanities is rooted in their belief that they have a greater potential for introspection and the development of meaning. The sciences, on the contrary, are cold and dispassionate. In the case where they are engaging they can seduce students, create doubts in their minds, or emphasize only partial aspects of human existence. For this reason they are dangerous. A survey by Bedford[30] suggests, that there is consensus by Søren Kierkegaard, Martin Buber, Karl Jaspers, and Jean-Paul Satre that the following subjects play major roles in existentialist curriculum: history, education, religion, literature, and fine arts.

Existentialist Method

Concerning how the subject should be taught existentialism views the current teaching-learning process as personal classroom tyranny or verbal manipulation because the teacher imposes the self on students who are obliged to submit to that teacher. Students are forced to submit to inflexible knowledge and evaluation of which the teacher is custodian. In this scheme the teacher is considered as an instructor. According to existentialists such a "teacher is devalued into a means for the transfer of knowledge and the pupil is devalued into some product of the transfer. Knowledge is sovereign and persons become means and product. How, then is knowledge to be transmitted? It is not to be transmitted but offered."[31] To offer means that the teacher should present multi-perspectives of the subject to bring about discussion. Hence, existentialism rejects the view in which the teacher is a confidant, provider, demonstrator, or model. To offer, from the point of view of the student, means that the student shall not just be an absorber of information, a receiver, and an imitator who tries to reproduce the teacher's life in his/her life. Rather, existentialism advocates a teaching-learning process in which teachers and students explore the truth together. For this reason, George Kneller infers that "in methodology, there is no question that the existentialist favor the Socratic approach."[32]

The Socratic approach is teaching by asking and questioning not telling and lecturing. The aim of this method is to engage both teachers and students in an open-ended exploration that examines the educational beliefs and assumptions of one another. It invites teachers to be ready to learn and to avoid making obsequious references to their status. One feature of the method is its conversational nature. As a dialogic undertaking it brings out the opinion of teachers and students in the dialogue. Also, the method is skeptical. That is, it begins with an acknowledgement of ignorance on the part of both teachers and students in the search for truth. Avowal of ignorance is not an insincere pretense but an expression of genuine intellectual humility. Furthermore, the Socratic Method is inductive or empirical in the sense that definitions are tested by recourse to experience. Finally, the method is deductive in that experientially tested definitions constitute the basis from which educational implications are drawn.

EXISTENTIALIST EDUCATION FOR TODAY

Educational Reform According to Existentialism

Existentialism's emphasis on the individual and his/her personal choices has put many philosopher-educators on edge as a theory that can result in educational anarchy. However, when one approaches this philosophy as an educational theory it has some pertinence for today in the area of teacher education.

The first area in which existentialist education can have an important impact is in the area of courses on method. A review of the syllabuses on method courses reveal that such courses put more emphasis on the organization of the subject matter, choices of activities that will leverage the topic, and promising teaching techniques to facilitate the teaching and learning process. The arrangement of the method does not take into consideration the human elements of free choice, anguish, or emotions that must necessarily interact with the subject matter proposed for learning and pedagogical techniques employed. Hence, existentialism suggests that human concerns must accompany structural concerns in the determination of educational method.

The second area in which existentialism can be pertinent is that of educational psychology. Psychology today treats students as 'objects' to be observed and measured. They are treated as determined beings because they can be statistically measured. Group dynamics also makes the teachers look like social engineers. The drawback of these approaches to education is that they do not take into consideration the exercise of freedom of choice and responsibility as well as the commitment of students to learning. Inasmuch as educational measurement always set out to establish what is 'objective', existentialist education cautions that to leave out the 'subjective' element in students will falsify the findings of any research.

Third, existentialist philosophy of education rejects the idea of a prefabricated human being. As a philosophy that advocates the idea that individuals create themselves through their choices, existentialism provides a base and starting point for discussing educational pluralism and multiculturalism. Pluralism in schools is the existence of different cultures, religions, and ideologies resulting in diverse educational and social goals that may conflict but without any one necessarily or justifiably overriding all others. Multicultural education, on the other hand, provides strategies for appreciating one's culture, developing critical thinking, and empowering students to learn about the culture of other students. In civilizations like the United States of America where there is room for each one to choose their orientation existentialist education can offer perspectives that enlighten the choice and acceptance of responsibility for those choices. Also, existentialist education rejects the idea of subordination of individuals to systems. By so doing it is not advocating the isolation of individuals. Rather, it is advocating the notion of individual-in-relationship as is evident in Buber's 'I-Thou' philosophy. The challenge of existentialism for modern education which insists on same subjects, same standards, and same lessons for students and teachers is that the aim should not be to bring about a collectivity or homogenous group. Heterogeneity should be the aim.

Existentialist education also has something to say in the area of school rules and regulation. Many existentialists today consider school rules and regulations as bureaucracies imposed on students. These rules enslave students and determine their growth into directions that are not of their choosing. School rules enslave students. Hence, existentialist educators will advocate and promote greater student participation in the drafting of school rules. Students' challenges of these rules should not be taken amiss since each student's individuality vis-à-vis the rules has to be respected. What is important here is that existentialism is an antidote to loneliness to which students who do not fit into a school system are pushed. Existentialism is a clarion call to take care of those who may be termed 'school misfits'. Existentialism is an antidote to the dehumanizing aspects of systemic education.

Inconsistencies in Existentialist Educational Philosophy

One problem with the role attributed to teachers by existentialists is that it contradicts existentialism's rejection of authority and standards. The overriding concern of existentialism is for the individual and the primacy of choosing the self. The presence of a teacher is problematic in this scheme. Morris captures this difficulty as follows:

The very presence of a second person [the teacher] immediately 'socializes' the learning condition and thereby compromises the possibility of his developing his own individualistic view of things. This difficulty may account for the relative silence of existentialism on so social an undertaking as education has turned out to be in the modern world[33]

Another problem concerns the impracticality of system. Existentialist educational philosophy emphasizes individuality. The logical conclusion to which this leads is that students should neither attend classes nor take examinations, and there should be no set curriculum. These extremes of existentialism make it a companion of anarchy. "Modern education is a mass enterprise. It is not possible to individualize the work of the school to provide specifics for each student. Moreover, we live in society. Students are living and will continue to live in society. External controls must exist of necessity. They are part of the socializing process through which all must go."[34] Modern education is an institutional expression of some culture organized to perpetrate itself across time. Because of this inherent sociological character of education the feasibility of individual curriculum at an extensive scale of a nation, for example, does not seem plausible.

Conclusion

Existentialist philosophy does not speak the language of scientific demonstration or logical dialectic. Education should be about the meaning of one's own individual life. A merit of existentialist education is that it is a plea for individuals to be serious about life. Existentialist education is not an activity of the mind alone but also of the emotions. In education teachers and students are engaged in a joint exploratory process. Teachers are not to impose on students but act as resource persons that students may or may not choose to use.

[1] Martin, V. M. (2003). *Existentialism*. In B. L. Marthaler et al. (Eds.). *New Catholic Encyclopedia*. 2nd Ed. Vol. 5. New York: Thomson Gale. p. 544.

[2] Wild, J. (1955). *The challenge of existentialism*. Indiana: University of Indiana Press. p. 57.

[3] Mayer, F. (1962). *New perspectives for education*. Washington, DC: Public Affairs Press. p. 112.

[4] Morris, V. C. (1972), *Existentialism in education. What it means*. New York: Harper and Row. p. 5.

[5] Mayer, *op. cit.,,* p. 6.

[6] Satre, J. -P. (1972). *Existentialism*. In Bedford, *Existentialism and creativity.* New York: Philosophical Library. p. 8.

[7] Satre, J. -P. (1948). *Existentialism and humanism*. London: Methuen & Co. p. 28.

[8] Kneller, G. F. (1971). *The challenge of existentialism*. In G. F. Kneller, (Ed.) *Foundations of education*. 3rd Ed. New York: John Wiley & Sow. p. 253

[9] Martin, V. M., *op. cit.,,* p. 545.

[10] Mayer, *op. cit.,,* p. 111.

[11] Depuis, A.. & Nordberg, R. (1964). *Philosophy and education. A total view.* Milwaukee, WI: The Bruce Publishing Company. p. 270.

[12] Knight, G. (1980). *Education and philosophy. An introduction in Christian perspectives*. Berrien Springs, MI: Andrews University Press. p. 72.

[13] Bedford, M. (1972). *Existentialism and creativity.* New York: Philosophical Library. p. 13.

[14] Bedford, *op. cit.,,* p. 24.

[15] Harper, R. *Significance of existence and recognition for education*. In A. M. Depose & R. Nordberg, (1964). *Philosophy and education. A total view.* Milwaukee, WI: The Bruce Publishing Company. p. 277.

[16] Mayer, *op. cit.,,* p. 131.

[17] Morris, *op. cit.,,* p. 116.

[18] Morris, *op. cit.,,* p. 117.

[19] Satre, J. -P., (1956). *Being and nothingness*. Trans. H. E. Barnes. New York: Philosophical Library. p. 555.

[20] Morris, *op. cit.,,* p. 119.

[21] Kneller, (1971), *op. cit.,,* pp. 254-5.

[22] Mayer, *op. cit.,,* p. 112.

[23] Mayer, *op. cit.,,* p. 126.

[24] Thomte, R. (1948). *Kierkegaard's philosophy of religion.* New Jersey: Princeton University Press. p. 201.

[25] Knight, G. R. (1998). *Philosophy and education. An introduction in Christian perspective.* 3rd Ed. Berrian Springs, MI: Andrews University Press. p. 77.

[26] Kneller, G. F. (1958). *Existentialism and education.* New York: Philosophical Library. p. 63.

[27] Samuelson, W. G. & Markowitz, F. A. (1988). *An introduction to philosophy in education.* New York: Philosophical Library. p. 49.

[28] Morris, *op. cit.,,* p. 129.

[29] Ozmon, H. A. & Craver S. M. (1999). *Philosophical foundations of education.* 6th Ed. Upper Saddle River, NJ: Prentice-Hall, Inc. p. 267.

[30] Bedford, *op. cit.,,* pp. 294-98. Also see Morris, *op. cit.,,* pp. 137-47.

[31] Kneller, (1971). *op. cit.,,* p. 261.

[32] Kneller, (1958). *op. cit.,,* p. 133.

[33] Morris, V. C. (1961). *Philosophy and the American School.* Boston, MA: Houghton Mifflin Company. p. 211.

[34] *Existentialism.*   www.edst.purdue.edu/georgeoff/phil_am_ed/EXISTENTIALISM.htm

CHAPTER 8

MARXISM AND EDUCATION

MARXISM AS PHILOSOPHY

Life of Karl Marx

Marxism is a doctrine derived from the teachings of Karl Heinrich Marx (1818-1883) and Friedrich Engels (1820-1895). Its peculiarity consists of an economic interpretation (historical materialism) of Hegel's dialectic. As such, it can be characterized as a re-enthronement of materialism against the renaissance of Hegelian idealism.

Karl Marx was born in Trier, Germany, in 1816 of Jewish parents. The family converted from Judaism to Christianity in 1816 not for religious reasons but out of expediency. Marx's father, an accomplished lawyer, could not enter the law profession legally as a Jew. Marx's Jewish background exposed him to prejudice and discrimination. This may explain why he questioned the role of religion in human affairs and advocated social change. Marx studied law in the University of Bonn. In 1836 he transferred to the University of Berlin where he read history and philosophy. In Berlin he was associated with the so-called *Doctorklub* whose membership was mostly made up of left wing or radical Hegelians. He later resigned from this group because he was dissatisfied with their purely theoretical attitude to politics, for example. An important contact he made in Berlin was with his theology teacher, Bruno Bauer. Bauer propounded a theology of need in which he explained that Christianity was not historical but a record of human fantasies arising from emotional needs. This concept of need will become for Marx a cornerstone of his dialectic. In 1841 Marx and his Hegelian colleagues were influenced by Ludwig Feuerbach's publication of *The Essence of Christianity*. In this work Feuerbach propounded and supported a theory of materialism against the idealism of Hegel. From this point forward Marx tried to put together Hegel's idealism and Feuerbach's materialism. Here, one finds the germ of Marx's dialectical materialism. In 1842 Marx became editor of the *Rheinisch Zeitung* and this brought him into close contacts with political, social, and economic problems. The conviction that issued form here was that theory must be the fruit of practice. Soon Marx's ideas were not well received by political authorities. In 1843, year of his marriage, Marx moved to Paris. At this time Paris was considered the center of socialist thought and of extreme groups that called themselves communists (from the French Communue).

In Paris Karl Marx assisted in founding the short-lived *Deutsch-Französische Jahrbücher or German-French Yearbooks,* became a member of a socialist group, and enlisted in a study of political economy. An important personal contact that Marx made in Paris and which was to stay with him throughout the rest of his life was his meeting with Engels. Friedrich Engels was a regular contributor to the Yearbooks. Expelled from Paris after a year Marx moved to Brussels where he spent the next three years organizing the German Worker's Union. Engels rejoined Marx in Brussels in 1845.

The Brussels period was marked by greater collaboration between Karl Marx and Friedrich Engels. Both put together their intellectual prowess to publish *The Holy Family* in 1845. In it they criticized the Hegelian theology of Bruno Bauer. Next they wrote *The German Ideology* (1845-46 and published in 1932) in which they exposed their concept of history. Marx also picked a bone of contention with the French socialist Pierre-Joseph Proudhon's *The Philosophy of Poverty* (1846). Marx's counter offensive was entitled *The Poverty of Philosophy* (1847). Marx was attacking Proudhon's support of the petty bourgeois. In 1847 Marx with the collaboration of Engels published *The Manifesto of the Communist Party,* which was a statement of the principles of the Communist League. In 1848 Marx was invited to Paris to be part of the post-revolutionary provisional government. As the revolution extended to Austria and his native Germany Marx decided to go back to his native Rhineland. His political activities at home earned him expulsion in 1849. He moved to London that same year.

Marx was now to spend the rest of his life in London. There he spent much time reading and writing articles that became the source of his meager finances. In 1851 and on the invitation of Charles Dana, Marx became the European-based correspondent for *The New York Tribune* contributing over 500 articles and editorials by 1862. Most of them were on politics and social analysis of agitations. He was dependent on Engels for sustenance.

The philosophy of Marx has variously been called dialectical historical materialism and scientific socialism.[1] Basically, it is a critique of experience like that of the proletariat and a critique of ideas like those of Hegel. What is peculiar to Marx's philosophy is that he does not consider problems about human beings, matter, knowledge, and so on by themselves. The unique stamp of Marx's philosophy is that he probes such problems in relation to other problems and in relation to their social, political, economic, and historical contexts respectively.

Salient Features of Marxism

Dialectic Materialism

Materialism constitutes the principle and foundation on which the whole of Marxist philosophy is construed. Materialism is the theory that the observable world or material nature exists on its own right independent of the thinking mind. In this light the materialism of Marx is post-Hegelian because for Hegel and idealism the existence of the material world is dependent on the thinking mind. For Marx it is the material world that gives the mind food for thought not thought that creates the world. Hence, Marxist materialism is not a denial of the existence of the mind. Rather, it is an assertion of the priority of matter. It is a repudiation of any non-materialistic interpretation of the world-process. Evidence for this is found in the writings of Marx and Engels who attributed passivity to the mind and activity to matter. Marx wrote,

> It is not the consciousness of human beings which determines their being, but it is, on the contrary, their social being which determines their consciousness.[2]

Engels in his treatise on Ludwig Feuerbach noted,

> We conceive the concepts in our heads once more from a materialist point of view as copies of real things, instead of conceiving real things as copies of this or that stage of the absolute concept.[3]

In brief, materialism is a denial that there is a Mind or Idea prior to Nature. However, this does not lead to a conclusion that human beings have no minds. In fact Marxism affirms that human beings have minds. But what the powers of the mind are is still obscure in this doctrine.

Dialectic is a Marxist concept of self-development. It is an amalgam of Hegelian dialectic and Darwinian evolution. Darwin discovered the law of development of organic nature. Marxist dialectic is a discovery of the development of human history. Dialectic, for Marx, is a theory that all things are dynamically interconnected, that change is universal, and that everything has within itself opposing forces (thesis and antithesis) whose movement necessarily changes it into something else (synthesis). Stated schematically dialectic is a process of development characterized by contradicting an existing state of affairs, followed by a contradiction of the contradiction. This second contradiction or third moment in the developmental process is an overcoming of the original existing condition.   An alternative view of the dialectic is to see it as a principle of reciprocity "where causes produce effects that react on the causes in such a way that the character of the causes may be modified or determined… In other words, the law of reciprocity states that a given set of conditions depends upon its antecedents and also upon the resulting set of conditions."[4]

Understood within the matrix of the Hegelian triad (thesis, antithesis, and synthesis) thesis and antithesis are mutually interactive – each is the cause and the effect of the other. The synthesis or new situation is created by and in the process of interplay of thesis and antithesis. The importance of stressing reciprocity and mutuality is to underscore the fact that Marxist concept of development or dialectic is not mechanistic or deterministic but dynamic in character. That is, in his consideration of development Marx does not have a place for a purposeful design or moral guide to development. Also, in light of Hegelian dialectic the Marxist concept of development or change is not to be understood in terms of growth or maturation. Rather, the synthesis is to be taken as the emergence of a new institution or form. Furthermore, unlike Hegel who considered the world-process closed Marx insisted it is a circularity that spirals. For Hegel the circle ends when freedom is achieved. For Marx the spiral will tip-off when socialism or communism is established. This is synonymous to the elimination of class contradictions or differences that are the fuel for the dialectic process.

Dialectic materialism is not an expression that was coined by Marx or Engels. It is a concept borrowed by Marx from Hegel. For Hegel the dialectic epitomized a process of self-development of Thought or Idea. This movement is reflected in the world by Thought process. For Marx dialectic exists first in reality, that is, in Nature and human history. Human thought is a reflection of the dialectic process in reality. Dialectical materialism is a Marxist 'science' of nature and history. It is a borrowed transformation or modification of Hegel. Marx, for example, rejects any Hegelian belief in any supernatural, immaterial, or theological entity. That is why Marxism is atheistic. In Marxism there is a reversal of Hegelian thought concerning the relationship of thought and reality. In this reversal one finds the rationality for Marxist materialistic conception of history. Dialectical materialism is the mainstay of Marxism and has dire repercussion for Marxist concept of history, human beings, and the nature of knowledge.

Marxist Anthropology

Active Human Nature

Marxist dialectic affirms the priority of Nature over mind. But what is Nature? According to Marx Nature does not exist without humans. This is not an affirmation of the non-ontological independence of Nature, lest Marxism becomes idealism. However, the statement is to be understood in two senses.

First, that nature exists for human beings. Second, that human beings are oriented toward Nature. According to Marx human beings are not self-sufficient beings. They need things other than themselves to survive. Human beings do not passively but actively transform nature to satisfy these needs. The difference between a human being and an animal is that the human being "consciously transforms a natural object to satisfy his needs" whereas for animals and other non-humans the action to satisfy their needs is innate or instinctive.[5] Engels clarifies this difference as follows:

> The normal existence of animals is given by the condition in which they live and to which they adapt themselves – those of man, as soon as he differentiates himself from the animal in the narrower sense, have as yet never been present, and are only to be elaborated by the ensuing historical development. Man is the sole animal capable of working his way out of the merely animal state – his normal state is one appropriate to his consciousness, one to be created by himself.[6]

The relationship of human beings to nature can be qualified as a conscious productive activity. From this elaboration one deciphers the salient tenets of Marxist anthropology.

Human beings are not contemplative beings but active beings in material production. As productive beings they do not work as monist but social beings. They produce in society for society. Hence, for Marx human beings are active social beings. Marx, in his Theses on Feuerbach, makes the point in one of his aphorisms thus, "But the essence of man is no abstraction inherent in each separate individual. In its reality it is the ensemble of social relationships."[7] Marx reiterates the point in his Critique of Political Economy. "Man," writes Marx, "is in the most literal sense of the word a zoom politikon, not only a social animal, but an animal which can develop into an individual only in society. Production by isolated individuals outside of society… is as great an absurdity as the idea of the development of language without individuals living together and talking to one another."[8] From this point of view Marxism is a strong critique of philosophies like existentialism, which hold the view that human beings are individualistic, and by nature self-centered. By focusing on the active life of human beings Marxism "takes the practical lives of human beings as the foundation of our ideas."[9]

Marxism also affirms that human activity is teleological. Its purpose is to satisfy human needs. In Marxism, therefore, human beings are beings with needs. Various means of production are needed to satisfy the different needs of humans. As human needs change so too will the means of satisfying them change. The first and basic need of humans according to Marx "is the production of the means which enable man to satisfy these needs."[10] From the point of view of the mutation of human needs and the processes of satisfying them one important conclusion follows: the human-Nature relationship is not static but developing. Human beings and the world are not finished products but are constantly changing, moving, and developing. Also, the satisfaction of human needs points to the fact that labor is the touchstone for human self-realization. Labor is also the medium for human beings to create the world of their choice. Lastly, labor should constitute the source of human display of talent, of bliss, and of making the world a home. From the point of view of needs the desire for human self-realization is not provoked by external stimuli. The need for self-realization and, therefore, for work is located in human striving to achieve their needs. Marx, thus, considers human beings from the viewpoint of their social productive involvement.

Alienated Human Beings

Human labor or productive activity is what gives meaning to life. However, within the context of capitalism human productivity has instead become a source of enslavement or dehumanization. "If his needs as a human being are to be satisfied by his productive activity, then truly he has been indentured by the capitalist, who, in defrauding him of his labor, defrauds him of his humanity."[11]

Marxist Epistemology

The thought that Nature and human history are in process is important for Marxist epistemology. Knowledge in Marxism is synonymous to knowledge of Nature and human history. "From this it follows that human knowledge, as a mirror of this twofold reality, is itself a process which does not and cannot reach a fixed and absolute system of truths."[12] It follows, therefore, that Marxist knowledge consists in an investigation of the histories of things and of the factors that bring about the change. Marxist epistemology rejects eternal and absolute truths to be learned and accepted. It advocates a relationship between human thought and the social context in which it occurs.

Going behind the appearances of nature produces knowledge of the principle underlying Nature. Knowledge consists of a discovery of the hidden phenomena that accounts for Nature that is apparent and observable. From this definition of knowledge it follows that Nature or "the real is a multi-layered structure, consisting of entities and processes lying at different levels of that structure. The empirical world with which we are familiar is on the surface level but is causally connected to 'deeper', ontological levels, and it is by virtue of these connections that we can use sense data, experience, and observation in constructing knowledge of the structures and processes of the real."[13] Knowledge is constructed and, therefore, the method of its acquisition is not passive but entails the creative involvement of the knower. People know not by an internal causation of thought by thought (meditation) but through an active inquiry into the laws of nature.

Marxist epistemology, unlike Hegelianism, is not interested in describing mere facts. For Marx knowledge should be knowledge of the laws or whys governing the movement of history so that the future can be predicted. Knowledge is recognition of the laws of necessity.

Concept of History

Marxist concept of history is described as historical materialism. Karl Marx tells us what he means by that in these words:

> In the social production which men carry on they enter into definite relations that are indispensable and independent of their will; these relations of production correspond to a definite stage of development of their material forces of production. The sum total of these relations of production constitutes the economic structure of society – the real foundation, on which rises a legal and political superstructure and to which correspond definite forms of social consciousness. The mode of production in material life determines the social, political, and intellectual life-process in general. It is not the consciousness of men that determines their being, but, on the contrary, their social being that determines their consciousness. At a certain stage of their development, the material forces of production in society come in conflict with the existing relations of production, or – what is but a legal expression for the same thing – with the property relations within which they have been at work before. From forms of development of the forces of production these relations turn into their fetters. Then begins an epoch of social revolution. With the change of the economic foundation, the entire immense superstructure is more or less rapidly transformed. In considering such

transformations a distinction should always be made between the material transformation of the economic conditions of production, which can be determined with the precision of natural science, and the legal, political, religious, aesthetic, or philosophic – in short, ideological forms in which men become conscious of this conflict and fight it out... No social order ever disappears before all the productive forces for which there is room in it have been developed; and new higher relations of production never appear before the material conditions of their existence have matured in the womb of the old society itself. Therefore, mankind always sets itself only such tasks as it can solve; since, looking at the matter more closely, we will be always find that the task itself arises only when the material conditions necessary for its solution already exist or are at least in the process of formation.[14]

It is now appropriate to analyze the above concept for better understanding.

The designation historical materialism can only be understood in the light of Marx's concept of mode of production. Mode of production is a polysemic expression that sometimes "refers specifically to production, sometimes to the economic process as a whole, and sometimes to social relationships, not only the economic and political but the ideological relationships as well."[15] Historical materialism designates social relationships, which according to Marx also includes political, social, and ideological relationships. Production is key to establishing these relationships. The system of production is at the base of social and political relationships. Productive relationship is social relationship. The stoppage of the production process is tantamount to the death of society.

Production is the relationship of two forces that have been called the Base (economic structure) and the Superstructure (political, ideological, and social structure). According to Marx economics does not simply respond to the policies dictated by the Superstructure and vice versa. Rather, there is a reciprocity and mutuality between economics and politics.

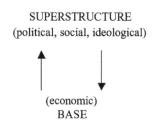

Figure 1: PRODUCTIVE RELATIONSHIP

Economics as the base (production in factories) brings about class-consciousness, unionization, and eventually political activity of the working people. This analysis indicates a multi-social level of relationship in the mode of production: intra-Base, intra-Superstructure, and inter Base-Superstructure relationships.

The relationships described by Marxism are neither mechanical nor static but creative and dynamic. Marx cites the example of the effect on the Superstructure outpaced by economic development. Economic changes send shock waves to the Superstructure. Politicians, social activists, and ideologists begin to adjust their activity and outlook so as to fit the new economic situation. Marx calls this the class conflict.

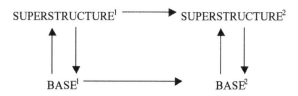

Figure 2: EFFECT OF CHANGE IN RELATIONSHIPS

In the case of class struggle one can describe the change as a 'lateral displacement' to another level.

Another wave of change may come about because of contradictions within one of the forces of production. Marx offers the example of a change of production from non-monopoly capitalism to monopoly capitalism.

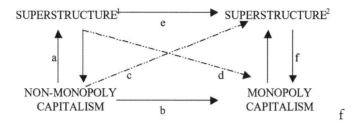

Figure 3: EFFECT OF CONTRADICTION IN PRODUCTION

The effects are explained as follows:

a. The Base-Superstructure relationship in the epoch of non-monopoly capitalism.

b. Changes in production result in changes in Base-relationships.

c. Vestiges of old production method still linger in new Superstructure

d. Vestiges of old Superstructure still influence the new Base

e. A new ideology begins to emerge.

f. A new Base-Superstructure relationship is established.

Conflict in relations of production and contradictions in the forces of production are responsible for the dynamism of historical materialism.

Although not used by Marx the expressions forces of production and relations of production have been respectively used by humanist Marxists (Edward Thompson and Raymond Williams) and structualist Marxists (Louis Althuser and Etienne Baliber) to explain the nature and dynamism of historical materialism. As noted earlier, Marx's purpose in investigating historical changes and development is not to describe the complexity of the change. Marx's purpose as a 'social scientist' is to uncover "the laws or tendencies guiding the social development."[16] It is a Marxist hypothesis that in the motley events and swirls of causal relationships this is the major motif or unique cause.

In order to arrive at the basic law that explains social change Marx offers the following analytical process:

- Critical analysis of problem
- Historical specification of problem
- Postulating the forces that generate development
- Generalization and confirmation of finding

In his analysis of social development Marx deciphered five historical epoch that chronologically are primitive communal, slave, feudal, capital, and socialist/communist. The final cause for social change is not found in philosophy, human brains, or insights into eternal truths. The changes can be explained by conflicts in the mode of production.

The materialistic conception of history can be summarized in the following theses statements:

- History starts with the proposition that the production of the means to support human life is the basis for all social relationships.

- Through their interaction with the forces of production human beings create history and meaning. As such, the meaning of the world is not naturally or supernaturally provided. Rather, the world is an objectification of human labor.

- History is created by human labor. As such it has no guaranteed outcomes. The future is not a known paradise or hell but an open question of which production is ultimately the determining element.

- Historical materialism emphasizes human agency and responsibility at the core of the creation of history.

Historical materialism underscores the economic foundation of Marx's philosophy.

MARXIST EDUCATIONAL PHILOSOPHY

Educational theories are founded on fundamental principles and basic assumptions derived from particular social, economic, or political philosophy.

Marxist educational theory is no exception. It is the result of Marxist social, economic, and political philosophy. The foregoing section presented the philosophical principles of Marxism. The present section uncovers how Marxist education built and developed its foundation on the principles of Marxism.

Timeline of Marx's Educational Thought

Marxist educational philosophy is embedded in its philosophy. Below is a timeline of how Marx's educational theory evolved within his philosophy.

1848	In the *Manifesto* Marx and Engels summarized the principles of education in a communist society: "Free public education. The abolishment of factory labor for children in its present form. The combination of education with material production."[17]
1867	Marx elaborated further on labor-education combination in *Capital*. Marx discussed education at a period after "the inevitable conquest of political power by the working class" and defined it as "technological education."[18]
1871	Two days after the fall of the Paris Commune on May 28th, 1871 Marx read papers commenting on the legacy of the Commune. He came to this conclusion after his reading. "All of the educational institutions were opened to the people, gratuitously, and at the same time all interference of Church and State were removed. Thus not only was education made available to all, but Science, itself, was freed from the fetters which class prejudice and governmental force had imposed on it."[19] Maurice Shore comments of this experiences as follows: "From this time on, Marx's attitude towards quasi-reformers and 'opportunistic' educational programs of liberal groups and moderate socialists became firm and overtly antagonistic."[20]

Polytechnic Education

The Factory Acts of mid-19th Century England demanded an alternation between schoolwork and factory work. Marx saw in this the seeds of future communist education. Marx incorporated this idea in his theory of polytechnic education that became his educational legacy.

Polytechnic education is an educational arrangement organized around the recognition and practice of labor. It is an applied orientation of instruction. It combined productive labor with instruction not as "one of the methods of adding to the efficiency of production, but as the only method of producing fully developed human beings."[21] The heart and strength of Marxist education is rooted in a combination of work and school. Participation in schoolwork and production constitute the dialectical ingredients of social betterment or the creation of a new civilization. The French Marxist, Paul Langevin, reiterates Marx's concept of integrated training as the basis of polytechnic education. According to Paul Langevin there must be in education

> an organic liaison between the school and its surrounding… The school should unite with nature and with life, often leaving the walls of the classroom to return laden with experience and with observation, to enrich itself with reflection and meditation, to learn how to record the expression and the representation of things seen, lived, or felt. It should feel itself constantly part and parcel of the outside world… Thus the child's field of vision will widen progressively along with his discovery of is immediate world. This will enable him to find his place there, as well as in an ever-widening circle. He will follow the true way of culture from the concrete to the abstract, from individuality to generality, from egocentric to altruistic interest. This is as true of his contact with men as it is of his contact with things.[22]

From the above, it follows that combining work-with-the-mind and work-with-the-hand is an essential and fundamental ingredient of Marxist educational theory. Marx advocated a school system that was not removed from but immersed in the problems of the local community. By linking instruction to productive labor the practical problems of life in the community become the entry port for student involvement in their local communities. Also, the student becomes familiar with the theory and practice of all the branches of production. For Marx, therefore, schools should be oriented outward to the world of production rather than turned in into itself in a process of realizing a pre-established utopia. Marx's proletariat education can also be described as a labor school or productive-study system.

Marx's integrated education is based on the role of labor and the concept of human nature, respectively. Labor is the first, central, and final ingredient of polytechnic education because according to Marx labor is the source of value. Without labor polytechnic education is worthless. Polytechnic education is also founded on a Marxist utopian conception of human nature and the communist society. "Marx envisaged that the individual under communism would enjoy the opportunity to achieve the all-sided development of his capabilities – a condition which, Marx claimed, was unattainable under capitalism because of the division of labor."[23] In a communist system Marx foresaw the disappearance of divisions and provision of an opportunity for uniform education in the theory and practice of production.

Aims of Education

The production process contained in it two promises: the liberation of the workers and a projected realization of communism.

Liberation of Workers

Polytechnic education aims at educating the 'whole person' in order to liberate him/her from the crippling effects of verbalism and vocationalism of current education.

Marxist education considered the combination of intellectual, physical, and polytechnic education into one educational system as the ideal of a rounded education. With this arrangement Marx hoped to revolutionize the existing 'academic' schools of the Tsarist gymnasium characterized by verbalism and intellectualism. The 'academic' schools or gymnasium led to formalism and also separated theory from practice – a real *bête noire* for Marx. Polytechnic education also aimed at overcoming the narrow and fettering effects of vocationalism. Vocationalism was a policy of "proletarization of education", that is, preferential treatment of workers or their children, with total disregard for their intellectual capacity. It was vocational training without any theoretical foundation. Marx and Engels were convinced that rigid professional specialization practiced by capitalism is dehumanizing. Specialization made special skilled workers vulnerable in the case that their skills become obsolete. Also, premature specialization also limited the occupational choices of the young. Marxist polytechnic schools liberate individuals by offering them broad general education and a multi-sided development that Marx claimed was not attainable under the division of labor in capitalism. Engels made the point clearly thus:

> The division of labor… which makes one person a peasant, another a bootmaker, a third a factory worker, and a fourth a speculator on the stock exchange will disappear completely. Education will give young people the chance of quickly attaining a practical mastery of the whole system of production. It will allow them to transfer in turn from one branch of production to another, in response to the requirements of society or their own personal inclination. Education will consequently free them from the one-sidedness that the contemporary division of labor forces on each individual.[24]

Marxist philosophy of education is against a one-sided development of person. Apart from the liberation of individuals the combination of mental and physical labor also has a utilitarian justification. The acquisition of skills was to respond to a specific historical situation, namely, the preparation of skilled workers in sufficient numbers to take over and control the factories.

Social Reconstruction

One thrust in Marxist philosophy is its fanatical conviction in the amelioration of the human condition. Marx foresaw a future in which the privation and restrictions of the present will change into situations of abundance and freedom; the hatred between capitalists and proletariat will, in the future, change to a universal brotherhood. In Marx's view the English Factory Acts contained the 'germ of the education of the future."[25] Like in sociology Marx postulates an educational system not geared toward the present but toward the future. Hence, the aim of Marxist education is not to serve as a temporary cure or transitory remedy. Marx insists that the finality of education is total societal reconstruction.

In his Thesis on Feuerbach Marx stated, "philosophers have only interpreted the world in various ways; but the real task is to alter it."[26] Marx foresees the alteration in terms of change in the frame of reference from capitalism to communism. This change will take place through a 'class struggle' between the bourgeoisies and the proletariat. In light of Marx's revolutionary absolutism many educators decipher change or social reconstruction as the goal of education. Marx does not conceive education as a weapon per se but as a way of preparing for the future. The change envisaged by Marx calls for education to take care of social consciousness. Hence, a sub-aim of social reconstruction is the formation of social consciousness. This involves a reorganization of the outlook of students.

Marx's faith in the ability of the working class to bring about change and faith in the power of mass education are rooted in his belief that human beings can acquire goodness, that is, that which they need to satisfy their individual needs. This conception of human beings calls for a different kind of education. The first object of education is not to 'stuff' ignorant students with information. Neither is it the object of education to train specialist. For Marx the primary office of education or the labor-school is for the rounded development of the person. Hence, another sub-aim in the social reconstruction process is human character formation. Society mirrors human character.

Marxist education does not wait for chance to produce an ideal society. The ideal society has to be worked for. Hence, the aim of education is to bring about piecemeal and dramatic change of society. Marxist education has a double aim, namely, the transformation of the world and the transformation of human beings.

Marxist Curriculum

One question that curriculum theory answers is: what should be taught? Marx's curriculum principles can be gleaned from his response to a question at the General Council of the First International.[27] At this assembly Marx remarked,

> Political economy and religion ought not to be taught in the lower grade schools or even in the higher ones; that is a kind of education that must rest with the adults; instructions in these fields should be given in the lecture hall, not in the school.

Only the natural sciences, only truths that are independent of all party prejudices and permit only one interpretation should be taught in schools.[28]

The curriculum principle that stands out of the above citation is that Marxist education shall not be a tool of party politics. Marx is very much opposed to utilitarianism in education. It is not the responsibility of education to serve political ends. The office of education according to Marx is to develop the intellectual powers and practical skills of students. Education must remain practical and applied. Lenin, Stalin, and Khrushchev will oppose this view of curriculum by Marx later. According to these later Marxists it is hypocritical to consider schools as neutral or apolitical institutions. For these objectors schools "must be of a kind and character capable of creating socialist men and women by erasing paternalistic policies instituted by the ruling class and intended to shape docile and obedient citizens."[29]

In his intervention at the First International Marx rejected religion as part of school curriculum. Many have characterized this rejection as an endorsement of atheism. However, from the standpoint of the evolutionary concept in Marx's dialectic the rejection can be viewed alternatively. If religion is considered as an unquestionable acceptance of truths stated by someone else as Marx understood it then its acceptance precluded any inquiry of the truth. Religion becomes the 'opium of the people' in the sense that it leaves no room for probing and reconstructing the truth. The method of religion contradicts the twin processes of Marxist education. Religion, in a way, causes 'stagnation' in science and the progress of peoples. So, from the educational perspective Marx's rejection of religion may not be considered as a rejection of religion *qua* religion. Rather, it should be considered as a curriculum principle that eliminates form the curriculum any subject that does not open the possibility of inquiry and reconstruction of knowledge.

Importance of Marxist Theory Today

Educational justification

Marxist educational philosophy revitalizes the question of the justification of education that all educators and providers of education must face. Offering reasons for the existence of school is a two-prong question: What is the origin of this system of education? What is its role in society? Marx's integration of personal and socio-historical development constitutes the explanation or justification for education.

Role of work in education

Marx's historical materialism has a human concern, namely, the welfare and progress of students. In his polytechnic system of education Marx noted the indissoluble link between the historical development of society, on the one hand, and the personal development of the individual, on the other hand. According to Marx the development of students is not a merely sequential process but a contextual process. The social environment is a generator of human development.

Marx is credited for underscoring the importance of the historical contextualization of education. No educational enterprise unfolds in a vacuum. John Donohue acknowledges that the awareness of educational context is important because "such historical awareness is needed in those who must safeguard the continuity of society by helping the young possess themselves of the cultural deposit."[30]

In prescribing work as part of the educational process Marx envisaged the production of real good. However, his integrated approach was driven less by economic reasons and more by educational purposes. In an effort to respond to the problematic economic situation of providing skilled workers for the economy Marx introduces students to learn the logical methods of production practically. In their practical immersion students learn to collaborate with others thus indissolubly building their social skills and character. Hence, the educational function of work in Marx is located at the epistemological and ethical levels, respectively. In Marxism work plays a humanizing not economic role. This view of work by Marx challenges the spirit with which apprenticeships or curriculum practical training programs are arranged.

Critique

Although Marxist education aims at educating the 'whole person' its functional approach ends up educating the person to be a functional unit of the production process. Hence, Marxist philosophy of education is a 'cog in the machine' philosophy.

Also, Marx's polytechnic education lends itself to be considered more appropriately from an interdisciplinary perspective. In this light, any study of an education system will have to focus on how societal influences shape educational provisions and how educational reforms aim at keeping society in check. Proponents of this kind of thought suggest that Marxist educational theory should be studied as sociology of education rather than as philosophy of education.

[1] Bowyer, C. H. (1970). *Philosophical perspective for education.* Glenview, IL: Scott, Freeman and Company. p. 237

[2] Marx, K. *Critique of political economy.* In Copleston, F. (1963). *A history of philosophy.* Vol. 7. Part II. Garden City, NY: Image Books. p. 83.

[3] Engels, Ludwig Feuerbach. In Copleston, *op. cit.,,* p. 83-84.

[4] Bowyer, *op. cit.,,* p. 238.

[5] Copleston, *op. cit.,,* p. 86.

[6] Engels, F. (1940). *Dialectics of nature.* New York: International Publishers Co. p. 190.

[7] Cohen, R. S. (1955). *The Marxist philosophy of education.* In N. B. Henry (ed.). *Modern philosophies and education.* The fifty-fourth Yearbook of the National Society for the Study of Education. Chicago, IL: The University of Chicago Press. p. 190.

[8] Marx, K. (1904). *A contribution to the critique of political economy.* Chicago, IL: Charles H. Kerr & Co. p. 268.

[9] Brosio, R. A. (2000). *Philosophical scaffolding for the construction of critical democratic education.* New York: Peter Lang. p. 83.

[10] Marx, K. German *Ideology. In Copleston, op. cit.,,* p. 87.

[11] Hakim, A. B. (1987). *Historical introduction to philosophy.* New York: Macmillan Publishing Company. p. 584.

[12] Copleston, *op. cit.,,* p. 89.

[13] Sarup, M. (1983). *Marxism, structuralism, education. Theoretical developments in the sociology of education.* London: Falmer. p. 23.

[14] Marx, (1904). *op. cit.,,* pp. 11-13.

[15] Sarup, *op. cit.,,* p. 24.

[16] Gonzalez, G. G. (1982). *Progressive education: A Marxist interpretation.* Minneapolis: Marxist Educational Press. p. 16.

[17] Marx, K. & Engels, F. (n.d.) *Manifesto of the Communist Party.* New York: International Publishers. p. 31.

[18] Marx, K. (n.d.). *Capital. The process of capitalist production.* Trans. Eden & P. Ceder. New York: International Publishers. p. 527.

[19] Marx, K. (n.d.). *Civil war in France.* Trans. E. B. Bass. Chicago: Charles H. Kerr Y Co. p. 44.

[20] Shore, *op. cit.,,* p. 68.

[21] Marx, K. *Capital.* P. 488.

[22] Langevin, P. *La Pensée.* In Cohen, *op. cit.,,* pp. 201-202.

[23] DeWitt, N. (1961). *Education and professional employment in the USSR.* Washington, DC: United States Government Printing Office. p. 79.

[24] Engels, F. (1847). *Principles of communism.* In Fitzpatrick, *op. cit.,,* p. 5.

[25] Shore, *op. cit.,,* p. 52.

[26] Marx, K. (1845). *Eleven thesis on Feuerbach.* In King, *op. cit.,,* p. 2.

[27] First International is the common and popular name for the International Working Man's Association founded by Marx in 1864 to defend the rights of workers.

[28] DeWitt, *op. cit.,,* pp. 119-120.

[29] Powers, *op. cit.,,* p. 144.

[30] Donohue, J. (1959). *Work and education. The role of cultural education in some distinctive theories of humanism.* Chicago, IL: Loyola University Press. p. 48.

EPILOGUE : TEACHING PHILOSOPHY OF EDUCATION

The guiding question of the foregoing chapters was: what should philosophy of education as an intellectual enterprise be doing? No one is born a philosopher of education. Each one starts out first as a student of philosophy of education. As we come to the end of our intellectual voyage it is worthwhile making a statement on how teachers should handle this starting point of educational philosophy. What should teachers of students of philosophy of education aim at? What ought they be doing? Two aims suggest themselves. Teachers should assist students to acquire the skills for establishing validity and to develop a philosophical attitude toward education.

Establishing Validity

Teaching is an activity aimed at assisting learners to achieve learning. The spirit with which such an activity is to be carried out should be one that respects the learner's intellectual integrity and capacity for independent judgment.[1] Hence, propaganda and indoctrination are not teaching because they do not genuinely engage the judgment of the learner. If teaching is a goal-oriented activity what should teachers of philosophy aim to achieve with their students?

A philosopher is not a scientist. Scientists are concerned with all kinds of nature, carry out relevant laboratory or field observation, and finally describe their findings. The philosopher, by contrast, is a systematic thinker whose business is limited to human thinking. The scientist demonstrates truth through scientific induction and mathematical (logical) proof. The philosopher establishes truth only through logical proof without much regard for sense experience. In the context of education the philosopher of education is not a grammarian who studies the rules of language. S/he is not a psychologist or sociologist who studies the ways in which symbolic thinking works. The area of thought in education that is the office of educational philosophers is claim to validity of education. Educators "are constantly making statements, passing judgment, taking decisions, and expressing preferences. In doing these things and many others like them we make the claim, explicitly or implicitly, that what we have said – our statement, judgment, decision or preference – is justified."[2]

Making such educational claims supposes that there are principles that justify such claims. It is the office of the educational philosopher to reach such principles. Any teacher of educational philosophy must aim at providing students with philosophical and educational tools that will assist these students to establish solid and valid principles of education. The practice of educational philosophy shall not be limited to an examination and description of educational phenomena but must also be extended to an assessment and evaluation of claims to validity. The discovery of principles hints teachers of educational philosophy the kind of knowledge and skill they should aim at cultivating in students. Hence, the students must be familiar with these criteria among others:

Plausibility:	Is the principle explaining the educational phenomenon it purports to explain?
Feasibility:	Is it operationalizable – logical?
Effectiveness:	Can the principle guide and stimulate discussion about the educational phenomenon?
Pragmatic:	Is the principle compatible with previously established valid principles?
Predictive:	Does the principle explain educational expectations?
Intersubjectivity:	Can other philosophers arrive at the same principle independently?
Inter -methodological:	Can the same principle be arrived at through different investigative methods?

Building Personal Philosophy of Education

Teachers make several decisions daily. This may include decisions on what to include in or exclude from lessons or test, what to emphasize with parents, and so on. Such decisions are not arrived at haphazardly. They are arrived at on the basis of what is good education and appropriate educational purpose. Whether or not a teacher knows that such decisions are made on the basis of a philosophy it is certain that the teacher decides on the basis of his/her conceptions of education. To avoid inconsistencies in the teaching of educational philosophy it is important for teachers to arrive at a genuine vision of education that will give significance to their work and the life of the students. Hence, teachers of educational philosophy shall not only aim at presenting students with a theoretical understanding of educational philosophy. As a practical component of teaching the teacher shall assist students to start developing their philosophy of education. Teachers of educational philosophy should guide students to seek ideas and impressions that can later become part of their educational philosophy. Teachers must emphasize the necessity of building one's educational philosophy because education has come to stay with humanity. Such knowledge will be useful to the students either as motivators in their present learning or later as educators, administrators of education, parents who must make educational decisions for their kids, or simply as concerned citizens.

Stephen Brookfield emphasizes the importance of developing a teaching philosophy which holds true for teaching education and any other subject. A personal reason for developing a teaching philosophy is that "a distinctive organizing vision – a clear picture of why you are doing what you are doing that you can call up at points of crisis – is crucial to your personal sanity and moral."[3] A teaching philosophy also has a strategic purpose which is to provide teachers with a sense that their "position is grounded in a well-developed and carefully conceived philosophy of practice… You are more likely to gain a measure of respect for your thoughtfulness and commitment, which is important both for your self-esteem and for your political survival."[4] Developing a teaching philosophy is also important for professional reasons. A teacher's commitment to a certain rationale of educational philosophy can boost the identity of the teacher and foster "the development of professional strengths among teachers."[5] The pedagogical import of a teaching philosophy cannot be overemphasized. A teaching philosophy "is about making some kind of dent in the world so that the world is different than before you practiced your craft. Knowing clearly what kind of dent you want to make in the world means that you must continually ask yourself the most fundamental evaluative question – What effect am I having on students and on their learning?"[6]

A philosophy of education, just as a philosophy of life, does not evolve overnight. It is constantly challenged, refined, and broadened by changing society, and the variety of people and ideas the teacher meets in the course of teaching or studying. Teaching philosophy of education should not only be limited to dispensing the content matter of a course. Teaching philosophy of education should constantly challenge the convictions of the teacher concerning the goals and purposes of education. Hence, teaching philosophy of education must have a formative purpose. Some methodological considerations for building a philosophy of education which teachers must let students grasp are structure, comprehensiveness, and selectivity. That is, students must learn to answer the following questions: How is the content of the educational philosophy organized? Is it complete or does it have loopholes? What is the line of argument? In teaching philosophy of education the teacher must bear in mind to set in motion the maturation process of thinking and building the educational philosophy of both the teacher and students.

[1] Scheffer, I. *Philosophical models of teaching.* Harvard Educational Review. Spring 1965 (35) 1, p. 190.

[2] Corbett, J. P. (1965). *Teaching philosophy now.* In R. D. Archambault, (Ed.). *Philosophical analysis and education.* New York: The Humanities Press, pp. 141-156.

[3] Brookfield, S. (1990). *The skillful teacher. On technique, trust, and responsiveness in the classroom.* San Francisco: Jossey-Bass Publishers. p. 16.

[4] Brookfield, *op. cit.,,* p. 17.

[5] Brookfield, *op. cit.,,* pp. 17-18.

[6] Brookfield, *op. cit.,,* pp. 18-19.

BIBLIOGRAPHY

Ackrill, J. L. (1997). *Essays on Plato and Aristotle.* Oxford: Clarendon Press.

Acton, H. B. (1967). *Idealism. In P. Edwards (ed.). The encyclopedia of philosophy.* Vol. 4. New York: The Macmillan Company & The Free Press. pp. 110-118.

Andermahr, S., Lovell, T., & Wolkowitz, C. (1997). *A concise glossary of feminist theory.* London: Arnold.

Alexander, H. & McLaughlin, T. H. (2003). *Education in religion and spirituality.* In N. Blake, P. Smeyers, R. Smith, & P. Standish (Eds.). *The Blackwell guide to the philosophy of education.* Malden, MA: Blackwell Publishers Ltd.

Almond, B. (1988). *Women's rights. Reflections on ethics and gender.* In M. Griffiths & M. Witford (Eds.) *Feminist perspectives in philosophy.* Bloomington, IN: Indiana University Press, pp. 29-41.

Avalos, B. (1962). *New Men for new times. A Christian philosophy of education.* New York: Sheed and Ward.

Baldner, S. (1999). *Christian philosophy.* Etienne Gilson, and Fides et ratio. www.nd.edu/ Departments/Maritain/ti99/haldner.htm.

Barnett, G. (Ed.). (1966). *Philosophy and educational development.* Boston, MA: Houghton Mifflin Company.

Barr, J. (1999). *Liberating knowledge. Research, feminism, and adult education.* Leicester, UK: National Institute for Adult Continuing Education.

Bauer, N. (2001). S*imone de Beauvoir, philosophy, and Feminism.* New York: Columbia University Press.

Bedford, M. (1972). *Existentialism and creativity.* New York: Philosophical Library.

Belth, M. (1965). *Education as discipline. A study of the role models in thinking.* Boston, MA: Allyn and Baton, Inc.

Berlin, I. (1969). *A dangerous but important activity.* In V. C. Morris (Ed). *Modern movements in educational philosophy.* pp. 9-13. Boston, MA: Houghton Mifflin Company.

Bogoslovsky, B. B. (1936). *The ideal school.* New York: The Macmillan Company.

Bonnett, M. & Cuypers, S. (2003). *Autonomy and authenticity in education.* In N. Blake, P. Smeyers, R. Smith, & P. Standish (Eds.). *The Blackwell guide to the philosophy of education.* Malden, MA: Blackwell Publishers Ltd.

Bowyer, C. H. (1970). *Philosophical perspectives for education.* Glenview, IL: Scoot, Freeman and Company.

Brameld, T. B. (1955). *Philosophies of education in cultural perspective.* New York: Dryden Press.

Bréhier, E. (1931). *Y a-t-il une philosophy chrétienne? Revue de métaphysique et de morale 38.*

Brookfield, S. (1990). *The skillful teacher. On technique, trust, and responsiveness in the classroom.* San Francisco: Jossey-Bass Publishers.

214

Brosio, R. A. (Ed.). (1994). *Philosophical studies in education.* Terre Haute, IN: Ohio Valley Philosophy of Education Society.

Brosio, R. A. (2000). *Philosophical scaffolding for the construction of critical democratic education.* New York: Peter Land.

Broudy, H. S. (1954). *Building a philosophy of education.* New York: Prentice-Hall.

Brown, C. (1969). *Philosophy and Christian faith.* Chicago, IL: Inter-Varsity Press.

Brown, J. N. (1940). *Educational implications of four conceptions of human nature.* Washington, DC: The Catholic University of America Press

Brubacher, J. (1969). *Modern philosophies of education.* 4th, Ed. New York: McGraw-Hill.

Brumbaugh, R. S. & Lawrence, N. M. (1986). *Philosophers on education. Six essays on the foundation of Western Thought.* Lanham: University Press of America.

Buetow, H. A. (1988). *The Catholic School. Its roots, identity, and future.* New York: Crossroads.

Burbules, N. C. *Deconstructing "difference" and the difference this makes to education.* www.edu. uiuc.edu/EPS/PES-Yearbook/96_docs/burbules.html

Butler, J. D. (1966). *Idealism in education.* New York: Harper and Row Publishers.

Butler, J. D. (1968). *Four philosophies and their practice in education.* New York: Harper.

Calkins, M. W. (1917). *The persistent problems of philosophy.* 4th Ed. New York: The Macmillan Company.

Cates, P. W. Faith *Christian ministries.* [on-line] www.faithchristianmin.org/articles/cpe. htm

Catholic School Office of the Diocese of Fargo. (2001). *A brief philosophy of Catholic education.* www.fargodiocese.org/cef/cathschools/theory/phil.html.

Code, L., Overall, C., & Mullet, S. (Eds.). (1988). *Feminist perspective. Philosophical essays on method and morals.* Toronto: University of Toronto Press.

Cohen, R. S. (1955). *On the Marxist philosophy of education.* In N. B. Henry, (Ed.). *Modern philosophies of education.* The Fifty-fourth Yearbook of the National Society for the Study of Education. Chicago, IL: The University of Chicago Press.

Congregation For Catholic Education, (1997). *The Catholic school on the threshold of the Third Millennium.* www.fargodiocese.org/cef/catholicschools/theory/csttm.html.

Conrad, D. R. (1976). *Education for transformation. Implications in Lewis Mumford's ecohumanism.* Palm Springs, CA: ETC Publication.

Copleston, F. (1963). *A history of philosophy.* Vol. 7. Part II. Garden City, NY: Image Books.

Corbett, J. P. (1965). *Teaching philosophy now.* In R. D. Archambault, (Ed.). Philosophical analysis and education. New York: The Humanities Press.

Counts, G. S. (1957). *The challenge of Soviet education.* New York: McGraw-Hill Book Company, Inc.

Cunningham, W. F. (1949). *The pivotal problems of education.* New York: The Macmillan Company.

Curtis, S. J. (1968). *An introduction to the philosophy of education*. London: University Tutorial Press Ltd.

Demaine, J. (1981). *Contemporary theories in sociology of education*. London: The Macmillan Press Ltd.

Demiashkevitch, M. (1935). *An introduction to philosophy of education*. New York: American Book Company.

Denton, D. E. (Ed.) (1974). *Existentialism and phenomenology in education*. New York: Teachers College Press.

Dewey, J. (1897). *My pedagogic creed*. www.pramatism.org/gnealogy/dewey/My_pedagogic_creed.htm

Dewey, J. (1910). *How we think*. Boston, DC: Heath and Co.

DeWitt, N. (1961). *Education and professional development in the USSR*. Washington, DC: National Science Education.

Donald, A. (1967). *Philosophy of education*. New York: Harper & Row.

Donohue, J. (1959). *Work and education. The role of technical culture in some distinctive theories of humanism*. Chicago: Loyola University Press.

DuBois, E., Kelly, G., Kennedy, E, Korsmeyer, C, & Robinson, L. (1985). *Feminist scholarship. Kindling in the groves of academe*. Chicago, Il: University of Illinois Press.

Dupuis, A. M. (1985). *Philosophy of education in a historical perspective*. Lanham, MD: University Press of America.

Dupuis, A. M. & Nordberg, R. (1964). *Philosophy and education. A total view*. Milwaukee, WI: The Bruce Publishing Company.

Eisenstein, H. (1984). *Contemporary feminist thought*. London: Allen & Unwin.

Elias, J. L. (1995). *Philosophy of education. Classical and contemporary*. Malabar, FL: Krieger Publishing Company.

Existentialism. www.edst.purdue.edu/georgeoff/phil_am_ed/EXISTENTIALISM.htm

Engels, F. (1847). *Principles of communism*. In S. Fitzpatrick, (1979). *Education and social mobility in the Soviet Union 1921-1934*. Cambridge, MA: Cambridge University Press

Engels, F. Ludwig Feuerbach. In F. Copleston (1963). *A history of philosophy*. Garden City, NY: Image Books.

Engels, F. (1940). *Dialectics of nature*. New York: International Publishers Co.

Fitzpatrick, S. (1979). *Education and social mobility in the Soviet Union 1921-1934*. Cambridge, MA: Cambridge University Press

Flanagan, F. M. (1994). *John Dewey*. www.ul.ie/~philos/vol1/dewey.htm

Flower, E. F. (Spring 1956). *In two keys*. The Harvard Educational Review 26(2) 99-102.

Frankena, W. K. (1965). *Three historical philosophies of education*. Aristotle, Kant, Dewey. Chicago, IL: Scott, Foresman and Company.

Fuhrmann, B. & Grasha, A. (1983). *A pra introduction to philosophy of education*. New York: J. B. Lippincott Company.

Greene, T. M. (1955). *A liberal Christian idealist philosophy of education*. In N. B. Henry (ed.) *Modern philosophy and education*. The Forty-fifth Yearbook of the National Society for Study of Education. Part I. Chicago, IL: The University of Chicago Press.

Griffiths, M. & Whitford, M. (Eds.) (1988). *Feminist perspectives in philosophy*. Bloomington, IN: Indiana University Press.

Groome, T. H. (1998). *Educating for life. A spiritual vision for every teacher and parent*. Allen, TX: Thomas More

Haight, R. (1990). *Dynamics of theology*. New York: Mahwah.

Hakim, A. B. (1987). *Historical introduction to philosophy*. New York: Macmillan Publishing Company.

Hans, N. (1958). *Comparative education. A study of educational factors and traditions*. London: Routledge & Kegan Paul.

Hart, C. A. (Ed.). (1936). *Christian philosophy and the social sciences, Vol. 12*. Washington, DC: The Catholic University of America.

Hartsock, N. (1983). *The feminist standpoint. Developing the ground for a specifically feminist historical materialism*. In S. Harding & M. Hintikka (Eds.). *Discovering reality*. Dordrecht: Kluwer Academic Publishers.

Heideggar, M. (1961). *A introduction to metaphysics*. Trans. R. Mannheim. New York: Doubleday and Company.

Hekman, S. J. (1999). *The future of differences. Truth and method in feminist theory*. Malden, MA: Blackwell Publishers Inc.

Held, V. (1993). *Feminist morality. Transforming culture, society, and politics*. Chicago, IL: The University of Chicago Press.

Hemming, R. P. & Parsons, S. F. (Eds.) (2002). *Restoring faith in reason*. London: SCM Press.

Heslop, R. D. (1996). *Analytic philosophy*. In J. J. Chambliss (Ed.). *Philosophy of education.. An Encyclopedia*. New York: Garland Publishing.

Hill, B. V. (1982). *Faith at the blackboard. Issues facing the Christian teacher*. Grand Rapids, MI: Wm. B. Eerdmans Publishing Company.

Hirschmann, N. J. (1992). *Rethinking obligation. A feminist method for political theory*. Ithaca: Cornell University Press.

Hocking, W E. (1918). *Human nature and its remaking*. New Haven: Yale University Press.

Hocking, W. E. (1959). *Types of philosophy*. New York: Charles Scribner's Sons.

Holland, N. J. (1990). *Is women's philosophy possible?* Savage, MD: Rowman & Littlefield Publishers, Inc.

Holmes, A. F. 1971). *Faith seeks understanding. A Christian approach to knowledge*. Grand Rapids, MI: Wm. B. Eerdmans Publishing Company.

Holmes, B. (1965). *Problems in education. A comparative approach.* London: Routledge & Kegan Paul.

Hooks, S. (Spring 1956). S*cope of philosophy of education.* The Harvard Educational Review 26(2) 145-8.

Horne, H. H. (1908). *The psychological principle of education.* New York: The Macmillan Company.

Horne, H. H. (1927). *The philosophy of education. Being the foundations of education in the related natural and mental sciences.* New York: The Macmillan Company.

Horne, H. H. (1931). *The new education.* New York: Abingdon Press.

Horne, H. H. (1939). *The philosophy of Christian education.* New York: Fleming H. Reuell Company.

Horne, H. H. (1954). *An idealist philosophy of education.* In J. S. Brubacher et al. (Eds.). The Forty-first yearbook of the National Society for the Study of Education. Part I. Chicago, IL: The University of Chicago Press.

Houston, B. (1996). *Feminism.* In J. J. Chambliss (Ed.). *Philosophy of education. An encyclopedia.* New York: Garland Publication.

Hughes, C. (2002). *Key concepts in feminist theory and research.* London, Sage Publications.

Humm, M. (1995). *The dictionary of feminist theory.* 2nd Ed. Columbus, OH: Ohio State University Press.

Hutchings, K. (2003). *Hegel and feminist philosophy.* Malden, MA: Blackwell Publishing Inc.

John-Paul II. (1998). *Encyclical letter fides et ration.* www.christlife.org/library/churchdocs/C_fides.html.

Joyce, B. & Weil, M. (1972). *Models of teaching.* Englewood Cliffs, NJ: Prentice-Hall, Inc.

Kant, I. (1938). *The fundamental principles of the metaphysics of ethics.* Trans. O. Manthey-Zorn. New York: The Macmillan Company.

Kaplan, A. (1998). *The conduct of inquiry. Methodology for behavioral science.* New Brunswick, NJ: Transaction Publishers.

Kelly, G. (1992). *Education, women, and change.* In P. G. Altbank and G. P. Kelly (Eds.). *Emergent issues in education. Comparative perspective.* New York: State University of Wisconsin.

Kendel, I. L. (1955). *The new era in education. A comparative study.* Boston, MA: Houghton Mifflin Company.

Keohane, N. O., Rosaldo, M. Z., & Gelpi, B. C. (1982). *Feminist Theory. A critique of ideology.* Brighton, Sussex: The Harvester Press Limited.

King, E. J. (1962). *World perspectives in education.* New York: The Bobbs-Merrill Company.

Khazanchi, D. *A philosophical framework for the validation of information systems concepts.* www.hsb.baylor.edu/ramsower/ais.ac.96/papers/Khazanch.htm

King, E. J. (1963). *The concept of ideology in communist education.* In E. J. King (ed.) *Communist education.* New York: The Bobbsmerrill Company

King, E. J. (1973). *Other schools and ours. Comparative studies for today.* 4th Ed. New York: Holt, Rinehart and Winston.

Kneller, G. F. (1958). *Existentialism and education.* New York: Philosophical Library

Kneller, G. F. (1971). *The challenge of existentialism.* In G. F. Kneller (Ed.). *Foundations of education.* 3rd Ed. New York: John Wiley & Sons.

Knight, G. R. (1998). *Philosophy of education. An introduction in Christian perspective.* 3rd Ed. Berrien Springs, MI: Andrews University Press.

Kretzmann, N. (1990). *Faith seeks, understanding finds.* In T. P. Flint (Ed.). *Christian charter for Christian philosophy.* Notre Dame, IN: University of Notre Dame Press.

Langevin, P. La Pensée. In Cohen, R. S. (1955). *On the Marxist philosophy of education.* In N. B. Henry, (Ed.). *Modern philosophies of education.* The Fifty-fourth Yearbook of the National Society for the Study of Education. Chicago, IL: The University of Chicago Press.

Langland, E. & Gove, W. (1983). *A feminist perspective in the academy. The difference it makes.* Chicago, IL: The University of Chicago Press.

Lodge, R. C. (1947). *Plato's theory of education.* London: Kegan Paul, Trench, Trubner and Company.

Lucas, C. J. (1969). *What is philosophy of education?* London: The Macmillan Company.

Lynch, L. E. (1968). *A Christian philosophy.* New York: Charles Scribner's Sons.

MacNabb, E., Popham, S., & Prys, R. (Eds.). (2001). *Transforming the disciplines. A woman's studies premier.* New York: The Haworth Press.

Makiguchi, T. (1989). *Education for creative living. Ideas and proposal.* Trans. A. Birnbaum. AMES: Iowa State University Press.

Marique, P. J. (1939). *The philosophy of Christian education.* New York: Prentice-Hall.

Maritain, J. (1940). *Science and wisdom.* Trans. B. Wall. London: Centenary Press.

Maritain, J. (1955). *An essay on Christian philosophy.* Trans. E. H. Flannery. New York: Philosophical Library.

Martin, M. J. (1994). *Changing the educational landscape. Philosophy, women, and curriculum.* New York: Routledge.

Martin, V. M. (2003). *Existentialism.* In B. L. Marthalar et al., (Eds.) *New Catholic Encyclopedia.* 2nd Ed. Vol. 5. New York: Thompson Gale.

Marx, K. (n.d.) *Civil war in France.* Trans. E. B. Bas. Chicago: Charles H. Kerr & Co.

Marx, K. & Engels, F. (n.d.) *Manifesto of the Communist Party.* New York: International Publishers.

Marx, K. (n.d.) Capital. *The process of capitalist production.* Trans. Eden & P. Ceder. New York: International Publishers.

Marx, K. (1845). *Eleven thesis on Feuerbach.* In King, E. J. (1963). *The concept of ideology in communist education.* In E. J. King (ed.) *Communist education.* New York: The Bobbsmerrill Company

Marx, K. *Poverty of philosophy.* Trans. H. Quelch (1910). Charles H. Kerr & Co.

Marx, K.. *German ideology.* In F. Copleston (1963). *A history of philosophy.* Garden City, NY: Image Books.

Marx, K. *Critique of political economy.* In F. Copleston (1963). *A history of philosophy.* Garden City, NY: Image Books.

Mayer, F. (1962). *New perspectives for education.* Washington, DC: Public Affairs Press.

McClellan, J. E. (1976). *Philosophy of education.* Englewood Cliffs, NJ: Prentice-Hall, Inc.

Midgley, M. (1988). *On not being afraid of natural sex differences.* In M. Griffiths & M. Witford (Eds.) *Feminist perspectives in philosophy.* Bloomington, IN: Indiana University Press, pp. 29-41.

Moore, T. W. (1982). *Philosophy of education. An introduction.* Boston, MA: Routledge & Kegan Paul.

Morgan, R. (1970). *Goodbye to all that.* In L. B. Tanner, (Ed.). *Voices from women's liberation.* New York: Signet.

Morris, R. K. (1956). *The philosophy of education: A quality of its own.* The Harvard Educational Review 26(2) 142-4.

Morris, V. C. (1961). *Philosophy and the American school. An introduction to philosophy of education.* Boston, MA: Houghton Mifflin Company.

Morris, V. C. (1966). *Existentialism in education. What it means.* New York: Harper and Row.

Morrish, I. (1967). *Disciplines of education.* London: George Allen & Unwin Ltd.

Nedoncelle, M. (1960). *Is there a Christian philosophy?* Trans. I. Trethowan. New York: Hawthorn Books.

Nettleship, R. L. (1968). *The theory of education in the Republic of Plato.* New York: Teachers College Press.

Noddings, N. (1995). *Philosophy of education.* Boulder, CO: Westview Press.

Noddings, N. & Slote, M. (2003). *Changing notions of moral education.* In N. Blake, P. Smeyers, R. Smith, & P. Standish (Eds.). *The Blackwell guide to the philosophy of education.* Malden, MA: Blackwell Publishers Inc. pp. 341-355.

Oryshkewych, O. E. (1966). *Education. The philosophy of education.* Vol. I. New York: Philosophical Library.

Owens, J. (1990). *Towards a Christian philosophy.* Washington, DC: The Catholic University of America Press.

Ozmon, H. & Creaver, S. (1999). *Philosophical foundations of education.* 6th Ed. Columbus, OH: Merrill.

Park, J. (Ed.). (1968). *Selected readings in the philosophy of education.* 3rd Ed. New York: The Macmillan Company.

Parker, F. H. (1971). *Faith and reason revisited.* Milwaukee, WI: Marquette University Press.

Pazmiño, R. W. (1988). *Foundational issues in Christian education. An introduction in Evangelical perspective.* Grand Rapids, MI: Baker Book House.

Peifer, J. F. (2002). *Idealism.* In B. C. Marthaler et al. (Eds.). *The New Catholic Encyclopedia.* 2nd Ed. Washington, DC: The Catholic University of America. pp. 296-302).

Perry, R. B. (1966). *Education and the science of education.* In I. Scheffler (Ed.). *Philosophy of education. Modern readings.* pp. 17-38. Boston, MA: Allyn and Bacon, Inc.

Peterson, F. E. (1933). *Philosophies of education current in the preparation of teachers in the United States. A study of four State colleges, twelve normal schools, and nine liberal art colleges.* New York: Teachers College Columbia University.

Phenix, P. H. (1959). *Philosophy of education.* New York: Henry Holt and Company.

Power, E. J. (1982). *Philosophy of Education. Studies in philosophies, schooling, and educational policies.* Englewood Cliffs, NJ: Prentice-Hall.

Power, E. J. (1996). *Educational philosophy. A history from Ancient World to Modern America.* New York: Garland Publishing.

Pratte R. (1992). *Philosophy of education. Two traditions.* Springfiel, Il: Charles C. Thomas Publishers.

Price K. (1962). *Education and philosophical thought.* Boston, MA: Allyn and Bacon, Inc.

Price, R. F., (1977). *Marx and education in Russia and China.* Totowa, NJ: Croom Helm

Ramos, A. & George, M. I. (Eds.). (2002). *Faith, scholarship, and culture in the 21st century.* Washington, DC: The Catholic University of America Press.

Redden, J. D. & Ryan, F. A. (1956). *A Catholic philosophy of education.* Milwaukee: WI: The Bruce Publishing Company.

Reese, W. L. (1980). *Dictionary of philosophy and religion.* Eastern and Western thought. New Jersey: Humanities Press.

Rice, S. & Burbules, N. *Communicative virtues and educational relations.* http://www.ed.uiuc.edu/EPS/PES-Yearbook/92_docs/Rice_Burbules.htm

Ryan, J. J. (1950). *Beyond humanism. Towards a philosophy of Catholic education.* New York: Sheed and Ward.

Sacred Congregation for Catholic Education, Catholic schools #4. In A. Flannery (ed.) 1975. Vatican Council II. *The Conciliar and Post-Conciliar Documents.* Vol. II. Northport, NY: Castello.

Sahakian, M. L. & Sahakian, W. S. (1974). *Rousseau as educator.* New York: Twayne Publishers.

Samuelson, G. & Markowitz, F. A. (1988). *An introduction to philosophy in education.* New York: Philosophical Library.

Sarup, M. (1978). *Marxism and education.* Boston, MA: Routledge & Kegen Paul.

Sarup, M. (1983). *Marxism, structuralism, education. Theoretical developments in the sociology of education.* London: Falmer.

Satre, J.-P. (1948). *Existentialism and humanism.* London: Methuen & Company.

Satre, J.-P. (1956). *Being and nothingness.* Trans. H. E. Barnes. New York: Philosophical Library.

Satre, J.-P. *Existentialism.* In M. Bedford, (1972). *Existentialism and creativity.* New York: Philosophical Library.

Sayers, S. & Osborne, P. (Ed.) (1990). *Socialism, feminism, and philosophy. A radical philosophy reader.* London: Routledge.

Scheffer, I. *Philosophical models of teaching. Harvard Educational Review.* Spring 1965 (35)1, pp. 190-200.

Schleiermacher, F. (1996). *On religion. Speeches to its cultural despisers.* Cambridge, MA: Cambridge University Press.

Seigfried, C. H. (2002). F*eminist interpretations of John Dewey.* University Park, PA: The Pennsylvania State University Press.

Shore, M. J., (1947). *Soviet education. Its psychology and philosophy.* New York: Philosophical Library.

Shumilin, I. N. (1962). *Soviet higher education.* Munich: Carl Gerber.

Siegel, H. *What price inclusion?* http://www.edu/EPS/PES-Yearbook/95_docs/siegel. html

Smith, D. (1988). *The everyday world as problematic. A feminist sociology.* Milton Meynes: Open University Press.

Smith, G. (1971). *Christian philosophy and its future.* Milwaukee, WI: Marquette University Press.

Smith, P. G. (1965). *Philosophy of education.* Introductory series. New York: Harper & Row.

Smith, T. L. (Ed.) (2001). *Faith and reason.* South Bend, IN: St. Augustine's Press.

Stromquist, N. P. (2000). *Contributions and challenges of feminist theory to comparative education research and methodology.* In J. Schriewer (Ed.). *Discourse formation in comparative education.* New York: Peter Lang.

Suppes, P. (1996). *The aims of education.* In A. Neiman (Ed.). *Philosophy of education.* 1995. Urbana, IL: University of Illinois at Urbana-Champaign, pp. 110-126.

Sweeney, L. (1997). *Christian philosophy: Greek, Medieval, Contemporary reflections.* New York: Peter Lang.

Thompson, M. M. (1934). *The educational philosophy of Giovanni Gentile.* Los Angeles, CA: University of Southern California.

Thomte, R. (1948). *Kierkegaard's philosophy of religion.* New Jersey: Princeton University Press.

Tozer, S. *Two texts in philosophy of education.* http://www.ed.uiuc.edu/EPS/PES-Yearbook/97_docs/tozer.html.

Tyler, R. W. (1980). *The curriculum. Then and now.* In Tanner D. & Tanner L. N. *Curriculum development. Theory into practice.* New York: Macmillan Publishing Co. p. 16.

Urban, W. M. (1930). *Metaphysics and value.* In G. P. Adams & W. P. Montagne (ed.). *Contemporary American Philosophy.* Vol. II. New York: The Macmillan Company. p. 375.

Wagner, D. *Total education. A faith inspired Catholic philosophy of education.* [on-line] www. saskschools.ca/-cathcurr/articles/totaleducation.html.

Ward, L. R. (1963). *Philosophy of education.* Chicago, IL: Henry Regnery Company.

Weiler, K. et al. (Eds.) (1995). *Repositioning feminism and education. Perspectives on education for social change.* Westport, CT: Bergin and Garvey.

Westcott, M. *Feminist criticism of the social sciences.* Harvard Educational Review. 49(1979), 4. pp. 422-30).

Wild, J. (1955). *The challenge of existentialism.* Indiana: University of Indiana Press.

Wilson, J. (1979). *Preface to the philosophy of education.* Boston, MA: Routledge & Kegan Paul.

Wingo, M. (1965). *Philosophies of education.* Lexington, MA: Heath.

Wynne, J. P. (1947). *Philosophies of education from the standpoint of philosophy of experimentalism.* New York: Prentice-Hall, Inc.

Lightning Source UK Ltd.
Milton Keynes UK
UKHW011103201020
371910UK00001B/224